A LASTING PEACE

A LASTING
PEACE

〜〜〜

Collected Addresses of
Daisaku Ikeda

New York · WEATHERHILL · *Tokyo*

First edition, 1981
Third printing, 1990

Published by Weatherhill, Inc., New York, with editorial offices at
Tanko-Weatherhill, Inc., 8-3 Nibancho, Chiyoda-ku, Tokyo 102, Japan.
Copyright © 1981 by Daisaku Ikeda; all rights reserved. Printed in
Japan.

Library of Congress Cataloging in Publication Data: Ikeda Daisaku. / A
lasting peace. / 1. Sōka Gakkai—Addresses, essays, lectures. I. Title. /
BQ8449.I384L37 294.3'928 / 81-14699 AACR2 / ISBN 0-8348-0166-3

Contents

v

Preface

In conversations I have had with leaders in various fields in all ten countries that I have had occasion to visit this year—the United States, the Soviet Union, France, West Germany, Italy, Austria, Bulgaria, Canada, Mexico, and Panama—the most impressive topic of conversation was always fervor for peace. Though internationalization is bringing the peoples of the world closer together, we still face grave problems and serious threats in connection with environmental pollution, dwindling natural resources, population growth, poverty, and spiritual desolation in the midst of material plenty. My travels have made me more convinced than ever that the only way to generate solidarity for peace under such circumstances is to stimulate grassroots exchanges among peoples on a level of mutual concern transcending politics, economics, and ideologies. In addition, my journeys reconfirmed the belief that the true way to stimulate the necessary mutual love and concern is the Buddhist way, which I first discovered in my youth and to which I have devoted myself ever since. I am certain of this because, among all the religions of the world, Buddhism is most tolerant and most firmly founded on the spirit of compassion and peace.

I am not in sympathy with the current tendency to separate religion from education, culture, and science and, as a result of excess emphasis on materialism, to disregard the significance of religion for society. Religion must not be separated from mankind's other fields of interest and endeavor. The relation between them is like the mutual interdependence of earth and plants. No matter how splendid the plants, if the earth in which they grow is barren or contains poisonous elements, no beautiful flowers or delicious fruit will be forthcoming. Conversely, the most fertile plain is a wilderness without green trees and flowering plants. A rich soil of religion is essential to the germination and cultivation of truly outstanding culture, education, science, and lasting peace. This is why I strongly advocate the restoration of religion to a place of importance in the lives of all people.

Human beings create culture in all of its ramifications. Similarly, in all civilizations and at all times, crises on levels ranging from education in the broadest sense to minor domestic matters arise because of the thoughts and actions of individual human beings. Buddhism, the quintessence of the spirit of the Orient, summons forth the light of compassion, wisdom, and courage existing deep with in all hearts.

For more than twenty years, my studies and practical activities have concentrated on interior revolutions in the minds of individuals leading to the salvation of all mankind and the creation of enduring peace through the Buddhism of Nichiren Daishonin, in which I and my associates believe. Part of my work in this connection has been discussing proposals for future culture, education, and peace with leaders and intellectuals in Japan and many other countries. In these endeavors, I have enjoyed the enthusiastic support of countless friends who share with me the firm conviction that the light of the Mystic Law of Nichiren Shoshu Buddhism will, like the sun dispelling night, usher in an age filled with the brilliance of hope, mutual love and respect, and peace in the twenty-first century.

In this book, some speeches, remarks, and advice to the young that I have delivered at conferences, universities, and other gatherings in Japan and elsewhere between 1971 and 1981 are here presented in collected form. Though these pages may err in observation and reflection, they represent my belief as a practicing advocate of the Mystic Law of Buddhism. I shall be happy if they are of assistance in bringing the light of that Law into a dark, confused society and, in that way, serve as a guide to peace for mankind.

In conclusion, I should like to express my deep gratitude to the editorial staff of John Weatherhill, Inc., for their excellent and painstaking efforts and to Richard L. Gage, translator and editor, and to translators Charles S. Terry and Burton Watson.

June, 1981

A LASTING PEACE

A Proposal for Lasting Peace

*Delivered at the Thirty-fifth General Meeting of Soka
Gakkai, held at Nippon Budokan, Tokyo, November 2, 1972.*

THE YEAR OF STUDY

This is the first general meeting to be held following the completion
of the Sho-Hondo (Grand Main Temple) at Taiseki-ji, head temple of
Nichiren Shoshu. On this beautiful autumn day, it is with the greatest
joy that I, together with nearly fifteen thousand representatives of
our nationwide membership, greet High Priest Nittatsu, who has
kindly come from the head temple. It makes me very happy to
extend a welcome to him; to Reverend Do'ō Hayase, general
administrator of Nichiren Shoshu; to priests from temples all over
Japan; and to our distinguished guests. I wish to express my deepest
gratitude to all of you for attending this meeting.

Nikko Shonin, the second high priest of Nichiren Shoshu, selected
the beautiful land at Oishigahara, on the lower slopes of Mount
Fuji, 682 years ago to serve as the site of our head temple and as the
point from which our great movement to propagate true Buddhism
would begin. On October 1, 1972, our long-cherished dreams of a
new main hall at the head temple were realized with the completion

of the magnificent new Sho-Hondo, the importance of which is intensified by its location in this sacred place. On October 7, the Dai-Gohonzon, the major object of veneration of all believers in Nichiren Shoshu, was transferred to its new home on the altar of the Sho-Hondo. From October 11 until October 17, a series of important and splendid ceremonies was held at Taiseki-ji under the leadership of High Priest Nittatsu, the sixty-sixth successor to this position. Fortunately, we were blessed with beautiful weather for all these services. I am convinced that it was the strong, pure prayers of all our fellow members and their constant self-sacrificing efforts that made this success possible. For that reason, I should like to take this opportunity to express my deep gratitude to you and, through you, to our membership all over the world. Once again, thank you for all you have done to help make our dream come true.

Miao-lo—or Myoraku as his name is read in Japanese—a great scholar and teacher in T'ien-t'ai (Tendai) Buddhism, said the good acts and resulting good fortune of those who serve the Buddha exceed the ten virtues of the Buddha; that is, their good fortune is very great indeed. In this connection, I believe that the human triumph manifest in the building of the new Sho-Hondo marks a record for human good fortune and glory. In addition, it represents the closing of one chapter in our efforts to spread our faith to all peoples. For these reasons, I am certain that it will remain an eternal symbol of our belief. I am equally certain that the heart-felt prayers for peace for mankind that are an integral part of the building will be a source of wonder and admiration for the generations that follow ours. Without doubt, the completion of the building is a sign of the brilliant work of those bodhisattvas of the Mystic Law who are prophesied to appear in our times. As such a sign, the great undertaking of building the Sho-Hondo probably enjoys the greatest approval from Nichiren Daishonin himself. Moreover, I know that the actual work on the part of his disciples must gladden the spirit of our teacher and former president, Josei Toda, whose request it was that we build the Sho-Hondo at the head temple. It is now our duty to intensify our devotion to the head temple Taiseki-ji, especially because it is the home of the Dai-Gohonzon.

The Dai-Gohonzon Knows No Discrimination

It is of the deepest significance that the Dai-Gohonzon extends its care to everyone and is by no means the property of any class or group. Nichiren Daishonin inscribed the Dai-Gohonzon to a man named Yashiro Kunishige, about whom virtually nothing is known. It is certain that in his own heart Nichiren Daishonin considered a common man like Yashiro Kunishige to be the ideal recipient of the most important of all our objects of veneration. The significance of this selection must not be overlooked. He did not inscribe the Dai-Gohonzon to the priesthood, the rich, the aristocratic, the scholarly, or the famous. He chose a humble man, a man of the common people. Consequently, Yashiro Kunishige was a representative of the masses who, oppressed by authority, are eager to learn the Law and willing to undergo suffering for the sake of greater knowledge in the Law. I believe this point is of utmost importance. We must never doubt the keen wisdom of Nichiren Daishonin, who understood completely the desire of ordinary people to live their lives to the fullest and to live them in peace. We must never forget that this is the fundamental meaning of the essential posture of the Buddhism of Nichiren Daishonin. Both priesthood and laity must advance in an intensified spirit of unity as we protect the Dai-Gohonzon and strive for the worldwide spreading of our faith for the sake of our own eternal prosperity and for that of Nichiren Shoshu.

A New Chapter

The personal faith, practical activities, and general history of each of us, as well as the tradition and history of Soka Gakkai, have reached a fulfillment in the new Sho-Hondo; and we now face the dawn of a new day. The sun is rising on the second chapter of our movement to spread our faith over the world and on a new period of world peace. The completion of the Sho-Hondo concluded the sixth of our seven-year plans for growth. We are now entering the seventh plan, which will end in 1979, on the eve of the fiftieth anniversary of the founding of Soka Gakkai. I call on all of you to strengthen the ties of faith that bind us together and, in a newly awakened sense of unity with this organization, to help write the second chapter in the history of the human revolution.

A Reliable Philosophy

Now I should like to explain briefly why we have designated 1973 the Year of Study. The first reason for our decision has much to do with the path Soka Gakkai will follow in the coming years. Until now the image of Soka Gakkai has been one of an organization of action. In other words, we have labored without rest in an urgent program to build the platform and framework for the worldwide propagation of our faith. It goes without saying that behind our efforts were the *Gosho*—the collected writings of Nichiren Daishonin—and the great doctrine of the value of humanity and human life. At the same time, without the mighty passion and energy that have prompted our actions, the great upsurge of the people that we represent and Soka Gakkai itself as it is today would never have been possible.

We have now entered a period of stability. Numbering in our group people from all walks of life, we are creating an ideological current that is reaching the shores of all countries. What path must Soka Gakkai follow if we are to meet the challenge of our next concerted manifestation of strength? I believe that our future actions must be based on a combination of profound thought and practical action. I am certain that our work from now on must be done with diligence and breadth of scope.

I do not want us to resemble either of two kinds of religions that have appeared in the past. In one of these, the religion itself was closely shut up in a sphere completely removed from the common people. In the other, the religion captured the hearts of the people for a while and therefore made explosively rapid progress. But, after a while, it died and passed into oblivion. I want us to face new problems and difficulties and to move steadily forward together with the people. Undaunted by the violent winds of trouble that buffet us, we must tread the path of a positive philosophy as we keep our eyes firmly fixed on the future. I want us to build a Soka Gakkai that is as firm as a great boulder. In doing so, I want us gradually to deepen our ideological knowledge while making practical application of our ideas in order to fulfill the wishes of the whole people, of contemporary society, and of our friends who will live in the twenty-first century.

Three of the great principles of Buddhism are teaching, practical action, and verification of one's belief. From our present standpoint, teaching is the philosophical basis of the Buddhism of Nichiren Daishonin. Practical action must be the direct application of this philosophical basis. It must be undertaken on the part of the person who actually practices the Buddhist Law. Finally, verification of one's belief takes the form of the majestic proof of the true Buddhism manifest in the life of the individual human being. I believe that a religion is only truly alive when it incorporates all three of these principles. Similarly, a human being can only be called a practicing Buddhist in the richest sense if he harmonizes these three elements in his heart in daily life and on wider social planes. Because this spiritual state can only be achieved if we realize the importance of theoretical knowledge as a basis for action, we have resolved to call this first post-Sho-Hondo year the Year of Study.

Spiritual Stability

The second reason for naming 1973 the Year of Study is connected with my desire to help each individual develop his potential. In addition to sponsoring an intensified study movement, I hope to make each of our members self-assured in an awareness that our practical actions are forerunners of a new age. But what will be the source of the needed self-assurance? And what will make that self-assurance unshakable once it has come into being? First, I believe that when we all act together as a united body, the self-assurance of the individual increases as a result of the whirlpool of energy generated by the mass. But self-assurance based solely on group support is ephemeral. Over and above assurance derived from membership in a larger body, the individual requires a firm basis enabling him to advance with the strength of his beliefs, even when he is completely alone. Where will he find such a basis? I am convinced that the answer lies in stabilizing one's inner thoughts and philosophy by means of sincere, devoted study of the Buddhist teachings of Nichiren Daishonin. Though of course in the coming years the general organization of Soka Gakkai will remain important, I believe that the relative importance of the individual will increase. Though the light each of us bears may be small, it is nonetheless potentially great. Brought together, our small lights can form a better and greater brilliance for all mankind.

As I often say, I want all our fellow members to feel not so much that they are included within Soka Gokkai as that Soka Gakkai is included within each of them. I think that this is the point of clear separation between true believers and those whose faith is shallow. I am resolved to rebuild our organization—and to ask you to help rebuild it calling on the help of only those people who are strong enough in faith to support the burden of the Mystic Law and of Soka Gakkai, even if the actual number of such people should be very small.

Courageous Philosophers of the People

The third reason for using the name Year of Study arises from the current state of human thought. Today thought is impoverished, and philosophy has fallen on evil times—in fact, in the West some people argue that philosophy ended with Hegel. As the nineteenth century drew to a close and the twentieth century began, societies everywhere tended to rely on rationalism, pragmatism, and practical politics to the extent that power relations alone controlled everything. The results of this trend have been dire. War has incessantly plagued the earth, our environment has fallen victim to dangerous pollution, and civilization itself has begun a march of death. This state of affairs has now become so widely recognized that it is a matter for discussion on the most ordinary levels. Furthermore, mankind's spiritual desolation has increased in intensity to an alarming degree. Indeed we have reached a crisis point, at which man seems to be suffering from spiritual pollution. One might go so far as to say that what was once referred to as the thinking reed no longer thinks.

In the midst of the flood of information, confusion, and violence that constitutes our society, mankind has begun groping for some unwavering basic point. At no time in the past has respect for human nature and human life been so greatly demanded, and at no time in the past has the human viewpoint been so emphasized. The tendency to regard these issues as vital matters related to life and all nature has become remarkably strong. Our time is one of maximum crisis and at the same time one of maximum opportunity for innovation. I am certain that this is the age when a complete turnabout will be made in man's fate and when it will be decided whether or not the world opens a road to lasting peace. Now that the United States and China have approached each other and Japan and China have reopened diplomatic relations, the next major issue of world attention will be dealing with the nature of the twenty-first century. In connection with this issue, man will—in fact absolutely must—begin a deeper examination of questions of philosophy and of the nature of life. In other words, we are entering a phase in which faith in the true Buddhism can spread to worldwide limits, a time when a truly religious movement can take place. In this age of spiritual turbulence, we as philosophers of the people, having abandoned the vanity of the world in the search for Buddhist truth, must now re-emerge into the world to initiate a movement of spiritual revival.

A New History

As a start in this direction, I have initiated a discussion of the theory of life with two intelligent young scholars. This discussion appears in the pages of our monthly magazine, *Dai-Byakurenge*. To be frank, I consider the issue of life one of the most difficult of all topics. This difficulty is infinitely greater when one must explain the philosophy of life in a fashion convincing to others. I had hoped to engage in more intensive discussion of this issue in the future, but several things have led me to think that the proper time to do so is now. Many members of Soka Gakkai studying the theory and philosophy of life have urged me to discuss it. For this and other reasons, though I am not yet certain of the form in which I shall develop the discussion, I am determined to challenge this unexplored world at the present. I believe that the attempt to come to grips with the all-important issues of the philosophy of life can be a hint to the opening of a new kind of history for succeeding generations.

Society today moves with awesome force. The volume of mass-communications information is enormous. In many fields—sports, leisure, and others—the general trend is toward broad scope and participation by an ever-widening segment of the population. Science is steadily advancing at an increased pace toward the discovery of new techniques. Nevertheless, in all this hasty transition, one senses emptiness. I suspect that this feeling arises from a lack of purpose, an absence of certainty about the meaning of all our activities. No matter how much we may speak of the value of human life and the respect due to it, there seems to be no foundation for such attitudes. Consequently, our words, after ringing empty in the ears of our listeners, pass on, leaving no lasting impression.

When I gave thought to finding a purpose behind everything, the issue of life presented itself to my attention. This issue involves many questions of great importance. What does it mean to live? What does dying mean? After death, does the life of the individual end? Does life go on to lead to rebirth? If a human being is reborn, what form does he take in his new life? As long as fundamental problems like these remain unsolved, society's advances are no more than meaningless roaring and noise. And people, having been caught up in this resounding, but empty, whirlpool, find, upon at last returning to themselves, nothing but futility.

I suspect that, from the end of the twentieth into the beginning of the twenty-first century, a movement will arise to deal with the ideas of life. Perhaps this movement will begin even earlier. But I am convinced that it is necessary to propound a theory of life now for the time when the movement arises.

Theory of Life as the True Heart of Soka Gakkai

In the postwar period, when former president Josei Toda set out to rebuild Soka Gakkai, he started with the theory of life. I, as his disciple, feel that it is my responsibility to develop my teacher's philosophy further and to present it to the world in a systematized form. Indeed, this may be my most important mission. Now that the Sho-Hondo has been finished, I am already dealing with the question.

Soka Gakkai begins and ends with the theory of life; in other words, Josei Toda's enlightenment of the meaning of life—experienced while he was in prison during World War II—is the starting point of our organization. But Soka Gakkai did not invent this theory: the Buddhism of Nichiren Daishonin itself is a philosophy of life. Soka Gakkai has inherited and is carrying on this philosophy. The *Gosho* (writings) of Nichiren Daishonin and the enlightenment of Josei Toda, who interpreted the *Gosho* as a philosophy of life, are the true essence of Soka Gakkai.

Three thousand years ago, in coming to grips with the sorrows of human life—birth, aging, sickness, and death—Shakyamuni Buddha opened a boundless world within himself. In order to make his meanings clear to the people of his time, he employed many learned contemporary allusions, parables, and ceremonies. Later, in China during the middle and late parts of the Zoho Era, through introspection T'ien-t'ai the Great became aware of the essence of the force of life embodied in the Lotus Sutra and systematized it into the famous doctrine of Ichinen Sanzen. Finally, seven centuries ago, Nichiren Daishonin appeared in Japan as the Buddha of the Mappo Era. His enlightenment consisted in the knowledge that the true source of life is to be found in the Mystic Law, Nam-myoho-renge-kyo. Making full use of the Lotus Sutra itself and of the teachings of T'ien-t'ai and of Miao-lo, Nichiren Daishonin brought this vital truth to the people in both his oral teachings and his written works.

Philosophy Based on Human Revolution

From what I have been saying it is apparent that the philosophy of life is the essence of true Buddhism and that the great advocates of this philosophy have devised ways to make this philosophy intelligible to different peoples in different ages. But the life theory is more than just a theory. The life of which I speak is based on power to transform a human life from one of boredom and suffering to one of radiant hope by altering the very inward fate of the person. The individual can revitalize himself when he is enlightened to the interaction between the microcosm, which is the life of a human being, and the macrocosm; that is, revitalization is possible when such enlightenment is a person's faith. The philosophy of life developed from actual experiences of revivals in which this kind of faith served as a basis.

Our own life-philosophical movement must begin at this point.

That is to say, the eternal and unceasing mission of Soka Gakkai is to lead people to an understanding of the Gohonzon, which is the basic law of union with the macrocosm and the life emanating from it. One of our most serious battles will be to live in harmony with the life philosophy, to allow the human revolution to take place in each one of us, and to continue studying the life philosophy of Nichiren Daishonin. In connection with the last point, our battle henceforth will demand diligent effort.

No one is outside the macrocosm of the Mystic Law. Moreover, no one is beyond the karmic law of cause and effect. Any person who makes light of the solemn life philosophy is simultaneously despising the life within himself. For these reasons, I believe that our movement for the life philosophy must shake the most profound levels of the mind of man and must ultimately give rise to a revolution in human consciousness. We must continue to advance toward this goal with a deep awareness that the century of life must inevitably come.

An idea gains the power to propagate and spread itself when it is linked with the inner feelings of human beings. For instance, the liberalism of Jean Jacques Rousseau became a source of the French Revolution because the idea itself found sympathy in the minds of the bourgeoisie. Similarly, the communist theories of Karl Marx swept over Europe with great speed because they struck home in the hearts of the laboring class. But our movement is not oriented toward any specific class; our purpose is to teach all human beings how to live in a way worthy of their humanity. Since what we have to offer can bring fulfillment even now in the dreadful vacuity of the twentieth century, it should be obvious that our movement can reach the greatest heights for the sake of all mankind.

The time has come for Soka Gakkai as an organization to dedicate itself anew to the wholehearted, mind-and-body task of bringing to society and to all mankind a clue to a way out of the tangled web of complicated elements constituting the world in which we live. In order to achieve this, we must directly face the field of life and its difficult, often unknown, but basic, problems. Of course, I entertain great hopes for contributions to world peace and happiness on the part of individuals in many fields who have trained their eyes to see the truth and who burn with the ardor of faith. At the same time, I feel that there is still a larger task for us. My hope is that the people as a whole will bravely instigate their own movement for the extensive study and practice of the life philosophy.

Because this movement will be a challenge to a world of which mankind as yet knows little or nothing, the road it must follow will be twisted and hard. But it is both the true road of the Buddhism of Nichiren Daishonin and the path of action voluntarily chosen by Soka Gakkai. Consequently, I believe that we must all follow this road with courage and with high spirits.

Buddhist Philosophy: Unwavering Faith for the Individual

Standing at a point where we have just completed the task of building the Sho-Hondo and are about to enter a new period, I should like to take a general look at our future. The year 1979 will be of the greatest importance to us because it is the seven-hundredth anniversary of the inscription of the Dai-Gohonzon. It will also bring to a close the seventh seven-year plan of Soka Gakkai. By that year, we hope to have five million members in our Study Department.

The following are our reasons for setting this goal. We want all of our members to make the Buddhist philosophy of Nichiren Daishonin their own bulwark of faith and, by achieving this spiritual support, to become Soka Gakkai members in the deepest sense. As a corollary of this desire, we want our members to learn to discuss the Buddhist philosophy of Nichiren Daishonin in contemporary language so that they can contribute to the spread of these ideas throughout society at large.

I have said that we want five million members in the Study Department by 1979; quality, not quantity, is our goal. It makes no difference whether we have five hundred thousand or two million members. Clearly, the meaning of a philosophical movement fades when the people conducting it are concerned solely with statistics. Similarly, the philosophy we want to study must not be one of mere words and ideas. We must all regard this philosophy as alive in the life of each individual. We must do our best to master it to the extent that we can influence contemporary society by discussing our beliefs in words intelligible to everyone.

Our Year of Study will not terminate with 1973. In fact, I think it would be excellent to regard all seven years between now and 1979 as Years of Study.

The Buddhist Cultural Course

At present it is only a proposal, but next year I should like to establish a course of studies that I tentatively call the Buddhist Cultural Course. The aim in setting up this course is to permit people to conduct systematic academic studies in Buddhism and to enable them to embark on extensive activities on a worldwide scale. This will entail the study of foreign languages. At the outset, I should like to accept applications to the course from all over Japan; but at first the number of students will be limited to fifty. A committee to study this question will be formed in the Study Department. I shall leave the composition of concrete proposals and policies to them.

Study is the backbone of faith and action. This has been the tradition of the Soka Gakkai Study Department, and it remains unchanged. At the same time, I think we must now attempt to take a more academic view of our learning methods. I trust that a number of outstanding people will emerge from the Buddhist Cultural Course and will go into the world to take part in the drive for peace. It is my hope that the entire Soka Gakkai will protect and guard the growth of these people.

Since the time of former president Josei Toda, we have continued to hold lectures for the general membership. As a matter of policy, the Study Department plans to open these lectures to people who are not members and who are not believers in Nichiren Shoshu. My wish is to develop the lectures into Buddhist seminars that will become important nuclei in the life-philosophy movement. With the combined efforts of the Buddhist Cultural Course, Buddhism seminars, and the other groups—local chapter seminars, study-discussion meetings, and youth-division meetings that have long been part of our study movement and whose natures I do not want to alter—I hope that we will be able to bring into being and maintain for a long time a study movement of a kind unparalleled in the long history of Japan.

Emphasis on the Right to Remain Alive

During the Students Division Summer Course this year, I said that all nations in the world would do well to learn from the Japanese constitution and abandon not only weapons but also rights to belligerence. I said this because, as a religious man, I feel it is my conscientious duty to do what I can to awaken the masses of the world to their right to remain alive. I realize that some people will criticize my attitude as an idealistic dream, hopeless of fulfillment, but I am nonetheless painfully aware of the urgent need to proclaim to all men their rights—and not necessarily in terms of politics—to live.

For that reason, I should like to instigate a worldwide movement to ensure the observance and protection of this most basic of all human rights. All peoples in all lands have this right, which ought to be inviolable. But at no time in man's history has it been so necessary to start a movement to awaken people to it.

I rely largely on youth to bring this movement to life. For that reason, in addition to calling it the Year of Study because of its importance to our life philosophical study movement, I should like to give next year the name Year of Youth, for it is in the hands of the young people that the future rests.

To the Twenty-third Century

The next seven years will tax the ingenuity of all our membership, because, during that time, we must strive to raise the qualitative level of our personnel. In achieving this aim, I must have the cooperation of all the leaders of our organization. Only in this way can we hope to preserve the Law eternally in the world of man and to extend our faith all over the earth. In connection with this drive to improve our membership, the following meeting will represent an important goal.

Summer Course, 1974

It is our hope to hold a meeting of three hundred thousand people at the head temple, Taiseki-ji, in the summer of 1974. At that time, we wish to engage in diligent study of Buddhist philosophy. As a gathering of the truest members of our organization, it will represent a step toward the worldwide dissemination of our faith. Each participant will become a symbolic treasure tower, since each of those three hundred thousand people will help to shed the light of the Mystic Law over the entire earth in the way that is worthy of the name of the Dai-Gohonzon as the ultimate source of life for all mankind.

Approximately three thousand believers from other countries attended the completion ceremonies of the Sho-Hondo. These are some of the many fellow members who have undergone great hardship to bring the overseas organizations to their present status. I feel that we must do everything we can to protect and assist these people.

The introduction of Buddhism into any land brings happiness and prosperity to that nation and its people. This is indicated by the fact that the transferal of Buddhism from India, the land of its origin, to China, Korea, Japan, Burma, and other parts of Southeast Asia produced cultural flowerings but never resulted in subjugation to Indian control.

The same is true of the Buddhism of Nichiren Daishonin, which was created to serve the needs of the Mappo Era. In the tradition of the Buddhism of Nichiren Daishonin, a great man of practical action and religious faith arises and devotes himself entirely to the nation and people from which he emerges. This is one of the meanings of the Bodhisattvas prophesied to arise in our age to serve mankind. I am attempting to make this point very clear, because there has been a tendency in the past to misconstrue the nature of the propagation of the Buddhist faith. Mistaken ideas develop because people sometimes try to see nonexistent similarities between our activities and those of Christian missionaries associated with the former colonial empires of European nations. Just as religion and government ought to be separate within a nation, so on the international scale as well, faith is purely a matter of belief. Matters of faith must remain separate from politics, and political matters must never intrude upon the sphere of faith.

Peace Festival in Los Angeles

The year 1979 will be of special significance. First, it will mark the seven-hundredth anniversary of the inscription of the Dai-Gohonzon. Second, it will be the twenty-first anniversary of the death of former president Josei Toda. As one goal—or perhaps only part of a larger process—in our drive for worldwide belief in Nichiren Shoshu, a proposal has been advanced to hold a World Peace Festival in Los Angeles that year. We want the festival to offer people a chance to pray for peace and to display the products of their spontaneous, free creativity. Such an event would be a fitting way to bring to a close our seventh seven-year development plan.

As an extension of this undertaking, we hope to select a scenic place in the United States and to build a temple there by 1990. That year will be the seventh centennial of the founding of Taiseki-ji. It is true that Taiseki-ji, as the home of the Dai-Gohonzon, will remain the most sacred place in the world for all Nichiren Shoshu believers. But, as our membership in the United States increases, it is only natural that a home temple in America be built to crystallize the wishes and prayers of our people there. George Williams, general director of Nichiren Shoshu Soka Gakkai of America—who is here today— has expressed a warm wish to be allowed to build such a temple. High Priest Nittatsu was made very happy by the proposal, because he regards the building of a head temple in the United States as important to world peace. These are our feelings on the subject, and we leave the planning and other details to our American fellow members. In the eighteen years remaining to them, they should be able to make adequate preparation. This project will impose no burden on the Japanese membership.

Before leaving this subject, I should like to express my thoughts about the advantages of building such a temple. The American membership will tend to regard the Buddhism of Nichiren Daishonin as exclusively Japanese as long as they must travel to Japan to visit a head temple. Such a situation makes Nichiren Shoshu an alien element in American society. To interpret Nichiren Shoshu in this way is wrong, because it narrows the bounds of Nichiren Daishonin's ideas and his compassion, which are intended for all people everywhere.

Establishment of a World Center

A similar project for the sake of Nichiren Shoshu believers in all countries involves the establishment of a culture center. At present we are considering Los Angeles as the location and are tentatively referring to the center as either the World Nichiren Shoshu Association or the World Nichiren Shoshu Center. As you know, the organization Soka Gakkai does not exist outside Japan. In the United States our membership is organized as Nichiren Shoshu Soka Gakkai of America, in France as Nichiren Shoshu Française, and so on. This means that all the groups are brought together organizationally under Nichiren Shoshu, though they are established in accordance with the laws of the lands in which they are located. We want to establish a center in Los Angeles as a place of unity and support for our membership all over the world. Taken in the wide view, then, our future in the remainder of the twentieth century entails two major landmark years: 1979 and 1990.

The Twenty-first Century: the Mystic Law as the Spirit of the World and of the Age

In 1990, we will commemorate the thirty-second anniversary of the death of former president Josei Toda. At the 1967 general meeting of Soka Gakkai, I expressed a desire to initiate another series of seven-year—we call them seven-bell—development plans beginning in the year 2001. I also said that we must leave the concrete details of these programs to the people who succeed us. But I should like to take this opportunity to make some general remarks about the probable current of events in the more remote future.

Josei Toda often expressed his conviction that two centuries would be required for the worldwide spreading of our faith. If we postulate the period between 1972 and 2000 as the first phase of the second chapter of this propagation, the second phase may be assigned to the years between 2001 and 2050.

In the initial phase, it is our most urgent duty first to put a stop to the current trend toward the destruction of mankind and then to build power for peace. In the second phase, it is my hope that peace, prosperity, and happiness will be brought to the peoples of Asia, who, in our own century, have experienced continuous oppression and suffering. Josei Toda himself expressed the same hope in this poem:

> To the peoples of Asia,
> So eager to see the moon
> Hidden behind the clouds,
> We will send the sunlight.

The third phase, between 2051 and 2100, will include the centennial anniversary of the completion of the Sho-Hondo. Marked by an event of such momentous importance, this period should see the life philosophy of Nichiren Daishonin become the spirit of the age and of the whole world. I have called the twenty-first century the Century of Life because I am convinced that a great life-philosophical movement will arise in its latter part. My most deeply felt request of the people who will come after us is that they make their century an age of truly profound respect for all life.

The Spirit of Peace Transmitted to Our Grandchildren

By the fourth phase, that is, between 2101 and 2150, we can hope that an indestructible foundation will have been laid for lasting worldwide peace. If this is achieved, we can trust that the fifth phase—to the conclusion of the twenty-second century—will see the completion of the second chapter of our move to bring our faith to all parts of the world.

It may well be that the second chapter of this great movement will begin in 2253, the millennial anniversary of the founding of Nichiren Shoshu, or in 2279, the millennial anniversary of the inscription of the Dai-Gohonzon. I am well aware that I am talking about times very distant in the future and that none of us will be here to know what is happening. My purpose in making this forecast is to express my dream and prayer that the spirit of peace of Nichiren Shoshu and of Soka Gakkai will live to inspire our grandchildren and their grandchildren.

From another standpoint, there is no reason to be wary of discussing things no more than two or three centuries away. In a recent tour of places of historical interest in Europe, I saw great churches that took three or four hundred years to build. Some of the houses in the towns and some of the furniture in the houses had traditions of two or three hundred years' use. Our goal of the worldwide spreading of Nichiren Daishonin's Buddhism amounts to the building of a foundation for the entire Mappo Era. Instead of hurrying to erect something shoddy, we must take our time to build solidly and well. Manifestly, ours is a task that will require several generations. We must do our work so that the people who come after us will clearly see the lines they must follow.

In this discussion of the future I am not making prophecies; I am not saying that this is the way things absolutely must be. Aside from the Gohonzon, there is no absolute certainty. Just before he died, Josei Toda remarked that, after his death, it would be all right to erase everything he had ever said. I feel exactly the same way. My true wish is to leave things in the hands of our successors, who will be wise enough to deal with their own problems. Still, I want you to understand the call that rises from the innermost heart of one man of faith living now and earnestly praying for the building of a society of peace.

Realization of Lasting Peace Is the Mission of the Religious Man

Now I should like to examine the problem of world peace in our society from the standpoint of religious concepts. The realization of lasting peace is the greatest problem borne by man today. No people has ever managed to remain completely apart from the disasters of war. The fires of war on this earth have never been completely extinguished in any historical age. Moreover, war is not a disaster besetting man from without. It takes place in the heart of man, and man is the principal performer in its tragedy. It is one of the ugliest aspects of human life, erupting and spreading to become a blot on all humanity.

Since man causes war, it should be within his power to halt it whenever he sees fit. The reason war is difficult to deal with is that men refuse to open their eyes to the world of life within each human being. Buddhism has resolved the issue of human life, and the ultimate essence of Nichiren Shoshu Buddhism—which exists for the sake of all people—is the Dai-Gohonzon. Since the Dai-Gohonzon is enshrined in the Sho-Hondo, which was built as a result of the ardent wishes of believers all over the world, we have called the new building a prayer hall for world peace.

Now that the Sho-Hondo is finished, our major task is twofold. First, we must bring the light of Buddhism to confused and suffering humanity and thus reveal the solution to the problem of life. Second, we must prove to the world the magnitude of the contribution we are able to make to the realization of world peace.

A look at the activities of Nichiren Daishonin shows that among his initial social undertakings was a demand for peace. It is not difficult to imagine that one of the things that inspired him to study Buddhism was a desire to find a way to bring salvation to the people living in the Mappo Era, a time when, as was predicted by Shakyamuni Buddha, warring has no end and the teachings of Shakyamuni himself lose their power. Nichiren Daishonin's determination to raise the people of his time from the misery and mire of their surroundings might easily be interpreted as a longing to bring about peace. Immediately after establishing his own Buddhism, he confronted the authorities in power with his *Rissho Ankoku Ron* (The security of the land through the propagation of true Buddhism). In this work, he warns about the dangers of internal treason and invasion from without; and he foretells the crises of war. He goes on to insist that the only way to protect the nation and the people from these dangers is to establish true Buddhist Law.

Realizing Peace: The Ideal of Buddhist Practical Action

The core of the message of the *Rissho Ankoku Ron* is this: on a national, international, or worldwide scale, the only way to bring about lasting peace is to establish the reign of the true Buddhist Law. This work, Nichiren Daishonin's first active approach to social problems, and the establishment of the Dai-Gohonzon, the embodiment of peaceful wishes for all people, were profound reasons for Nichiren Daishonin's appearance on this earth. In these things he showed that the ideal and true spirit of practical Buddhist action in society is the realization of lasting peace for all mankind.

The most horrible of war's aspects is probably not the cruelty and evil of its effects, but the fact that it brings to the forefront the vilest, most atrocious elements of human life. War strips loftiness and respect from humanity and, through its wicked actions, covers man with filth. It is only natural that Buddhism, the aim of which is to guide all people to the highest, purest realms, is bound to oppose war directly. By a like token, the Buddhist believer who is eager to practice his faith in the truest way regards it as his mission to pour his entire soul into the task of building peace.

When we turn to the concrete issue of how to create lasting peace, we come to the problem of the nature of permanent things. Some people will regard the very mention of permanence as nonsensical, since in a world where things change as rapidly as they do today, nothing can be said to last forever. No matter how assiduously one strives to create peace that lasts under the conditions prevailing now, there is no assurance that such peace will persist in succeeding generations.

But in one very important respect, the present differs from the past. Long ago, thinking and ways of living were generally confined within the limits of nations. Today this is no longer the case. Our awareness and our very ways of conducting day-to-day life are directly connected with many countries. Throughout the past, probably the only people who could entertain as wide a view of life as we can now were those living along the ancient Silk Road connecting the Occident with the Orient or those conditioned by the social structures of something like the ancient Roman or the more modern British empires. Rapid advances in modern transportation, communications, and technology have made possible numerous and smooth exchanges of information, knowledge, goods, and even people. Consequently, many peoples now live on a highly international or worldwide plane. I believe that this fact has profound significance for the history of mankind.

Circumstances Making Lasting Peace Possible

By expanding the power of munitions to a horrendous extent, modern technological advances have made it imperative to work out a plan for lasting peace: if we fail in this, we inevitably face global destruction. On the other side of the coin, however, these same technological advances, by expanding the life awareness of people to a worldwide plane, have created circumstances conducive to the establishment of lasting peace. The decision we must make under these conditions is very clear. The supreme problem facing man today is the development of a policy whereby the horror of war will never again darken the globe. To this end, we must concentrate the best of human knowledge and effort.

Of course, we face a number of very important problems at this time: environmental pollution, overpopulation, insufficient food supplies, human relations in an increasingly administration-oriented society, use of leisure time, and many others. But all efforts devoted to the solutions of these difficulties will be no more than houses built on sand unless we resolve the one great problem of warfare, for this is the question that threatens us with imminent extinction.

Trap Inherent in the So-called Peace Mood

Some people may think that there is small reason to consider peace an urgent issue now, when recent relations with China have taken a turn toward a mood of pacificism and when so many people in Japan seem desirous of peace. But I see a trap in this mood of peace. Today, while everyone in Japan is intoxicated with restored diplomatic relations with China, the Diet is deliberating a fourth defense budget. Now, as before, power theories sway international politics, and the fangs of war are in a constant state of sharpened preparedness. In the attempt to establish true peace one must never take one's eyes off international politics.

Often peace is considered no more than the termination of hostilities. Indeed, in many cases, it is only after experiencing war that human beings truly appreciate the blessedness of peace. Similarly, a person rarely appreciates the happiness of good health until he has been sick and has once again regained physical well-being. If warfare can be compared to sickness, people have nothing but applause for the men who work out techniques for bringing about an end to fighting (curing the illness). Political use of technology to end a war and surgery employed to cure a patient are met with immense praise. But the important thing is not so much the cure, as remaining healthy and not falling victim to sickness. It is more important to create conditions in which war does not occur than to bring about the termination of fighting already taking place. Peace ought not to be thought of as the brief period of respite between wars. Instead it ought to be the perennial condition. My most profound wish is that we create a society and a world where this is true.

Since the result of both approaches is peace, it might seem to make little difference whether an end is put to warring or whether social conditions are devised in such a way that warfare cannot occur. But this interpretation is erroneous, because the efforts demanded to create such a society must be developed in a completely new dimension. Ways to peace have often consisted of methods for controlling war by mutually reducing arms preparedness on the level of diplomatic negotiations. But truly lasting peace cannot be brought about in this way. I am convinced that the only way to create lasting peace is to exert maximum efforts to build a high-level spiritual foundation by means of which to overcome the three human evils giving rise to war: greed, animosity, and ignorance. These evils—in modern terms we might call them ignorance on the levels of material possessions, social desires, and emotional impulses—are fundamental characteristics of life. They can never be eliminated. Moreover, on a certain plane, they perform vitally important roles in the maintenance of life.

Building a Communal Spiritual Foundation

When a person is controlled by these three evils, however, the greater their power, the more horrendous the effects they produce. Instead of being subjugated to greed, animosity, and ignorance, one must establish a spiritual support giving sufficient power to control and overcome them. The truth of this is evident from the practical actions of our daily lives. Everyone has desires, but if we allowed our desires to run away with us, society would crumble. For this reason we have rules that everyone must follow. In abiding by these rules, the individual is able to control his desires and impulses. The thing that supports the rules is an awareness of membership in a communal body—society itself. This sense of membership is equivalent to a recognition of the equality of other people and mutual respect for their humanity. In order to build lasting world peace, we must first establish a spiritual foundation of communality. Only when we have done this will we be able to compile rules by which to limit our actions; only then will these rules have enduring validity. Obviously much effort has gone into drawing up rules for action on the stage of international politics; but since no coherent foundation exists on which the rules may rest, mutual agreement about them is impossible. The rules themselves become impossible to apply or observe.

In my view, religion is the only thing that can succeed in building a communal spiritual foundation. Patently the religion that can achieve this must not foster divisions in terms of race or nation. On the contrary, it must possess philosophical universality to unite the peoples of the world. In short, it must be a world religion. It must not be a vulgar faith of escape from reality or of devotion to the fulfillment of the demands of greed, animosity, and ignorance; nor must it attempt to reject these aspects of life on a conceptual basis. Instead it must recognize and accept human life for what it is and, in this way, forge lofty ideals and a sense of mission. The religion that can build the foundation of spiritual communality that is needed today must be capable of sublimation to a higher level. The religion that fulfills these requirements, the true world religion based on a life philosophy strong enough to sublimate to a still higher plane, is the Buddhism of the Three Great Mystic Laws, the Buddhism of Nichiren Daishonin.

Accomplishing the Human Mission

I do not believe that the secure foundation of spiritual communality I have in mind can be achieved outside the realm of the Buddhism of Nichiren Daishonin. Furthermore, we must never forget that the creation of that foundation is our religious mission. But it is more than that. We are members of the society and of the world in which we live. Consequently, we would be wrong to feel that our duty is done if we merely fulfill our religious mission and leave our social missions to others. In the fullest meaning, our religious mission can only be realized when we carry out our duties as members of human society. In spite of differences in belief, peoples can join hands for the sake of peace and the preservation of the dignity of humanity if they act conscientiously and in good faith. If this kind of cooperation is possible, I am convinced that we ought to combine our strengths and advance together toward our goal.

For us to become entirely bound to our own religious ideas and to sacrifice our missions as human beings to them and stand by with folded arms as the earth hurtles to destruction would be doing little more than repeating the attitudes that led to the disastrous religious wars of the late medieval period of European history. When the opportunity arises, for the sake of establishing lasting peace and terminating warfare on this earth, Christians, Muslims, Buddhists, and members of all other religions must be willing to meet and talk together. I am fully prepared to join such a concerted effort.

Destroying the Myth of the Sanctity of the State

As I have said, the major role of religion is the creation of a foundation of spiritual communality. It follows that religion must produce spiritual bonds to link all peoples. In connection with this, I should like to make some remarks about the nature of the state, not in terms of religious doctrines, but in relation to self-evident ideas arising from the dignity of life.

As you know, it is primarily the states that wage wars. Some few exceptions to this assertion might be made—for instance, tribal battles in undeveloped societies or resistance movements in enemy-occupied lands—but such cases are rare. Generally speaking, war is a criminal act committed by states. If this is true, why are such acts permitted and often even enthusiastically supported? The answer is to be found in the controlling power of the erroneous myth that the state is worthy of the highest esteem. Under the influence of this mistaken idea, material wealth, human life, and the products of civilization are violently sacrificed to states. From ancient times, people of great minds have held that the dignity of life is the true essence of humanity. But in spite of all admonitions, today this dignity is being crushed for the sake of states. At last, however, the idea that the respect for life is the ultimate truth and the esteem of state no more than a myth willfully created by people in power is becoming widely recognized.

Defining the Idea of the Dignity of Life

Buddhism is clearly based on the idea of the dignity of life. It is the religion that strives to give this idea expression in actual experience. Because Buddhism is founded on this belief, it is the task of all of us as Buddhists to take the lead in destroying the myth of the sanctity of the state and to create a world in which the dignity of life is the controlling idea. In such a world, under no pretext would the state be entitled to threaten others or to demand sacrifice of innocent human lives. In fact, obligatory sacrifice of this kind must be forbidden. As concrete measures to achieve this end, nations must abandon military preparedness, give up the right of military conscription, and absolutely refrain from warfare of all kinds. As people of religious faith and as human beings, we must fulfill our mission and strive for these goals and ultimately for the establishment of lasting peace.

Although accumulations from the past have played their part, it is our generation that has created the current desperate situation. For us to pass it on unaltered to succeeding generations would be irresponsible in the extreme. To do so would indicate similar, and perhaps greater, irresponsibility on the part of leaders in all fields. We must not allow human history to end with our age; it is our duty to solve as many problems as we can before handing the task to our children and grandchildren.

I should like to refer to the passage "On the Selection of Time" from the *Gosho*: "Multitudes of streams form an ocean. Particles of dust accumulated to form Mount Sumeru. When Nichiren first pronounced faith in the Lotus Sutra, he was no more than a drop of water or a particle of dust in comparison with the population of Japan. If two, three, ten, or even billions of people recite and propagate the Lotus Sutra, they will indubitably form a Mount Sumeru of Enlightenment or make a great sea of Nirvana. Nowhere else should you seek the road to Buddhahood."

This section in Nichiren Daishonin's writings is famous as a restatement of the principle on which we base the worldwide propagation of our faith. In other words, this propagation begins with the drop of water and the grain of dust mentioned in this passage. But the grain contains the inherent power to grow into a mountain; and the drop, the power to become a great sea. As we now turn to a new stage in the propagation of our faith, each of us must be as a grain of dust or a drop of water. All human beings share a common foundation of humanity. Our movement is rooted in this foundation; and for that reason, each of us possesses the inherent power to grow into a mountain of Enlightenment and a sea of Nirvana. One person who is truly aware of the meaning of his own life will produce another person with similar awareness. These two will become three, and then ten, and so on. This is the one way to Buddhahood. Each of us must engrave this truth on his heart. And, transforming the obstacles in our path into growth rings of happiness, we must march boldly forth—like the true Bodhisattvas that we can become—toward the triumph of our faith. I trust that all of my companions in faith agree with me.

Creative Society

*Delivered at a General Meeting of the Kanto Young Men's
Division of Soka Gakkai, held in Tokyo, March 4, 1973.*

Let me begin my remarks by congratulating you on this fine meeting
of the Kanto Young Men's Division.

The Sho-Hondo has now been completed, and we have embarked
on the second chapter of our mission. In this phase, you will be
expected to fight bravely for the realization of our goal. In saying
this, I am not making a request of you. No request was made of me
years ago, when it came time for me to face my responsibility. I
simply accepted the torch from my predecessor, the former president
of Soka Gakkai, and I have continued to bear it high to the present
day. The achievement of our goal of *kosen-rufu* is not something
that you do because you have been requested to. You must do it
because you realize that you are Bodhisattvas of the Earth and because
you realize that striving to reach our goal is both your own mission
and also part of the activity of eternal, universal life.

People who lack self-determination and the willingness to practice
faith actively cannot carry out this task and cannot be courageous
warriors in the second chapter of our movement. They are not the
stalwart children of the true Soka Gakkai. In the *Gosho* it is said,
"Nichiren does not call cowards his disciples" (*Gosho Zenshu*, p.

29

1282). The second phase of our movement is a stage of intense religious practice for the sake of *kosen-rufu*. It demands people with deep, strong faith. We are now in a period in which cowards cannot do our work.

In the song of the Young Men's Division, you sing:

> Even if our companions may fall,
> We shall not forget our oath.
> We shall not forget our oath for the revolution.

I want you to remember that song and to sing it proudly as you become brave champions of the Law. Develop spontaneity and an active outlook in yourselves and join me in the forward drive for our revolution and for the further strengthening of our organization, which, though consisting of many different persons, is one in mind.

Perhaps there are still failings in our organization. I rely on you to take the lead in rectifying them. I have named this year the Year of Study and the Year of Youth, because I intend to leave our organization in its second phase entirely up to you. I shall expect you to take care of everything. In the future, when you see *kosen-rufu* achieved through your efforts, I want you to be able to smile with satisfaction.

A New Festival Spirit

I should like to say a few words next about the youth meeting, into which you have poured great energy. Festivals are part of ancient Japanese tradition. Even though, in modern times, their numbers have greatly decreased, I am sure that you remember how, when you were children, you experienced those exciting days, enlivened by the beating of the festival drums, so that you were unable to pay attention to school work because your minds were completely distracted by thoughts of the fun you would have later.

Of course, festivals are essentially religious in origin. Ritual *kagura* dancing and other artistic performances were intended to greet the divinity. The saké offered on such occasions was shared by gods and human beings. In addition, however, festivals and other annual ceremonies were closely related to productivity in the agricultural society. The entire population of a village came together to pray for bountiful harvests. By doing this, they strengthened the unity of the community. In brief, festivals were religious occasions that contributed to the building and improvement of regional society and provided amusement for farmers and their families after their hard work in the fields. At the festivals, everyone took part; everyone was equal as they drank, danced, talked, and made merry before the deity. The significance of the festival was to be found in the deepening of community ties among all the people of the region, who took part in the festivities on a footing of complete social equality. Festivals established a seasonal rhythm. Even though, with the passing of time, some were used to support the authority of the state and others degenerated into mere shows, we must remember that their original importance was the opportunity they gave for contacts among human beings living in a given region.

I believe that we ought to re-evaluate the traditional festival, especially since, at present, too many of the relations existing among members of our society are of an irritating, unpleasant nature. I place great importance on the festival, not as a religious observance, but as a chance for people to come together in a body. For this reason, I suggest that the Youth Division ought to devote attention and effort to turning their general district meetings into festivals.

But your festivals must not be noisy or boisterous. Instead, they should be based on study and filled with youthful desires for mutual development and refinement. By taking this approach, you will be able to give new life to an ancient festival tradition.

The three main pillars of Soka Gakkai in the second phase are Community, Youth, and Study. The development and improvement of the Youth Division meetings will enable you to carry out the Year of the Community, the keynote of the second decade, and to develop the three pillars of our organization in a unified way.

Our Ultimate Goals

I should now like to spend some time discussing the ultimate goals of our faith. These goals are expressed in the Japanese terms *issho jobutsu,* the attainment of Buddhahood during the lifetime of the individual human being, and *kosen-rufu,* the universal propagation of our faith.

Though the two aims are separate, since *issho jobutsu* is an ideal to be attained on the individual level and *kosen-rufu* a goal to be reached on the level of all of society, practical activities for the sake of both are a single entity and must be performed in harmony. The relation between the two goals may be compared to the movement of the earth, which rotates on its own axis while revolving around the sun. But I am sure that you understand this, as I have explained it many times in the past.

In addition to realizing that these two states are our goals, you must also fully understand the meanings of the terms if you are to know how to act for the sake of their fulfillment. If you lack such understanding, you will remain confined to the fruitless world of mere words. To provide you with the understanding you need, I shall now turn to specific definitions of these terms.

The ordinary modern man who has no knowledge of Buddhism believes that *jobutsu,* the attainment of Buddhahood, necessarily means dying. But such an interpretation arises from ignorance, and we need not concern ourselves with it now.

People with a slight knowledge of Buddhism, following the provisional teachings of Shakyamuni—that is, the teachings preceding the Lotus Sutra—believe that the attainment of Buddhahood means transformation into a special being inconceivable to the imagination of the ordinary mortal, a being endowed with mystical powers and an awe-inspiring, holy form. For example, it is said that the body of the Buddha is characterized by thirty-two traits and eighty distinguishing marks. But, upon learning that some of these traits are arms extending below the knees and froglike webbing between the toes and fingers, very few people today would want to possess them.

In the Amida Sutra, the most widely known of the provisional teachings, the Pure Land of Paradise for those who have attained Buddhahood is described as a world of happiness, unclouded by sorrow or suffering, but inhabited by men only. There are no women in that world—in other words, it is something like the meeting we are holding now. But this meeting is tolerable because it lasts for no more than two or three hours. I am certain that you would find eternity in a world without women—no matter how free from suffering it is—boring. I doubt that any of you would be eager to go there. I have selected extreme illustrations. But the point I want to make is this: people who regard the attainment of Buddhahood as something that is, to a lesser or greater extent, different from the actual world in which we live are likely to fall into delusions of this kind.

The attainment of Buddhahood, as taught by Nichiren Daishonin, is completely different. According to his teachings, all life exists in ten worlds, the paramount of which, the Buddha World, includes the nine others. Buddhahood is not something removed from the ordinary nine worlds of agony, joy, grief, anger, and so on. The nature of Buddhahood is an awareness of the real existence and basic nature of the greater life on which rest all the other nine worlds of life. To be unaware of this is to wander among the transmigrations of the lower nine worlds.

What is the nature of the greater life at the basis of all other life? Nichiren Daishonin identified it as Nam-myoho-renge-kyo and embodied it in the Gohonzon. A person who, by chanting the Daimoku to the Gohonzon, comes to realize that his own life is identical with the greater life identified as Nam-myoho-renge-kyo has already entered a state of Buddhahood. This state is called momentary Buddhahood (*setsuna jodo*), the state in which a human being attains Buddhahood while still in his mortal body (*sokushin jobutsu*). This teaching is the ultimate of the Buddhism of Nichiren Daishonin.

But, at this point, a different problem arises. If the person has already attained Buddhahood by chanting the Daimoku to the Gohonzon, he has reached his goal. There would seem to be no further need for conducting Gongyo devotionals or chanting the Daimoku. Unfortunately, however, it is not all that easy.

When the Gongyo and the Daimoku have ended, the life of the individual returns to the nine worlds of ordinary mortal living. It is in this sense that the Buddhahood attained through chanting the Daimoku is momentary. But persistent devotion in chanting and performing the Gongyo allows the profound life of the Buddhist World to become more firmly fixed in the life of the individual. A lifetime of regular devotion to these observances of religious faith enables the Buddha World to become as mighty and indomitable as a great tree grown from a tiny seedling.

Karma as a cause of happiness or unhappiness may be mutable or immutable. One of the things that helps make karma immutable is habitual practice. The way to make the Buddha World an immutable element in karma is to attain momentary Buddhahood regularly by the daily, unfailing practice of Gongyo and chanting of the Daimoku. When the immutable karma resulting from these practices becomes a profoundly and firmly established part of life, the individual dwells in a world of everlasting happiness transcending life and death.

At the summer training course last year we studied passages from the *Kanjin no Honzon Sho* (The true object of worship), where we saw that the theory of the ten worlds reveals life as constantly changing. Life never remains still. If one departs from the state attained by faith in the Gohonzon and by chanting the Daimoku, Buddhahood is lost at once. Even though the state has been built over years of devotion, by a person who has reached a high position of leadership in our organization, the minute that person is separated from the Gohonzon or ceases to chant the Daimoku, Buddhahood stops, as electric current ceases to flow when a switch is turned off.

But a lifetime of devoted religious practice makes the Buddha World the keynote of the individual's existence. A journey of as much as a thousand miles must begin with the first step. I believe that the theory of *issho jobutsu* can be stated in this fashion: accumulated instants of momentary Buddhahood attained by a mortal person firmly establish Buddhahood as the prevailing state of the life of the individual.

In the tenth chapter (*Hosshi-hon*) of the Lotus Sutra occurs this passage: "Let it be known that these people are free to be born wherever they wish." Nichiren Daishonin explains the text in this way: "This passage means that Buddhahood exists only in our benighted minds. When the life and death of the nine worlds attain their true, immutable nature, they are unrestrained in themselves. Chanting Nam-myoho-renge-kyo brings total freedom" *Gosho Zenshu*, p. 789). The words "our benighted minds" refer to the perplexities of the nine worlds. The Buddha nature—that is, the understanding of the true natures of all things—cannot exist outside the nine worlds. In other words, there is no enlightenment outside those worlds. "When the life and death of the nine worlds assume their true nature, they are unrestrained" means that, illuminated by the

Gohonzon, even the life of the nine worlds is capable of completely free, unrestricted activity.

But the life of the nine worlds is constantly changing. How can it be made completely free? Total freedom is possible, because this life is then firmly planted in the certainty of the Buddha World. It ceases to be controlled and tossed about by the nine worlds and becomes capable of controlling those worlds independently. When subjected to this control, the nine worlds themselves leave the shadow of delusion. Made manifest by the light of the Mystic Law, which is the law of the universe, the nine worlds glow with the brilliance of pure life. This great life exists within our mortal flesh. It is the purpose of chanting Nam-myoho-renge-kyo to uncover and reveal this life.

In all the many explanations of attainment of Buddahood found in the *Gosho* of Nichiren Daishonin, it is consistently said that the true meaning of such attainment is the opening of the palace of one's own life and the revelation of the ultimate truth enshrined there. This ultimate life is Buddhahood. Nichiren Daishonin does not teach that we ought to seek for ideal forms in some remote place. What we seek is to be found within ourselves, as we survive the realities of human existence. The realization that this is true constitutes the Buddha World. Failure to realize this and to look forward to a future blessed state is the condition of the ordinary, unenlightened mortal.

The ultimate goal of religious faith is the opening of the palaces of our lives to manifest our true selves and to develop our abilities to the maximum. But it is essential to realize that Buddhahood is not the outcome of having attained a certain, definite state. Always acting on the basis of the life of the Buddha World and freely controlling the life of the nine worlds, while living in our sorrow-filled modern society, is what I believe Buddhahood to be.

You are all young. You have many hopes and ideals for the future. By telling you that the Buddha World is to be found in you as you are now, I am not advising you to be resigned to the conditions of actuality as they are. We must learn that even ideals for the future must not be isolated from actuality. We must not turn our backs on reality. Keep your eyes on actuality, come sincerely to grips with the world, and work independently to reform things. Your hopes for the future are to be found in ceaseless reform and creative activity. By following this course, you will endow everything in yourselves with great value. I want you to remember this in your creative work of reforming society and our civilization and in your own individual battles for your human revolutions.

On a deeper level, this Buddhist principle is the basis for an eternally, constantly advancing revolution. I want you to remember always that maximum happiness and fulfillment are to be found in an independent life filled with continual challenge.

Many people—perhaps including a large number of you—tend to believe that happiness consists in having and realizing ideals. I suspect, however, that the true human condition is to feel emptiness and desperation when an ideal has been realized and there is nothing to take its place. My hope for you is that, remaining firmly faithful to the great principle of the Buddhist Law, you will live boldly and in a constant process of further development and growth.

The Buddha World as a Source of Creative Energy

Now I shall turn to the extremely difficult issue of defining the nature of the life of the Buddha World. The difficulty of solving this problem is increased because, whereas the worlds of Hell, Animality, Anger, and so on are easy to understand, since they occur directly in everyday life, the life of the Buddha World is different. Earlier I said that the life of the Buddha World is at the base of the lives of the other worlds, which it can control freely. At this point, I should like to say boldly that it is the fundamental source of energy for the creation of values.

In his *Sanju Hiden Sho* (Treatise on the threefold secret), Nichikan Shonin (1665–1726) says, "Kegon is the teaching of death; the Lotus is the teaching of life." On a deeper level, he says that even "this teaching is one of life in the hands of believers in the Lotus Sutra." In these remarks, he gives ultimate expression to the truth that the Lotus Sutra is a philosophy that invigorates all beings. The basic meaning of Buddhism is to make creative use of everything, one's own life and the lives of others as well. One of the three meanings of the word *myo* (mystic) given by Nichiren Daishonin in his *Hokekyo Daimoku Sho* (Treatise on the Daimoku of the Lotus Sutra; *Gosho Zenshu*, p. 940) is to revive. This means that, because of its vigorous creative power, the Mystic Law is able to revive human beings.

Tsunesaburo Makiguchi, the first president of Soka Gakkai, investigated many different philosophies before he turned to the Buddhism of Nichiren Daishonin. From its inception, Soka Gakkai has been devoted to inspiring the creation of values in the individual. And this is the ultimate teaching of Nichiren Daishonin. There are many other ways of expressing it, but I think the thing most needed in our age, when the pressure of a scientifically-oriented civilization threatens to crush humanity, is best described as "creative power."

In his book *Ningen o Kaeru* (Changing humanity), Akio Moribe, a prominent Japanese thinker, says, "It may be that today Japan is experiencing a psychological isolation in which accumulating creative powers are being suppressed within the individual. These powers threaten to give rise to a tremendous explosion, which will not take the form of a political or military revolution of the kind seen in some of the underdeveloped nations. Instead it will be a human revolution in which the masses give creative expression to their talents. When this takes place, a people of a larger scale, a people who no longer tend to copy others, will emerge. The true reason for living and the true value of human life are not the desire for ease and security—Nietzsche called this kind of thing the spirit of the camel—but creativity and a constant challenge of the unknown."

I wish to call your attention to Moribe's comment that, in Japan today, people are striving for a human revolution in which they can give expression to their talents. This attitude may seem to be no more than a minority opinion, but I am convinced that all people of sensitivity share it, even though they may not give it oral expression. Furthermore, adopting the policy represented by this attitude is the only way to revive our society. In the final analysis, the philosophy of the Mystic Law—in more concrete terms, the Dai-Gohonzon—is the one thing that points clearly to such a revival.

A Creative Society

If we assume that the goal of religious faith for the individual is a constant process of value-creating, how shall we describe the society that we are striving to build—that is, the society of *kosen-rufu*? In the past, I have described it in various ways; and, in the future, I shall continue to try to elucidate its nature from many angles. But, in brief, I think I can call it a creative society. It will be a society in which all human beings can live in a truly human fashion, in which everyone is constantly improving himself. We are striving, not for an insipid, dry, formalized society, but for one with limitless possibilities for creative development. I am convinced that this is the true image of the society of *kosen-rufu*.

In past ages, people have imagined utopias of the future and have worked toward their realization. There are people now who are willing to sacrifice the present for the sake of a glowing future world. Although dreaming of utopias has probably helped the oppressed masses, the ideal society advocated by Buddhism is not of that kind. Furthermore, Buddhist teachings make it clear that a standardized utopia is not the ideal that mankind pursues. In fact, in standardized societies, oppression of the people becomes deep and strong. Our age symbolizes the suffering of people in such a society. The hippies, or flower children, who, having abandoned everything offered them by our overcontrolled society and expressed their longing for the primitive life, were an accusation against the excess standardization of our civilization. The important thing is for each person to play a meaningful role and to make full use of his creative powers. In summary, attainment of Buddhahood for the individual is evoking one's inherent Buddha World and making it a rich, unfailing source of creative energy for a brighter society. Developing this energy within the individual and manifesting it in society are the purposes of the practical activities of Soka Gakkai.

One of our basic principles is the concept of the indivisibility of man and his environment (*esho-funi*). Our drive for *kosen-rufu,* the universal propagation of our faith, is directed toward the creation of an environment in which each person can give maximum play to his creative forces. *Kosen-rufu* is our way of directing all these creative forces outward to society. The process of attaining Buddhahood for the individual and of carrying our faith to all people is an unending revolution on the individual, social, and cultural levels. It requires

CREATIVE SOCIETY · *39*

constant sustenance from the Mystic Law, the original source of life.

With this truth in mind, I hope that all of you will continue daily Buddhist training and go on with your work for Soka Gakkai and the attainment of *kosen-rufu*. The *Gosho* says, "Life has an end. Yet you should not be grudging with it. Your ultimate objective should be the Buddha land" (*Gosho Zenshu*, p. 955). This expresses our view of humanity. I want you to keep this golden teaching always in mind as you continue your courageous struggle with ever-increasing strength and flexibility.

Torchbearers of
the Philosophy of Life

*Delivered at the Fourteenth General Meeting of the Students
Division of Soka Gakkai, held in Tokyo, March 11, 1973.*

~~~

Intellectual Systems for the Sake of Mankind

I should like to say a few words about the attitude I think you ought
to take to your studies. I am sure that all of you are busy with your
school work. You must be. We do not want members of the Student
Division to fail courses and repeat years in school. After all, your
whole family, society in general, and the age in which we live are
waiting for you to graduate and take an active part in the front rank
of our activities. You must cherish the materials you study: they are
a rich heritage of the devoted labor of many learned men, subtly
woven into a refined intellectual system. Nonetheless, you must realize
that, no matter how highly systematized, all of this subject matter
has been extracted by human reason from the activities of the throbbing cosmos and universal life. Consequently, learning must be used
to elucidate the workings of all of life and society and for the sake of
increasing human happiness. Even though our intellectual knowledge
is not the same thing as the activity of the universal life, we will see
that our learning is great and discover that we can use it as energy for

the further development of life if we view it in the light of Buddhist philosophy.

You must not merely accept the knowledge placed at your disposal. You must assimilate it; you must become an incarnation of the intellectual systems with which you come into contact. If you fail to do this, you will master a learning of death, instead of a learning of blazing life. An important question now arises: How is it possible to make oneself the kind of person who is an incarnation of learning? Enabling you to do this is one of the most important contributions of Buddhism. Unless you sincerely strive to build your personality along these lines, you will be unworthy to be a true member of the Students Division, and you will never be the kind of intellectual who uses his learning and culture for the sake of humanity.

True Learning Found among the People

If I may digress for a moment, I should like to share with you something I heard the other day. A recent radio broadcast described the experiences of a country doctor, who said that he had originally planned to work in a research institute, but that family conditions had forced him to become a country doctor—a title that he deeply resented at first. Later, however, as he learned that coming into direct contact with human beings is a highly valuable experience, he came to consider "country doctor" a term of respect and affection. He went on to say, "Human beings must be openhearted and frank; they must not be too concerned with outward appearances. I want to be a doctor who enjoys the affection and trust of his patients and who is worthy of that trust in all things.

"It is no longer possible for me to work as a doctor in a big hospital, where patients are seen only during office hours and dismissed from the mind until their next visits. Under such circumstances, doctors go home at the end of the day. I am with my patients all of the time. My family shares the sorrows and joys of my patients. Such experiences give me a reason for living. A doctor can only perform his role as he should when he knows his patients and their families thoroughly.

"To medical students who come to me for advice about the future, I say that they must either enter a research institute and devote themselves to intense study or become a country doctor. This is the best way for a doctor to live and work.

"Because of the nature of my work, I am often present at time of death. Recently I have been struck by the different ways in which people approach the end. Some suffer and resist to the last. Some are unaware that death is near. The use of sophisticated antibiotics in modern medicine sometimes prolongs life beyond the limits that were possible in the past; and the brain is destroyed first, with the outcome that the ill person never realizes he is dying. Other people, who feel that they have done their life's work well, depart peacefully. I have come to see that the way a person meets his final moments vividly tells whether that person has lived a fulfilled life. Realizing this, I want to exert my best efforts and all of my strength throughout my lifetime."

This man's experiences as a country doctor, proud of his calling and living with and learning from his patients, show me that the finest kind of human life and the highest learning are to be found among the ordinary people. Each of you will probably follow a different course in your future life. But, no matter what course you take, and no matter what high position of leadership you attain, I want you always to consider yourselves one with the masses of ordinary people. I hope you will walk hand in hand with the old and the unhappy along the path leading you to become what I would like to call authorities in the sincere and compassionate study of humankind.

Remember, even if they become famous, receive all manner of decorations and awards, and win the blessings of power and wealth, people whose lives have been hollow and false must face misery at the end. Whatever the outward appearances, the person who is true to his principles throughout his life is certain to be victorious and raise a song of triumph when the final hour comes.

I have heard that, at the instant of death, all the events of a person's life suddenly flash through his mind. If these fleeting images cloud the heart of one person with tears of regret, they enable another to meet death with the joy of satisfaction. Such a person will have been true to the best goals of human beings. His death is a victory; and this victory proves that, while alive, he went boldly forward and that his actions made a real contribution to the world and to the universe.

Altruism Means Self-perfection

What is the source of the tide of joy flooding the person who lives a victorious life and whose death is also a victory? According to the French philosopher Henri Bergson, joy is creation—more specifically, the creation of life. The gist of his book *L'énergie spirituelle* (Mind Energy), in which he gives a splendid description of the relation between joy and creativity, is that the more creative a life, the stronger the joy that fills it. This joy can grow to the extent at which it gives rise to a great storm of emotions.

If creation means the bringing into being of something that has not existed before, the creation of life means producing new life. This act expands the circumstances of the self and of others and enriches total universal life.

The universe in which we live is the source from which life is born and bred. It has given life to all the entities on our planet. The life that we enjoy at this moment is a treasure, resulting from the unlimited creative action that is in itself the great universal life. Human beings participate in the greater creative act. For instance, scholars discover truths and from them devise intellectual systems. Artists create things of beauty. Both kinds of work are joy-giving participation in the greater creative action of the universe.

In the same book, Bergson comments that, if victory in any and all fields is creative activity, the reason for human existence is the creativity in which any and all human beings participate, not just the scholar and the artist. This is creation of the self by the self, the making of much from little, the extraction of something from nothing, and the continual enriching of the world. The human personality grows and develops as an outcome of this kind of effort.

Bergson mentions a creative act in which all human beings can participate: the creation of the self by the self. Our Buddhist goal is the constant clearing of the road to revolution and perfection of the self. Buddhism finds the way to growth for human beings in the life of the

masses of ordinary people. In other words, from the Buddhist standpoint, creation of the self by the self means sharing the sorrows and
joys of others and striving to strengthen the life powers of those
around the self. Altruistic actions are the way to self-perfection.
Buddhism clearly reveals the overflowing source of power for the
life-creating act that we call altruism.

In *Ongi Kuden,* it is said that happiness means sharing joy with
others (*Gosho Zenshu,* p. 761). True joy is evoking happiness while
engaging in creative activity with other people. Life-creation will
become possible for all of you when you decide to—and actually
begin to—put all you have learned to use for the sake of the masses of
ordinary people. Naturally, then, you should study each field of
learning in which you engage in such a way as to apply your knowledge for the sake of general happiness. In addition, I hope that you
will accept as your mission a lifetime of effort at discovering ways to
help others summon from the depths of their beings and show to all
the strength and joy of life.

Courageous Faith

Last year while I was in France, a young man told me the interesting history of a newspaper called *Le Canard Enchaîné*. This name
—which means literally the chained duck—is defined as slang
for a third-rate newspaper but I was told that it refers to a duck
that, though quacking in complaint all the time, is powerless
because it is in chains. *Le Canard Enchaîné* has a circulation of five
hundred thousand. Because of the courageous policy it has followed
since its inception, this paper has played a vital historical role and
continues to be important in modern society as a kind of conscience
for Europe. It will tolerate no falsehood but insists on publishing
only the truth. This characteristic gives considerable authority to
even its shortest articles.

The banner of *Le Canard Enchaîné* bears the following motto:
"La liberté de la presse ne s'use que quand on ne s'en sert"
(freedom of the press is useless unless people make avail of it). The
purchasers and readers of the paper relish taking avail of freedom

of the press. Many of them are proud to be able to cite an early date from which they began reading *Le Canard Enchaîné*. The passion for freedom persists to the present; continuing to be largely anti-government in tone today, the paper resists all attempts to crush it. Among the anonymous contributors to the newspaper are people from the central organs of the government. Sometimes the paper prints items on government and business affairs that have not been officially released. Once the information has appeared in *Le Canard Enchaîné*, it is too late for officials or businessmen to do anything about the leakage. Though it calls itself by the pejorative term *Le Canard Enchaîné*, this paper is outstanding because it gives the people the truth; and it is very proud of its role. It accepts no advertising but relies entirely on subscriptions for financial support.

The fascinating and moving history of this newspaper reminds me of the circumstances in which the members of the Soka Gakkai Students Division live. Around us there may be scorn and even oppression, but your greatest significance as human beings and as young people is to go on living in such a way as to proclaim the truth of the philosophy of life and to maintain faith in all we do. This is the characteristic trait of the young, faithful Buddhist believer.

The struggle to maintain faith is the great battle of the young; winning that struggle is the only way you will be able to build a new century. A famous passage in the *Kaimoku Sho* (The opening of the eyes) says, "This I will state. Let the gods forsake me. Let all persecutions assail me. Still I will give my life for the sake of the Law—whatever persecutions I might encounter, so long as men of wisdom do not prove my teachings to be false, I will never accept the practices of the other sects. All other troubles are no more to me than dust before the wind" (*Gosho Zenshu*, p. 232). This passage reveals the great mission entrusted to you young people.

A thorny path lies ahead of us. I may fall by the wayside, but tens of thousands of you will take up the torch of the philosophy of life and continue the struggle. If I do not entrust you with this mission, my life is meaningless. Here, today, I give the future of Soka Gakkai and the attainment of *kosen-rufu* into your hands.

Education Centered on Faith

As I have often explained, I want all of you to expand the range of your education to the maximum. According to *Ongi Kuden,* "The ninth chapter of *Fahuawenju* says, 'Believing without doubt is faith; seeing clearly is understanding' " (*Gosho Zenshu,* p. 725). This means, of course, that faith is belief, without doubt, in the Gohonzon. But it goes further, to tell us that understanding is seeing clearly the principles of the Gohonzon, the philosophy of life, and the principles and power of the Law. It is for the sake of such understanding that education is essential.

Another passage in *Ongi Kuden* adds: "The sixth chapter of *Fahuawenju* says, 'People of moderate abilities first destroy all doubt and enter the way of Mahayana when they hear the Buddha explaining parables. This is called faith. Going further, they actually practice the teachings of Mahayana. This is called understanding' " (*Gosho Zenshu,* p. 725). To do away with doubt and recognize correctly the basic meaning of the Mystic Law, faith is necessary. But to put the teachings of the Mystic Law into actual practice, understanding is required. In brief, this passage teaches that true Buddhist practice demands study centered on faith.

I believe that a desire to improve is sufficiently characteristic of young people as to be virtually synonymous with youth. In a book entitled *Gakumon no Susume* (Encouragement of learning), the noted Japanese educator Yukichi Fukuzawa (1835–1901) said, "No one is born noble or base. No one is born poor or rich. Only people who have learned things through devoted study become noble and rich. Those who fail to do this become poor and base." Fukuzawa's interpretation can be applied to our study and faith. You are devoted to Buddhism, the greatest philosophy in the world. If you truly master its learning, you will be more than rich and noble; you will become great and worthy of maximum respect.

Your must delve deeply into Buddhism, but I further want you to study avidly as many other fields as possible. Unless you do this, people will not respect you, and you will be unable to grow into powerful leaders. In recent history, science has taken maximum precedence, and politics have overshadowed philosophy. This is the cause of the lamentable spiritual breakdown and inhumanity of our society. The only solution is for philosophy to assume the lead over both science and politics. Our own salvation is to imbue philosophy with the strength to do this.

I shall conclude by expressing my deep-felt wishes for your good health and for courage in our struggle and by offering the following passage from the *Gosho*: "It is my wish that my disciples become the offspring of the lion king and never be ridiculed by a pack of foxes" (*Gosho Zenshu*, p. 158).

On Being Creative

Delivered at the Third Entrance Ceremony of Soka University, held in Hachioji, Tokyo, April 9, 1973.

This university belongs to all of you. It must not be an ivory tower, isolated from society. Instead, it must be a tower of hope with boundless possibilities for the unfolding of a new era in history. I want you to adopt this attitude toward the university and to bear in mind always the need to devote thought and effort to doing whatever you can for the happiness of humanity.

Today I should like to examine the influence the university has exerted on society from the historical viewpoint. I do not intend to delve into an abstruse, abstract theory of the role of the university. I am not qualified to make such a talk, nor is there any need for one. I intend only to give a few examples of the ways in which the university—or, on the broader scale, learning in general—has been a compelling force in history.

Emergence of the University in the West

All of you are familiar with the cultural awakening that took place in the fourteenth and fifteenth centuries in Europe that is called the

48

Renaissance. This was a time when the long-dormant spirit of humanism awakened to inspire in painting, sculpture, literature, and the other arts a long series of works glorifying man. Europe was then greeting a new dawn. I am certain that I am not the only person who senses a crystallization of human joy in the artistic creations of the Renaissance.

This important epoch in European history was no mere accidental revolution in art and literature. The way had been prepared by a quickening that arose from the depths of the European culture. This quickening took the form of a revival of learning during the twelfth century, which, though less well known, was actually just as important as the Renaissance of the fourteenth and fifteenth centuries. Historians sensitive to its value call this movement the Renaissance of the Twelfth Century. It was during this period that the European-style university came into being.

In the Middle Ages, higher education was limited to the seven so-called liberal arts—Latin grammar, rhetoric, logic, arithmetic, astronomy, geometry, and music—which were considered necessary to the reading of the Bible for an understanding of God's natural laws and for the management of common law to support regal authority. Arithmetic and astronomy were needed for calculating church history, and music for church rituals. The other branches of learning were applied in law and politics.

In about the twelfth century, to these studies were added—especially in Spain and Italy—mathematics, philosophy, geography, and law, all of which were imported from the Islamic world. Among these imports were things that had been known to the ancient Greeks and Romans but that had been forgotten in medieval Europe. Other elements had been brought by Muslims and Italian merchants from India and the East. With the acquisition of this heritage of ancient—though new to Europe—learning, there took place an irrepressible drive to absorb still more, newer knowledge and to accumulate and systematize it.

Young people in search of knowledge broke from the bonds of the monastic schools and sought new repositories of learning. It might be said that the educational profession arose in response to their demands, with the formation in Paris and Bologna of organized bodies of teachers and students. This formation constituted the emergence of the European university.

The word "university" derives from the Latin *universitas,* one of the meanings of which is a society or guild, or a number of people in a group. In other words, the university is basically a united group of teachers and students, not necessarily buildings or an educational system. It began with connections among people. The university at Paris originated largely for research and reorganization of theology. The university at Bologna concentrated on law. Both institutions were sources of revised thought on traditional ecclesiasticism and were the scenes of increased modern, rational learning and knowledge, which was to be applied in rules governing the new kind of commercial transactions developing at the time.

The Need for a Profound Philosophical Heritage

The spiritual core of the quest for learning was humanism. I believe that the growth of the bourgeoisie and the increased vigor of commerce made possible the development of an intellectual class outside the framework of the aristocracy and topped by the university. This class created the ripe opportunity for the Renaissance. A steady examination of the human condition, combined with a desire for learning in search of truth, gradually stimulated a revival of the arts, which became a eulogy to man. The Renaissance would have been unable to alter the course of history if it had been merely a shallow movement in literature and the arts. It was epoch-making because it rested on human self-awareness, freed from the restraints of the older society and endorsed by profound scholarly assurance.

The work of Leonardo da Vinci reveals the effect of the new learning. The perspective he employs in his paintings is based on knowledge of geometry, and the study of anatomy and actual dissections gave him information for his delicate drawings of human beings and animals.

Reflecting on the influence of the twelfth century, we can see that the accumulation of learning and knowledge since that time made possible the brilliant works that we attribute to the Renaissance. The point I want to make is this: The elements that have the power to influence history result from human thought and the tide of life. To flourish, grow, and have wide effect, a civilization requires a profound philosophical heritage at its base. Without such a heritage, a civilization cannot produce geniuses. And, even if it were able to produce them, the geniuses would find no place to manifest their talents. Furthermore, a social structure built on the ethic of power alone cannot influence human life deeply or leave a brilliant historical record.

People often tend to grasp only the glorious, superficial products of history. They copy styles, respect established traditions, and attempt to use them as basic principles of action, while ignoring the deeper causes that made possible the achievement of such glories. I believe that the failure to look more deeply into historical phenomena explains the failure of past attempts at reformation. Action that exists for nothing but the attainment of the immediate goal must ultimately be idle and futile.

The University as a Basic Current of Civilization

The university is a repository of intellectual heritage. The quality and significance of the research and education carried out there can determine the fate of a nation, a society, or an entire civilization. Where learning flourishes, the people flourish. The ancient civilizations demonstrate the truth of these statements. At its peak, the world of Islam had many centers of learning, as did India in the heyday of Buddhism. The ancient Indian Buddhist university of Nalanda, which had an area of tens of square kilometers, dates back more than twelve hundred years. It reached its zenith between the fifth and seventh centuries. Larger in scale than most modern universities and much older than the universities of Europe, Nalanda was a spiritual center for both India and the whole Orient. Many Chinese students are known to have gone there to study. Uncovering several study rooms and dormitory rooms, recent excavations made it clear that, at one time, Nalanda could have accommodated as many as ten thousand students. The Chinese priest Hsuan Tsang (600–664), who visited Nalanda, recorded his impressions in the *Ta T'ang Hsi Yu Chi* (Great

T'ang record of western countries). Excavations have unexpectedly verified the material in this book. Nalanda developed and propagated the principles of Mahayana Buddhism for centuries, until it was finally destroyed by invading Muslims.

It is possible to trace the current of influence of this university in the great flow of Buddhist teachings from India to China and then to Japan. Recalling the thousands of Buddhist priests who once earnestly discussed Buddhism, debated important points, and then took what they had learned back to their home countries for practical application, I am convinced that Nalanda must indeed have been a fountainhead of Oriental spiritual culture worthy of the respect of the whole world. I want all of you to believe that, by deepening and expanding the profound aspects of your learning, you too can become part of such a great cultural fountainhead. Be firm in your conviction that the deep currents of the sea are stronger and more precious than the decorative swirlings of surface waters.

Ancient Seats of Learning Based on Humanism

Respect for humanity must be the basis of all institutions of learning. I have already shown that humanism was the foundation of the universities of the Renaissance, but something similar can also be said of more ancient institutions of learning that cannot accurately be described as universities in the modern sense. Plato's Akademeia in the grove of Akadomos is a case in point. In the Athens of his time, the Sophists acquired considerable influence through their rhetoric and their professional, purely pragmatic approach to teaching—they imparted to students only such knowledge as was needed to get ahead in the world. Socrates, who advocated the search for truth as the ideal, opposed the Sophists. Confronting the sunset of the Grecian world, he attempted to reform Athens on the basis of a philosophy devoted to understanding the truth about human nature. For this reason, he took a stand against philosophers who taught only pragmatism and reliance on systems. Furthermore, he devoted himself to a learning that would remain valid eternally. For Socrates, the market, the street corner, the banquet, or any of the places where human beings gathered were proper places for transmitting his beliefs to young people and combating what he considered to be corrupt teaching practices. He conducted true dialogues and training in what amounted to a university without school buildings.

Inheriting the basic beliefs of Socrates, Plato established his Akademeia. Though he employed a definite locale, the kind of education he conducted there was of the humanistic kind that Socrates had favored. In Plato's day, it was customary in Athens to take mealtime as an opportunity for discussing all kinds of affairs. Plato followed this practice in teaching. In addition, he conducted lively symposiums on philosophical and humanistic subjects during strolls with his students.

The attitude reflected in dialogues between students and teachers can be seen in the search for truth conducted by Plato and his followers. It was the pride of the Akademeia that teacher and student together strove to attain one truth. Though entrance requirements were strict, and even though it included certain aristocratic elements, the institution rested on a foundation of faith in freedom and a desire to reform society through philosophy. Men and women studied together, and the school was vigilant against any attempts by secular authority to encroach on its academic freedom. Established in about four hundred B.C. and in operation until it was finally closed by a Roman emperor, for approximately nine centuries, the Akademeia was a major force in Western spiritual education and, through its methods of dialogue and cooperative search for truth, had a great influence on history.

The teaching method of Shakyamuni, the first historical Buddha, is a still older example of the thorough application of the dialogue. Shakyamuni employed questions and answers to impart to others the content of his enlightenment about the fundamental laws governing mankind and the entire universe. Almost all of the sutras are written in a dialogue form in which Shakyamuni comes into direct contact with human suffering and reveals the truth about his own enlightenment. In later times, vast amounts of Buddhist doctrinal material were compiled, but it must be borne in mind always that human contact leading to refinement of the moral character and the search for truth lies at the basis of it all.

The Renaissance plea for a return to the learning of Greece reveals something about the great influence of Plato's Akademeia. In a similar manner, the humanistic teachings of Shakyamuni have left an imprint on virtually all of Oriental history. I believe that the basic power to exert such an influence is found in one primary aim: to base all efforts in the name of the search for truth on humanity and to elucidate basic human nature so as to inspire moral refinement. Any learning or search for truth that does not have humanistic roots is doomed to be abstract, futile, shallow, and fruitless.

At present the world stands in danger of losing sight of the basic elements of human nature. I hope that all of you will take pride in the role of education as guide and pioneer on the road of historical progress and that you will walk the way of learning and the search for truth in the hope of bringing about a truly humanistic reform of society.

Increased Spiritual Freedom

Having made these remarks about the nature of the university, I should like to make the following request of you: strive to be creative. The name of this institution—Soka University—means a university for the creation of values. This in turn means that the basic aim of our university is the creation of the wholesome values needed by society. Such values must be either offered to or returned to society. Consequently, each student here must cultivate his creative abilities in the effort to make contributions to a richer future.

A mere bright idea is not necessarily creative. But the production of even bright ideas requires a fairly firm foundation of basic knowledge. Creative work in the fields of scholarship and learning is much more demanding. It is like a mountain pinnacle: it cannot exist without a broad, deep, firm foundation.

The university is the suitable place for the evolution of such a foundation. Unfortunately, though most universities today are blessed with conditions enabling them to do so, they generally overlook the need to direct learning toward the ultimate goal of creative activity. They are not places where people are trained to have creative personalities. I want Soka University to be different. I want it to become an institution brimming with creative vitality, and I want it to introduce fresh air into society.

The spiritual soil must be rich for the cultivation of creativity. This means that spiritual freedom is essential. Independent thought and creative work are impossible under conditions of oppression or distortion. Inexhaustible creative thinking is possible only when the spirit is free to roam over a wide field.

But spiritual freedom does not mean spiritual license. True development can take place only in the presence of both expansive liberty and high-level self-discipline. Spiritual freedom does not give one the right to think and act completely as one wishes. My interpretation of true spiritual freedom is the opportunity to grow by means of dialogue to an expanded field of vision and ultimately to an elevated insight in the nature of things. Both in Plato's Akademeia and in the ancient Buddhist university at Nalanda, there was freedom. But there was also stern confrontation with the truth. There was creative thought. And, precisely for these reasons, the Akademeia and Nalanda evolved rich spiritual heritages.

In short, to increase spiritual freedom, strict training is required. Both Oxford and Cambridge are private universities where much has been achieved in the field of learning and where many famous and important scholars have been trained. In both schools, a strict educational system is followed now as in the Middle Ages. But, in both cases, students are given a high degree of freedom to expand spiritually and to prepare themselves to make their contributions to society.

What is the source of the energy that enables man to increase his spiritual freedom and broaden his range of activities? In asking this question, I inevitably return to the more fundamental issue of the true nature of man and to the philosophy that brings forth, develops, and elevates latent human talents.

Please remember that all the educational institutions I have mentioned had a backbone of humanistic educational philosophy. Free development of learning and rich cultural flowerings arise from a direct contemplation of and an attempt to develop life and humanity. I am convinced that this is the key to creativity. I hope Soka University will always aim for the perfection of humanistic learning and for high scholastic achievement. I want all of you to advance in your studies and in the search for truth, so that you will be able to become sources of power in a great reformation of society. I propose that you determine to become creative human beings worthy of the name of Soka (Value-creating) University. If this kind of determination can elevate its already fine tradition, I am convinced that Soka University can become an important, refreshing element in the modern world of Japanese university education, which is now in a state of chaos.

Pride and Devotion

To change the subject slightly, last year I made a fruitful trip to England, where I shared enthusiastic discussions with the famous historian Arnold J. Toynbee on a wide range of topics, including history, philosophy, art, science, and education. At our first meeting, I was suprised by the way Mr. Toynbee and his wife greeted me. He said, "I am grateful that you have visited my alma mater, Oxford." And she said, "I am grateful that you have visited my alma mater, Cambridge." It is true that I went to England at the invitations of these two universities. But I had not expected to hear such initial words from Mr. and Mrs. Toynbee. Their greetings, however, showed me how much pride and devotion they felt in Oxford and Cambridge.

In Japan, national universities are frequently more prestigious than private ones; but in the United States and Europe, the opposite is often the case, as is illustrated by Oxford, Cambridge, and Harvard, all of which are private institutions. The graduates of such schools are usually very proud of and devoted to their alma maters. When they succeed in their careers, they contribute sizable sums to their universities, which are thereby enabled to improve facilities and services. Please do not worry; I am not saying that you must hurry to become famous so that you can make contributions to Soka University.

Even though as institutions of learning they have a public role to play, private universities are unrelated to national authority. Fundamentally independent, they may seek to train people and make educational achievements for the sake of the realization of their own articles of faith. Because they are autonomous, private universities are the product of the action of all the people who operate them and study in them. In this sense, they differ from government or state public schools. The very concept of the university began with private institutions. The university emerged spontaneously and was not created to be the servant of governmental needs.

I want all of you to play your parts in the creation and perfection of Soka University. Do not think of your education here as the mere accumulation of learning. Do not regard the university as a passport to a good job. As long as you are here, engage in lively dialogues with your teachers and help evolve a university that is vibrant and warm. You have much to do in this creative building process, since Soka University is new and its traditions and teaching styles are not yet firmly established. I shall be observing what you do and shall always be ready to offer whatever assistance I can.

And when you have left Soka University, continue to think of your alma mater with pride. Watch over it and be willing to offer it enthusiastic support. Perhaps I am a little premature in talking about graduation to a newly matriculating class, but I want you to understand my heartfelt wish that you always and in all places be proud of your school. Have the kind of feeling Mr. and Mrs. Toynbee displayed when they thanked me for visiting their alma maters.

This will be a university that you have all built yourselves. You ought to be proud of it and to be grateful to people for admiring it. If you become this kind of a person, nothing could make me, as the founder of Soka University, happier.

A New Restoration

In a sense, modern civilization has reached a turning point. Can humanity survive? This is the ominous question facing us. The threat of armaments to peace and a mistaken faith in progress seem to be propelling mankind forward in a march to death. What should we do—what can we do—to enable mankind to survive? Englightened scholars are now debating this issue assiduously.

I cry out that what we need in such a time is another true restoration of humanity. I do not mean that human beings are the center of the universe or in any way omnipotent. The restoration I have in mind must enable human beings to live in harmony with all of our other fellow living creatures. People must cease being the servants of machines and must once again be the servants of human beings. The restoration I have in mind would help us find a way to achieve this.

It must be a neo-renaissance, requiring concurrent, immediate renaissances in the fields of philosophy and learning. Without doubt, if human beings devote attention to a new desire for learning and take a far-sighted view of their condition, a new philosophy enabling man to survive will be forthcoming. Such a philosophy will not only fulfill the negative role of permitting survival but will also sponsor the building of a new civilization that can be a eulogy to humanity. Soka University will have fulfilled its purpose if it can contribute substantially to the attainment of this goal.

The task is not an easy one. Definite conclusions cannot be reached in a short time. Clearly, the creation of this new civilization demands persevering, repeated, strict debates and determination over a long time. But, if all the people associated with Soka University now and all those who will be associated with it in the future—who will no doubt share our thoughts on this point—will cooperate in a single-minded effort, our goal can be achieved. Live a rich, full student life, not only as representatives of this institution but also as its honored founders and creators. Let your experiences here serve as a spring-board to a richer life after graduation.

From now on, education will be my major work, for I want to lay firm foundations in this field for the three decades following my death. Leading the people of the twenty-first century to peace and happiness is my sole concern. Because I feel this way, I request that you accept responsibility for the future of mankind. From the bottom of my heart, I request the members of our faculty to do all within their power to make fine human beings of our students. I shall conclude my remarks by expressing my hope for and pride in the part that Soka University will play in the future of mankind.

Scholastic Philosophy
and Modern Civilization

*Delivered at the Second Takiyama Festival of Soka
University, held in Hachioji, Tokyo, July 13, 1973.*

In the remarks I delivered concerning the origin of Soka University
at the opening ceremonies on April 9, I touched on the spirit of the
Renaissance, from which modern civilization grew. I explained how
the startling flowering of the Renaissance was not the result of sudden
mutation, but was the outcome of the inevitable tide of the times and
of constant, inconspicuous, upward human strivings over a long preceding period. Further, I said that the buds from which this flowering
developed had already started growing in the winter of the Middle
Ages, or the Dark Ages, as they are often called.

At present, the trees around this university are gleaming with new
green leaves. The buds from which those leaves grew did not suddenly
develop in the springtime. Preparations for them were steadily being
made during the severe cold of winter. The true origin of budding
takes place in the winter, but the trees put forth their misty, fresh
greenery only in the spring. Something very similar can be said about
human life. The inconspicuous daily efforts all of us are making now,
during the early period of the growth of this university, as well as our
many trials and errors, are preparations for a brilliant future flowering
of world culture.

Scholastic philosophy is often thought of as verdureless. Today, I should like to shed some light on that philosophy, in order to show that it, too, represents a period in which a persistent process of budding was taking place for the sake of the civilization of the succeeding age. I want to do this, because a sure understanding of the facts of the vivid transitions in the history of the past is the key to the history of the future.

Birth and Background of Scholastic Philosophy

Scholasticism is a general term for the philosophy that flourished in Europe during the twelfth and thirteenth centuries. The word *schola*, which refers to the schools attached to the monasteries of the time, is, as you all know, the source of the English word *school*. Often considered no more than an official philosophy, Scholasticism is sometimes called the handmaiden of theology, because it advocated the authority of Christian doctrines. Undeniably, philosophers and thinkers known by the name "Scholastics" strove to justify faith in the teachings of the Bible.

For this reason, European medieval philosophy in general, including Scholasticism, has come to be regarded as a dark valley between the brilliant peaks of Greece and Rome and the equally brilliant mountain range of the Renaissance. This interpretation has been advanced by modern rationalist philosophers, but is it correct? Now that modern rationalism has reached an impasse, as we enter a new age, what evaluation should we make of Scholasticism? Answering this question is the main theme of my talk today.

First we must take into consideration the conditions of the age and society in which Scholasticism was born and cultivated. European medieval philosophy can be divided into two main stages. The initial stage, which lasted from the first century of the Christian era until the eighth and ninth centuries, was patristic philosophy, named in honor of the Church Fathers, who wrote works explaining the teachings of Christianity.

Christianity first spread throughout the Roman Empire. After the collapse of that empire, it spread to the world of the Germanic tribes, who were then making their first major appearance on the stage of history. In other words, in this early period, the Church was in an active missionary phase. The primary duty of the Church Fathers, the nucleus of the missionary activity, was to systematize the teachings of Christianity and find a way to adapt them to the traditional ways of thinking of the Romans and the Germanic tribes. Consequently, during this stage, establishment of all-pervading faith was emphasized. Some of the outstanding Church Fathers include Justin, Tertullian, Origen, and Saint Augustine, who was famous as a universal philosopher. In the well-known phrase that is considered to be a summary of Tertullian's philosophy—"It is impossible, therefore I believe"—it is possible to see a crystallization of patristic philosophy as the advocate of absolute faith.

In *The City of God,* Saint Augustine laid an ideological foundation for the system of rule of the Catholic Church by teaching that, as the City of God made manifest on earth, it would continue eternally, even after the fall of Rome, the City of Man.

The age of patristic philosophy came to a close when Christianity was firmly established throughout Europe. The period between the ninth century and the Renaissance was the age of Scholasticism. The causes for the emergence of this philosophy must be analyzed from many angles; but some important elements can be stated simply: unification of Germanic society under Charlemagne, withdrawal of the forces of Islam, the Carolingian renaissance, and what today is called the rise of the arts and learning. The church and monastery schools that I mentioned earlier as the *schola* were instituted with the encouragement of Charlemagne.

When the age of missionary activity and development was over, with the opportunities presented by the flourishing of art and letters, a deepening and a formalizing of the doctrines of Christianity were required. Augustine and others of the Fathers had already perfected the basic doctrines. The problems in this later period were to prove them, to order them in relation to each other, and to systematize them.

Medieval Europe inherited the seven liberal arts—grammar, rhetoric, dialectic, arithmetic, geometry, astronomy, and music— from ancient Greece and Rome. The problem that scholars faced in the period before the Renaissance was to connect these seven arts with theology. The great influence exerted by Aristotelian philosophy by way of contacts with Islamic society made it essential to touch not only on individual sciences but also on basic human issues, such as the relationships between reason and the revelations of the Bible, between intellect and faith, and between philosophy and theology.

Separation of Intellect and Reason from Faith

Outstanding figures in the Scholastic movement were John Scotus Erigena, in the ninth century; Saint Anselm and Saint Abelard, in the eleventh century; Albertus Magnus, Thomas Aquinas, and Duns Scotus, from the end of the twelfth to the thirteenth century; and Roger Bacon, a forerunner of modern natural science, in the late thirteenth century. I do not intend to cover today the major aspects of the history of this philosophy, one by one, for the entire four centuries. I shall, however, abstract a few basic issues and, with the addition of some reflections, examine the general current of development from a modern viewpoint.

Erigena, who was born in Ireland and who spent his active life in Paris, is called either the First Father of Scholasticism or the Charlemagne of Scholasticism, because he laid the foundation for European medieval Scholastic philosophy just as the great emperor laid the foundations for medieval politics.

Erigena's philosophical basis is summed up in this proposition: True religion is true philosophy; at the same time, true philosophy is true religion; consequently, philosophy rejects skepticism in relation to religion. This proposition certainly holds true in the case of Buddhism. The major Scholastic conviction of the oneness of religion and philosophy and of faith and reason and the desire to prove that conviction are clearly revealed in the intention expressed in Erigena's proposition.

It must be recognized that, from its inception, Scholastic philosophy was seriously restricted by the need to provide intellectual and rational verification for faith; that is, it was indeed a handmaiden to theology. The absoluteness of faith was a major premise for all of the Scholastic philosophers, including Anselm, who said, "I believe because I do not know."

Thomas Aquinas and Duns Scotus

Nonetheless, subtle shifts in nuance occurred with the passing of time. For instance, Thomas Aquinas said: "Faith, within the limits apprehensible by reason, ought to be in concordance with theology. But, not all of the sphere of faith is necessarily acknowledged by reason. Therefore, in the area where reason cannot reach, truth can only be grasped by faith." His position, a subtle swing from the standpoint initially adopted by Scholasticism—that faith and reason are one—can be interpreted as a slight step in the direction of skepticism toward Christianity.

By the time of Duns Scotus, we have already reached a clear separation between reason and faith. He said: "Nothing restrains the Divine Will. It is free. It is something transcending reason. Reason, therefore, can neither perceive it nor discover its foundations. Theology is not a thing of reason but is solely a thing of action."

Though the process of change did not shake the faith of the Scholastic philosophers, it did impart to reason a special position, in which it was free of bondage to faith and theological doctrines. As a result of reason—once it had been placed in this new position—modern philosophy developed, learning flowered, and, as a consequence of learning, contradictions in the doctrines of the church were exposed. This shook the very teachings themselves; and, in this sense, the germination of the modern age and the modern world was gradually being accomplished within Scholastic philosophy.

The Middle Ages and Their Distinctive Culture

This discussion shows that it is possible to interpret Scholastic philosophy as more than the handmaiden of theology and the symbol of the Dark Ages: it can be seen as the point of origin of the modern world. But still deeper inquiry shows that, in this very trait, Scholasticism represents an illustrious period in which a great culture glowed.

As I have mentioned, it is the modern rationalist philosophers who describe the European Middle Ages as a time of darkness between the ancient and the modern periods. But this is an inappropriate description, since the Middle Ages produced a distinctive culture, in no way inferior to the cultures of the ancient and modern worlds. Essentially, it is in this culture that I see the germination of the modern world.

Stressing this point makes it possible to interpret modern civilization as a period of latter-day confusion and dehumanization caused by the decline of medieval Christian civilization.

In the truest meaning, the European Dark Ages lasted from the first century and the fall of the Roman Empire until the ninth or tenth century. During this time, the great Germanic migrations took place, social law and order were destroyed, and commerce came to a halt. An age that is forced to undergo constant pillage and slaughter can truly be called dark. But, from the ninth into the tenth century, social stability was achieved, people applied themselves diligently to productive activities, and the trend toward creating a new culture began to gain impetus. All of this was greeted by the age of Scholastic philosophy.

The churches and cathedrals that survive in many European towns and cities today were built or begun in the age of Scholasticism. Great memorials to the civilization of the Middle Ages, such works of Gothic architecture as Notre Dame, Chartres, and the Cologne Cathedral, were not built by political authority. Instead, they were the outcome of the application of the techniques and wealth assembled and put to use by religious faith.

Moreover, these buildings remain today as symbols of European cities, the histories of the peoples, and European civilization in general. In Paris, any number of buildings as noteworthy as Notre Dame from an architectural point of view could be cited—the Louvre, the Arc de Triomphe, the Eiffel Tower, and so on. But these are only remnants of the glory of monarchs or of people of the priviliged classes. As a crystallization of a culture, supported by the hearts and minds of the ordinary citizenry, they cannot approach Notre Dame in importance.

Just as the cathedrals, soaring examples of Gothic architecture, are physical symbols of the flourishing culture of the Middle Ages, so Scholasticism itself symbolizes the elevated spirit of that same period. The flourishing of learning gave birth to numerous such centers of education as those in Paris, Bologna, Oxford, and Cambridge, where teachers and students gathered to form universities. Indeed, the university of today is a heritage from the age of Scholasticism.

The things studied by the Scholastic philosophers—and of course taught in the universities—seem somewhat naive and mistaken in the light of modern knowledge. For instance, the Scholastics believed that knowledge is not something gained from observation but something written down by such ancient philosophers as Plato, Aristotle, and Euclid. Scholastic scholars engaged in subtle demonstrations for the sake of systematizing knowledge, proving doctrines of theology, and organizing what they knew. For this reason, they earned the name "followers of the complicated philosophy." Nonetheless, even when these faults are admitted, we cannot fail to recognize the important contributions that Scholasticism made on a more fundamental level.

Contributions of Scholastic Philosphy

First and most important is Scholasticism's clear guide to human behavior in life. This guide was drawn up on the basis of a complete, comprehensive world view. The Spanish philosopher Ortega y Gasset, in his book *Mission of the University,* refers to this point in a most interesting way. "What is called 'general culture' today was something very different in the Middle Ages. It was not an ornament for the mind or mere character training. It was, on the contrary, the system of ideas, concerning the world and humanity, which man at that time possessed. It was, consequently, a repertory of convictions which became an effective guide for his existence."

Although this passage deals with general culture in university education, its significance goes beyond college courses, for it is an important pronouncement on the basic nature of the kind of culture that human beings ought to possess. At present, what is called culture has a very vague content and is what Ortega y Gasset calls an "ornament for the mind" or at best "character training." True culture, however, is a "system of ideas concerning the world and man" (or human existence) that enables a person to guide himself from within.

In another passage, Ortega y Gasset says, "Life is chaos, a tangled and confused jungle in which man is lost. But his mind reacts against the sensation or bewilderment: he labors to find 'roads,' 'ways' through the woods, in the form of clear, firm ideas concerning the universe, positive convictions about the nature of things. The ensemble, or system, of these ideas is culture in the true sense of the term; it is precisely the opposite of external ornament. Culture is what saves human life from being a mere disaster; it is what enables man to live a life which is something above meaningless tragedy or inward disgrace."

In the Middle Ages, Scholasticism was the source of this kind of culture. Earlier I said that one of the significances of Scholasticism was the preparations it made for the development of learning in the modern world. But I call Scholasticism a peak of the civilization of the Middle Ages not for this reason alone but also because it was the source of the kind of culture described by Ortega y Gasset. Although the role it plays in preparing for the succeeding age is an important part of the contribution of a culture, I believe what it does for the people of its own time and for their improvement is more important still.

Of course, Scholasticism did not deliberately deal with questions of humanity and its improvement. As I said at the opening of my talk, its real aims were to endorse faith by means of reason, to unify the branches of learning under theology, and in this way to strengthen the authority of the Christian faith and the doctrines of the Church. In effect, however, what Scholasticism did was to fuse Hebraism and Hellenism, which Europe had inherited separately from the ancient world; incarnate them in itself; and thus forge a true Europe and a truly European view of humanity.

A Prototype of European Civilization

In terms of cultural history, Scholasticism played an important part in marking the decisive epoch of transition from a Mediterranean to a European culture. Of course, the political, economic, and industrial conditions for this change had been in preparation earlier. In the vital spiritual and intellectual fields, however, it was during the age of Scholasticism that Europe broke away from dependence on Mediterranean civilization.

From the time of its origin until the eighth or ninth century, Christianity's major stage of activity was the ancient world around the Mediterranean. The centers of primitive and early Christianity were Alexandria, Cappadocia, and Rome. Saint Augustine was born and was active in Hippo, in Numidia, which is now part of Algeria.

The expansion of the field of authority of Islam in the seventh and eighth centuries put an end to the cultural supremacy of Mediterranean civilization. The followers of Islam seized control of the Mediterranean Sea, and Christianity was shut up within the continent of Europe itself. Later, Charlemagne effected unification of the Germanic world, and even though the area broke up politically after his death it continued to move in the direction of cultural unity.

Through many vicissitudes, including the Renaissance, the Reformation, and modern nationalism, European civilization has developed and disseminated itself throughout the world to become what can be called the civilization of today. Essentially, it was completed in the twelfth or thirteenth century in the age of Scholasticism, which is the basic spiritual prototype of modern European civilization. Further, the continued fundamental importance to learning of such places as Paris, Oxford, and Cambridge—all centers of Scholastic study— indicates that the original spiritual current of that philosophy continues to flow.

The long series of historical developments that began with Scholasticism has produced some gross, disfigured, and ugly forms and now faces a tragic ending. The loss of humanity and the distortions of civilization symbolized by environmental pollution are obvious to all. The university, once a source of cultural creative energy, is at the brink of destruction. It is no exaggeration to say that the traditional university is about to lose its position of leadership as a place of learning and human development.

At this passing of an old age and opening of a new one, a novel university is needed. Perhaps the form of the university is of secondary importance. The vital thing is that it represent a new philosophy, the flourishing of a modern Scholasticism in the best sense. Such a new philosophy of human revival is one that is based on true religion and centered on true faith, one that unites all fields of learning, reason, emotion, desire, and impulse and puts each in its proper place. We must build a true culture that will clarify man's place in universal life and blaze a trail to show man how to live in the dense, chaotic forest of today.

Forming such a university is equivalent to bringing together human beings determined to find the required kind of philosophy and to put that philosophy to practical use. People and ideas, not buildings and facilities, make up a university. Any place where people with a philosophy that enables them to cope with the chaos of life come together—any place that is a source of energy to influence the age and to create culture—is a university in the richest sense.

Today Scholasticism has crumbled, because the religion on which it rested has lost its power. Perhaps no other age in history has lost the religious spirit to the extent that ours has; and no other age in history has been in greater need of salvation. We face this fact, and we must continue to live with it. We must be aware that our most pressing tasks today are to establish a philosophy that can cope with and take the lead in the current situation and to found a new religion as the basis of that philosophy.

What is the mission of a university whose pride it will be to bear the responsibility of the future? With the firm conviction that all of you already have the answer to this question in your hearts, I conclude my message.

Banner Bearers for Peace

Delivered at the Fifth NSA (Nichiren Shoshu Soka Gakkai of America) Students' General Meeting, held in Hachioji, Tokyo, October 9, 1973.

I should like to offer my sincere congratulations on this fifth NSA Students' General Meeting, held in the fruitful autumn, when the scenery of Japan is at its richest and most beautiful. This meeting is more than a gathering of students from Japan and the United States. It has the significance of—and indeed it symbolizes—the unity of people devoted to the Mystic Law, the highest wisdom of the world, and to the future of mankind. Transcending considerations of national boundary and race, this meeting of young Buddhist scholars is a great undertaking, of a kind probably unprecedented in the three thousand years of the history of Buddhism. For this reason, in addition to expressing my respect for all of the participants, I entrust to you my hopes for the future of the world and of humanity.

Although I have often discussed such things in the past, I should like to take this opportunity once more to express my views about guideposts for your future and for your whole lives. The discussion must inevitably involve the nature of the twenty-first century, or, more precisely, what we must strive to make of the twenty-first century. I believe that it will be a period that we should describe as the Century of Life. It will be a time when the philosophy of life, having become the source of all other philosophies, revolutionizes human beings from within. Respect for humanity will be embodied in all fields of endeavor, and man's wisdom will be required as the ultimate support. People of sensitivity now are coming to realize that, without such wisdom, further development is impossible and the very survival of man is in jeopardy.

In the twentieth century, the world has been controlled by the struggle between communism and capitalism, both of which are philosophies and interpretations of mankind made solely in economic and social terms. Prejudices and hatred caused by the conflict between these two incomplete ideologies have, as you know, resulted in the dehumanization and environmental destruction of our civilization. Now man is demanding a spiritual support that goes deeper and higher than communism and capitalism. I am convinced that only a way of thinking based on the philosophy of life can meet this demand.

You, who have taken your stand firmly in the life philosophy of Nichiren Daishonin, are the pioneers of the twenty-first century. From the bottom of my heart, I hope that you will strive to build new ideals based on that philosophy in all of the fields in which you specialize.

Learning is essentially a system applied to various fields and built on the basis of laws discovered from long-accumulated knowledge. It has emerged from human wisdom about daily life. In its truest sense, learning is deeply rooted in intimate connections with daily life, where it has grown and bloomed. In other words, learning is not merely knowledge: it is wisdom. But, because of the explosive growth of industrial society and the accompanying categorization and specialization of the modern age, learning has abandoned the study of humanity and human wisdom and has come to exist for the sake of knowledge alone. Modern learning can do nothing in the face of such perversions in our civilization as the threat of nuclear weapons, environmental hazards, and spiritual corruption. Indeed it was the pursuit of knowledge for its own sake that created such evils as these.

It is time for learning to reawaken to an awareness of its true, original mission. Jean Jacques Rousseau has said that, among all the various kinds of human knowledge, man's knowledge of himself is the least advanced, even though it is the most useful.

These words are pertinent to our age. I believe that Buddhism has made the clearest study of human nature and that, inspired by the wisdom of Buddhism, learning can return to its role as the study of wisdom. This is the only way out of the labyrinth in which modern learning finds itself. Learning of this higher kind can guide us in making the next century a century of life.

Education is the spreading of the fruits of learning and the support on which learning rests. On this point, too, I have a suggestion to make. I propose the establishment of an International Organization for Educational Cooperation to serve as a generating power in the creation of spiritual fortresses of peace in the hearts of men.

The three traditional Western branches of government are the legislative, judicial, and executive. For a long time, I have insisted on the addition of a fourth, independent branch: the educational branch. Education performs the vital role of cultivating the individual human being. In addition, it must bear the responsibility for teaching each individual absolute respect for life. It must not be controlled by political authority. It is true that UNESCO exists for the sake of international cooperation in educational, scientific, and cultural endeavors. The ideal of that organization is the building of peace. But, under the present national-power structure, UNESCO, like the United Nations itself, is subjected to considerable political influence.

I believe that the matter demanding first priority is that of establishing an independent education branch of government and creating a worldwide, peace-oriented, educational organization. Such an organization must be free of political control.

I hope that all of you who are involved with the educational process—teachers, parents and relatives who are instructors in the home, students of both senior and junior levels, and experienced educators—will help build an International Organization for Educational Cooperation that will contribute to the realization of truly worldwide peace and sponsor harmonious cooperation all over the globe. Further, I hope that all you members of the student divisions—the Japanese members, of course, but especially the American members—will be leaders in this movement.

As students with plentiful knowledge, pure emotions, and youthful enthusiasm, you must bear the banner in the building of peace. I have chosen this occasion as the most appropriate time to make this statement about an International Organization for Educational Cooperation, because I believe that you will undertake the task. My earnest request is that you now make the first significant step toward using your wisdom to abolish war and eliminate violence as you serve as envoys of peace in the construction of the new century.

The Global Family

Delivered at the Tenth General Meeting of NSA
(Nichiren Shoshu Soka Gakkai of America),
held at Taiseki-ji, Fujinomiya, October 11, 1973.

Today I am participating in this meeting along with visiting citizens of the United States, a nation that prides itself on liberty and independence. Socrates once said that he was not an Athenian and not a Greek, but a citizen of the world. And I, too, have a strong awareness of being a citizen of the world. I have shaken the hands of and engaged in conversations with people from many lands. With all of them I observed the same warm, human truths. In the eyes of all—Europeans, Africans, Asians, and Americans—I have seen the same tears and the same light. I intend to continue my journeys around the world until my death, because I believe that the kind of negotiations that we need now are not political ones between nation and nation, but life negotiations among individual human beings.

I wish to assign to this conference the significance of a great undertaking for the raising of the curtain on a global family. Surely in the three thousand years of Buddhist history, nothing has happened like this gathering of three thousand citizens of the United States here at the foot of Mount Fuji. I wish to declare to all mankind that this is an unprecedented event and a sublime page in the glorious opening of a brilliant history.

It can be said that the birth of the United States altered the history of the world. People from many lands, fleeing from political oppression, left their native countries to seek an ideal land on the American continent. Their way was difficult. Many pages of their history are stained with the blood and sweat of struggle.

The battle for American independence in 1776 was more than a political revolution. It was a fight to ensure equality among peoples and their innate right to liberty. In breaking with absolutism and feudalism, it was later to have an important influence on the French Revolution and was thus to change world history still further. Although I hear of many difficulties facing the United States today—difficulties symbolized by David Riesman's words, "poverty amidst affluence"—I am convinced that the noble, precious spirit of independence and freedom still lies at the bottom of the hearts of all American citizens.

I should like you to realize that Buddhism is an unending source of energy for a free spirit. It is likely that many young people who have been greatly disturbed by our times have found regeneration in this spiritual strength and in the effect it has on the modern urban desert.

The Buddhism of Nichiren Daishonin does not belong solely to the Japanese, just as it does not belong solely to the Americans, the English, the French, or the people of any one country. It is the jewel within the life of each person and the Buddhism for each individual everywhere. Followers of Buddhism naturally make contributions to their own societies and nations, each person according to his own means and abilities.

People of many races have come together to form the United States. I hope that America will demonstrate proof of the right to the pursuit of happiness, equality, and liberty into the twenty-first century—which will be rooted in a worldwide religion.

A truly great religion must be the ally of any suffering person, no matter what his nation or race. In the *Gosho* of Nichiren Daishonin it is said that ". . . one person has attained Buddhahood, and then following him, all people equally can attain Buddhahood" (*Gosho Zenshu*, p. 564). All people are equal as human beings. In American democracy I sense a spirit that agrees with the spirit of Buddhism.

Perhaps this is because the Buddhism of Nichiren Daishonin is both Oriental and Occidental in basic nature.

I hope that all of you, my American comrades, will take this conference as a dawning of a new chapter in human history and that, manifesting the frontier spirit of the Mystic Law, you will join together in a congenial body to struggle for humanity, the world, and peace.

Global Unity of Mankind

*Delivered at the Thirty-sixth General Meeting of
Soka Gakkai, held in Osaka, December 16, 1973.*

At the present time we face a sharp social parting of the ways. The time has come when we must abandon faith in materialism and economic growth and embrace faith in humanity and life itself. For this reason, we have decided to call 1974 the Year of Society. I am positive that Soka Gakkai's Year of Society can point the way for a year of basic human values.

The World in 1974

Today the outlook is very bleak. The petroleum crisis, triggered by the conflict between Israel and the Arab nations, and the aggravation of the already chronic, malignant inflation threaten the world with a depression comparable to the one that began in 1929 and was a causative factor in the outbreak of World War II. Almost all thinkers on these matters agree that Japan will be severely hit by the 1974 depression, especially because it depends on imports for petroleum and indeed for most other raw materials. If the petroleum crisis continues to worsen, by the spring of 1974, the Japanese economy will suffer a grave upset. For the past several years, Japan's annual economic growth rate has remained in the vicinity of ten percent. Now, however, some people foresee a zero economic growth rate or—if worse comes to worst—an economic recession for the coming year. Japan must be prepared to withstand the gravest financial setback since the end of World War II. For an economy that has been based firmly on belief in progress, this will be a crisis on a truly national scale. But it will be the ordinary people of Japan and the small and medium enterprises that will be forced to bear the brunt of the blows.

Signs of serious trouble are already manifesting themselves. Big businesses have been unethically cornering certain commodities. Prices have started rising abnormally, consumers have been frantically buying staple goods out of fear that they are going to be scarce, small and medium enterprises have been failing, and financially stricken people have resorted to family suicide as the only way out of a desperate situation. The cruel and savage air enveloping the Japanese islands calls to mind the dark period during World War II and the immediate postwar years.

The depression of 1929 played a significant part in the germination of conditions leading to World War II. It is often said that history repeats itself. And for me, one of the most frightening aspects of the current economic situation is the possibility that it might contribute to the outbreak of another hot war. The fires of strife have not yet died down in the Middle East. Nor have the boundary problems between China and the Soviet Union been settled. Tension continues in Latin America and in the Asian countries that are Japan's neighbors. Obviously, from a political as well as from an economic standpoint, 1974 will be a year of trials.

Some concerned individuals are most pessimistic. They argue that Japan has pursued a mistaken course up to the present time, and they feel that there is no measure that can alleviate the crisis. Japan is now reaping what it has sown in its greedy concern with its own stability and prosperity. There is nothing but withdrawal on all sides, with no bulwark to protect us from the wave of troubles threatening to crash down on our heads.

Another line of thought holds that the leaders of Japan have erroneously concentrated all of their attention on economic prosperity and have been unconcerned about the welfare of other nations and people. A thinker from another country—a man whose opinions I deeply respect—has deplored what he calls Japan's continued spiritual isolationism. I agree with his description of the Japanese attitude and insist that if our nation is to play a meaningful part in international society, we must break out of such isolationism.

I do not mean to imply that we ought to overlook economic difficulties; but I am convinced that the most important problems we face involve fundamental issues like the nature of mankind, the optimum way for human beings to live, and the contributions Japan can make to the welfare of other peoples of the world. Dealing with them now may seem like going the long way around the issue, but these problems must be solved before we can hope for improvements in other trouble areas.

Fundamental Change of Attitude

The history of human progress is marked by a series of changes in ways of thinking. Mankind has constantly sought new goals and has used these as starting points for further development. The Ptolemaic theory that the earth is stationary and that the heavens rotate gave way to the Copernican theory that the earth itself moves. In the twentieth century, the emergence of Einstein's theory of relativity has been another great change in our way of thinking.

But if there have been several such major changes, they have not occurred without opposition. Human beings tend to settle into patterns to which they become accustomed. As the resulting habits of thought and action take root and solidify, reactionary force tends to inhibit breaking away in new directions. This is true both of individuals and of society.

The Japanese people have long been accustomed to one very deeply ingrained thought pattern: they view the world solely from their own standpoint. Of course, most individuals put themselves in the center of their worlds and see other people through their own eyes; but it is important to try to see oneself with the eyes of others. The individual must see that the world does not center on him, just as man once learned that the solar system does not center on the earth.

The case with nations is similar. At no time in its history has Japan been more in need of a change of viewpoint. It is imperative that it now cease to see itself through its own eyes alone and try to discover what it looks like to other peoples and nations.

The imperative change in our way of thinking must be a fundamental alteration* of our basic approach to all things. Aberrations in basic approaches to life have led Japan to its present desperate state. Who is responsible? Today the nation is a confused mélange of conflicting egoisms. Some people live for nothing but their own privileges and advantages or those of the cliques and factions to which they belong. In pursuing nothing but economic gain, some Japanese have incurred the scorn of the foreign nations with which they deal. Professors concerned with their own academic standings ridicule the ordinary people. So-called critics use their finest phrases to praise themselves. Those who consider themselves members of some other kind of elite take unfair advantage of people outside their privileged group. It is now time to hold a mirror up to the Japanese people and allow them to re-examine themselves.

Never before has it been so urgent for the leaders and people of this nation to reorient their own fundamental approach in a correct direction. But they cannot do this as a result of shallow reflection or superficial changes in approaches to practical affairs. It is the force of life that supports all human thinking, and a fundamental change of our attitude toward that force is needed. What modern man needs most is a return to the life-oriented philosophy that is the core of Buddhism.

Guarding the Rights of All Peoples

The thing that disturbs me most about the present is not so much the economic depression as the frightening resemblance between the present state of affairs and the conditions that prevailed toward the end of the Weimar Republic, from which Nazism emerged.

* Translator's note: In referring to this fundamental alteration, President Ikeda employs the term *ichinen,* which literally means "one thought," but which in Nichiren Shoshu Buddhism indicates the instantaneous, ordinary human thought in which the entirety of universal life is contained.

Although many aspects of Nazism deserve severe castigation, perhaps its greatest fault was the way it trampled on the spiritual freedom and the very dignity of life of people who differed with or rejected Nazi opinions. Whenever I have an opportunity, I remind all the people I come in contact with that respect for the dignity and spiritual freedom of humanity is at once the heart and the mission of Buddhism. As the crisis of our times grows more serious, I am convinced that we must reaffirm as a basic article of faith our determination to support spiritual freedom, the dignity of man, and true democracy. Following are some of the concrete steps that we must take to this end.

First, we must further devote ourselves to the protection of the present Japanese constitution and especially of Article Nine, which forbids the use of military action and rejects the right of belligerence. I intend to stress this, especially with the youth and student divisions.

The second step is related to spiritual freedom. Obviously, we must do all we can to ensure our own freedom of religion and faith. But in addition, should it ever become apparent that the authorities are trying to use violence to rob others of their spiritual freedom, even if the philosophies and faiths of those people differ from ours, we must offer them all the protection we can in the name of the dignity of man. Because this is the unaltering Buddhist view of humanity, I insist that we must afford our protection to those whose religions are different from our own and even to those who reject religion altogether. I want to impress on all of you my conviction that this protective attitude is part of our mission as we embark on the Year of Society.

In the first chapter of the *Rissho Ankoku Ron* (The security of the land through the propagation of true Buddhism) of Nichiren Daishonin there is a short passage that has startling pertinence to conditions today: "When a nation becomes disordered, it is the evil spirits which first show signs of rampancy. Because these spirits become rampant, all the people of the nation become disordered" (*Gosho Zenshu*, p. 19), I think this passage shows how necessary it is in times of trouble to turn an attentive ear to the teachings of a great philosophy with a venerable history. In *Ongi Kuden*, another of Nichiren Daishonin's writings, "evil spirits" are explained as those things that rob humanity of life, the beings who deprive us of fortune.

They are, in other words, those forces within humanity that destroy life itself and deprive us of happiness. In more modern terms, they represent the demonic nature of life. The state man is in when he is completely under the control of his own ego is best expressed as demonic in this sense. When the demonic nature of a human life runs rampant, that life represents the condition described as "evil spirits in turmoil."

The world "land" in the title refers, of course, to land in the usual sense, but it also means something very close to the word "society." Whenever the total unity that ought to exist between man and his natural environment is upset, at the root of the trouble it is possible to see the operation of the human ego—or, more fundamentally, the operation of the demonic nature of life. As a result of this upset, all people are driven into turmoil; and the entire land is pushed toward destruction. Turmoil of the evil spirits is becoming increasingly violent in present society; and, unless the people have an understanding of these spirits and their place in the basic nature of life, the misery of the land cannot be alleviated.

Forum of Mankind

In overcrowded modern cities, open plazas where human beings may relax are certainly desirable. But they cannot be provided in the absence of bold urban-redevelopment programs. The task of creating physical plazas remains in the field of politics. We as individuals cannot undertake massive urban-redevelopment projects to give modern man physical places of refreshment and rest, but we can generate an ambiance of cooperation and oneness in humanity. Because this ambiance will play the kind of refreshing yet stimulating role for the spirit that the plazas, squares, and forums of the world's cities have played in the physical life of man, I call it the Forum of Mankind.

The people of Japan are not familiar with forums and plaza. From the practical viewpoint, they would doubtless regard it as extremely wasteful to tear down buildings and clear space that was not intended for housing projects to relieve the pressure in overpopulated cities or that was not at least intended to serve the needs of transportation.

But from the viewpoint of the Westerner, the apparently wasteful

plaza has long been an important part of city life. The agora was indispensable in the ancient Greek city-state, for it was there that citizens
met to transact business, relax, and debate issues of all kinds. The same
is true of the forums in Roman cities. In medieval European cities as
well, church and official government buildings—the heart of city
life, in other words—were always built around a plaza.

Because of the many physical functions they serve, plazas and
forums become a core around which there grows up a sense of oneness among the people who come into these places in a spirit of independence, equality, and freedom. It was exactly this spirit that assisted
the Greeks in resisting the Persian empire, whose citizens were no
more than slaves of an autocratic ruler, insignificant parts of a whole.
The Greeks were proud of their freedom; and the spirit that bred it
was related to the agora, the plaza that was the heart of much of Greek
daily life.

The case of medieval European cities is to some extent similar.
There is a general tendency to think only of the confining aspects of
the feudal system when considering the European Middle Ages. It
must be remembered, however, that the feudal system itself was
based on contracts between free individuals. And it was urban spaces,
especially the plazas, that liberated men from the more restricting
elements of the system and helped them develop a free society. People
with an awareness of freedom, independence, and equality managed
medieval cities; the plaza came into being in answer to the need for a
place where these citizens could communicate with one another. It
seems true that plazas helped cultivate the human spirit, but the
important fact is that the human spirit itself was the starting point
from which plazas originated.

Let us look at the situation in Japan. Japanese history is not devoid
of analogues of the European plaza. Towns in the immediate vicinity
of temples and shrines were once sacred zones where people gathered.
The thickly wooded groves surrounding the main halls of temples
and shrines and the spacious open zones in front of palaces and castles
were in a sense plazas. The immense inner and outer gardens of the
Meiji Shrine in Tokyo are examples of this. But, as one critic points
out, such Japanese places differ fundamentally from the traditional
European-style plaza. The Japanese zones I have mentioned are

intermediary regions between places that are considered secular and other places that are considered sacred. An intermediary zone is intended to inspire in the people assembling there a sense of solemnity. It is supposed to allow them to cleanse their hearts and minds of the dirt of the secular world.

The Forum of Mankind, the spiritual plaza where all people can come together in peace, must not reject humanity in this way. I want us to develop a forum—that is, a spiritual atmosphere—where people can come together to debate issues, enjoy themselves, and relax with independence, freedom, and equality. I want our forum to be one of abundant rest and human revival. Today the power of the government grows, and human beings are reduced to mere ciphers in an administrative society. Even in Europe, where the idea of forums as forces in social behavior originated, such spaces are becoming no more than a formality.

Consequently, I urge that we replace the physical forum with a spiritual attitude exemplifying freedom, cooperation, and human warmth. Unlike the agorae of the Greek city-states, the forums of the Roman cities, or the plazas of medieval cities, the Forum of Mankind would be unlimited in time or space. It would extend to all humanity.

My opinion is that today man urgently needs to revive his inherent feelings of warm concern for his fellow human beings. I once read something that illustrates the kind of emotion that I am convinced we must stress. It is said that for several hundred years all written material in Poland was in Latin. The first known document in vernacular Polish was found in the archives of a monastery. It dates from the thirteenth century and relates how a farmer watching his wife at work at a gristmill said: "Let me have that. I'll grind a while; you rest." This simple statement comes across the ages to show the kind of warmth and concern that we must have for one another. And I believe that we can find that feeling in Buddhism. Indeed, when all people have true humanity—the strong love of human beings that is the meaning of Buddhism—the Forum of Mankind will come into existence in country after country throughout the world.

The task before us is to create a spiritually united body of human beings, representing the kind of assembly of truly free people that the ancient Greeks confidently thought they had developed. We who have been blessed with the refreshing and revitalizing water of faith in the philosophy of life will, I am certain, be the forerunners in the accomplishment of this task. I want all of us—and I am convinced that you agree with me—to go forward toward the pioneering and building of a Forum of Mankind, filled with peace and life.

Buddhist Law and Society

In the *Hakumai Ippyo Gosho* (On the gift of rice) there is a passage that explains the relationship between the Buddhist Law and society. "In contrast, the sixth chapter of the Lotus Sutra reads, 'No affairs of life or work are in any way different from the ultimate reality.' In discussing the underlying significance of these quotations, Miao-lo taught that the first two sutras are profound, but still shallow when compared to the Lotus Sutra. Whereas they relate secular matters in terms of Buddhism, the Lotus Sutra explains that secular matters ultimately are Buddhism."

All other sutras argue that the secular world of society and the Buddhist Law are to be thought of as separate and that Buddhism is to be found deep within the secular law of society. In other words, society depends on Buddhism. In the Lotus Sutra, however, society and Buddhism are a single entity: society is Buddhism. The Lotus Sutra, the ultimate of all Buddhist teachings, goes further than saying that the relationship between Buddhism and society is very close: it insists that the two are one.

Now I should like to discuss the Four Sufferings of life—birth, aging, sickness, and death—from the standpoint of the oneness of Buddhism and society. As you know, the main purpose of Buddhism is to confront and overcome the suffering caused by birth, the sadness of growing old, the pain of illness, and the fear of death. Shakyamuni left his father's home in order to confront the Four Sufferings, which are an essential, inevitable part of life.

Human beings do, however, avert their eyes from the reality of the Four Sufferings and devote themselves to the pursuit of empty glory, wealth, and power. Unless a person solves the problem of the transience and instability of his own life, all the glory and power he achieves, no matter how proud and dazzling, is built on sand and must inevitably pass away without a trace. They are only illusion. What solutions does Buddhism offer to the problem of the Four Sufferings? Hinayana Buddhism teaches that one must return one's life to *ku* (void); thus releasing oneself from the revolving wheel of transience and of birth, aging, sickness, and death; and in this way enter the state that is called Nirvana.

Mahayana Buddhism, on the other hand, finds a constant element within the heart of the inconstancy of transmigration. In the very depths of life itself, Mahayana establishes a realm that is not subject to the transience of life and death, a realm that is immovable and indestructible.

Put to practical application, the teachings of Hinayana must lead to rejection of the actual world. Mahayana—especially as expressed in the Lotus Sutra—accepts actuality for what it is. By perceiving and manifesting the source of life in reality, the Lotus Sutra frees us from the dominion of ceaseless births and deaths; establishes an unshakable, true humanity, liberated from transmigration; and gives constancy to all human endeavors. More than any other teaching, the Lotus Sutra comes into direct confrontation with reality and provides a revolutionary philosophy to change reality for the better.

I have been implying that only the Lotus Sutra offers this revolutionary philosophy. This is true for the following reason. Although the other sutras tend to lead toward the revolutionary reconstruction of reality, they fail to make clear the philosophy needed for the reworking of human life. And this is the key to the entire issue. The ultimate philosophy-of-life revolution finds one constant reality deep within the inconstancy and change of transmigration. That one thing is the perception of the Law of Nam-myoho-renge-kyo. The Lotus Sutra clearly states that people who strive for enlightenment through learning and realization will attain Buddhahood and that each of the Ten States of Life contains within itself all of the other nine. When the nine states—all but the Buddha state—perceive the Mystic Law inherent within themselves, they transcend the sufferings of birth, aging, sickness, and death and become immutable. In figurative terms, I might describe this process as the original sun rising above the horizon of inconstancy, changing a gloomy world of darkness into a glittering world of dancing gold and silver waves.

Put simply, what I am saying is this: the faith in which we believe does not exist apart from real human society, and it does not pursue a realm of transcendent enlightenment. Indeed, our faith must do neither of these things. Our philosophy is one that commands us to allow our faith to bloom in the mire and grime of real human society.

If the products of all human society—culture, social activities, economics, politics, and education—are to become valuable manifestations of human life, they must derive their force from the philosophy of the Lotus Sutra. The Lotus of the Law does not bloom in some remote heaven. It sends its roots deep into the soil of this real world and flowers in profusion here, where we are. True Buddhism does not try to avoid the issues of birth, old age, sickness, and death. It confronts these problems and enables human beings to earn the status of teachers in social and cultural life.

When society and culture run counter to the wholesome wishes and duties of mankind, they fail to protect human life as they ought to do. This in turn intensifies the effects of the Four Sufferings. Under such circumstances, society and culture become authoritarian or oppressively formalistic. When this happens, Buddhist wisdom and compassion must undertake the mission of revitalizing and revolutionizing society.

The *Gosho* of Nichiren Daishonin says that Buddhism is the body and the world the shadow. When the body bends, the shadow must bend too. This should give us an idea of the decision that each of us who cherishes Buddhism must make independently in relation to our task of revitalizing present society. From the bottom of my heart I urge you to strive toward the accomplishment of this task with wisdom, perseverance, and steadfastness.

We can put no faith in people who are tossed about on the roaring waves of society like rootless grasses. We must all be aware that the only people of value are those who have their feet on the ground and who act with faith, responsibility, and sincerity.

Importance of a Happy Home

The most basic organizational unit linking the individual with society is the family, which includes most of the social functions—education,

GLOBAL UNITY OF MANKIND · 87

economics, politics, and various cultural elements. Protecting and cultivating the home and ensuring that it is always a place of lasting happiness and purity are ways to bear witness to the true nature of Buddhism in society. A steady record of success in the home helps build a social reformation. On the other hand, if the home is not a strong spiritual fortress, the principles of Buddhism cannot be expected to manifest themselves.

In emphasizing the importance of the home, I am not falling in line with the trend currently popular in Japan for everyone to be concerned entirely with his own domestic affairs. I speak in these terms because I want the home to develop into an open unit capable of having positive effects on society. The home is the point of junction between the greater social organization and the individual human being; but only when it is peaceful and pleasant can it continue to make creative contributions to society, and only then can society itself grow on a firm foundation.

Revolution with a Difference

We must bear in mind the fact that our movement is a still an unrealized religious revolution of a kind the world has never seen before. Of course, throughout history there have been countless revolutionary movements. In virtually all of them, a leadership of professional revolutionaries took control of activities, while the people lent support and economic assistance from the sidelines.

In the classical situation, revolutions have been carried out within a double structure. The leaders, who received economic support from the more or less inactive people, sacrificed their own private lives and devoted themselves twenty-four hours a day, every day, to the revolution. Undeniably, the communist revolution, in spite of its leaders' insistence that it was a mass movement of the laboring classes, conformed to the classical double structure, in that a group of professional revolutionaries assumed leadership and initiative in its undertakings.

The field of religious movements offers similar examples. For instance, Christian missionaries do the actual missionary work, while the people in their home countries support them with money. In Buddhism, as well, it has not been uncommon to find priests who have given up their own home lives to spread the faith and to be supported by contributions from laymen.

One of the results of this system has been a separation between the revolutionary leaders and the masses of the people. Since the leaders lived and worked for nothing but the revolution and dwelt, figuratively, in isolation from the real world of experience, it was difficult for their theories to coincide closely with the emotions and ideas expressed in the daily lives of the people. Such leaders' theories often suffer one of two fates: either they end up as no more than empty, meaningless plans on paper or they become wild idealism. When either of these two kinds of theories is put into actual practice, it tends to become radical and even to cause great bloodshed. Some revolutionary leaders have preferred to suffer annihilation rather than see the honor of their cause stained. We have known examples of such revolutionaries, and we realize that the ultimate cause of their actions is a tendency inherent in the double revolutionary structure.

But the peaceful revolution of Nichiren Shoshu denies and rejects the double structure. We must persevere in a revolutionary movement that makes significant use of spare time in the lives of the people themselves. Adopting this approach, we can bring about a realistic revolution intimately related to the acts of daily life. Unlike the traditional professional revolutionary, we do not sacrifice our own ways of living to our movement. Instead we make both our work and our homes the objects of our attention and the scenes of our activities.

This is one of the reasons why we insist on placing great importance on the home and place of work. Another reason is the very nature of Nichiren Daishonin's Buddhism, which was formulated for the sake of ordinary people. In continuing the tradition of imparting the meaning of our faith to others, we do not need to assume—indeed, we must not assume—the detached attitude of the professional revolutionary. We must be aware that failing to devote proper attention to home and home life and to work and place of work is an evil that can hinder the accomplishment of our revolutionary task. If we make strong fortresses of our homes and our places of work and if we go on from there to carry out our great task with composure and devotion, we will perfect the system of our movement and make it something unique in world history.

My heartfelt request of you is this: I want each of you to live every day with a smile on your face and with the determination to make the home a haven of peace, from which we can all expand our efforts toward the fulfillment of our mission. I want the peaceful and happy home to become one of Soka Gakkai's permanent policies, and I want each member of our organization to devote maximum effort to making the home an unshakable testimony to the power and value of our faith.

Global Unity of Mankind

Our thinking must move outward to ever-widening fields. We must begin with the individual and then proceed to the family and to the small society surrounding the family. From there our thoughts must advance to include the members of the geographical, historical, and cultural society in which we live—in our case, the society of Japan. But we must not stop here. We must expand our horizons to include the global family of mankind.

Humanity is one, but it contains immense variety. This variety offers us a chance to put our differences to good use, in expanding our field of vision as we stand firm in our common humanity. No matter how different our languages, physical traits, manners, customs, or cultural traditions, we share humanity in common. In the coming year, we must strive to contribute to a society built on an awareness of our single world citizenship. In this sense I hope that what we are calling the Year of Society will also be a year of mutual understanding and positive exchange among peoples with different ways of life. I am vividly aware of the need to make our Year of Society an opportunity to spread our message of peace to other nations.

Some preparatory steps have already been taken in this direction. The range of the activities of Nichiren Shoshu organizations in many parts of the world has been amazing. In May 1973, the European Institute of Nichiren Shoshu was established. This was followed in August by the founding of the Pan-American Nichiren Shoshu League. On December 13, the Southeast Asian Buddhist Cultural Council was independently formed. By way of response to these steps taken by Nichiren Shoshu organizations, the name of the former Overseas Headquarters has been changed to the International Headquarters of Nichiren Shoshu. In addition, we are planning the establishment of an organization designed to contribute to the advancement of world peace; this organization has temporarily been named the Nichiren Shoshu International Center. An independent corporation, the International Center will help our international organizations to develop in many different fields.

Each of the overseas organizations is at a different stage of growth. Motives for adopting Buddhism, national characteristics, and ethnic factors further vary the nature of each. Consequently, no one central organ can enforce directives or maintain control over all of these groups. Each must advance independently on the strength of the feelings and the sense of responsibility of its own members. Respect for the individual natures of various peoples is part of the spirit of the universal propagation of our faith. What I have said about the growth of overseas organizations applies as well to local Japanese organizations. The Nichiren Shoshu International Center should itself adopt as one of its fundamental policies a respect for the independence of overseas organizations and should strive to encourage and support that independence.

At present, each of the overseas organizations taken separately has too few members and is too small to engage in extensive activities. In this connection, Soka Gakkai of Japan, as a sister organization, will have to help its overseas groups to grow as much as possible.

As you all know, our fellow members in many parts of the world are intensely dedicated to religious truth and have a great sense of mission and responsibility in the spreading of the faith. In general, the Japanese people tend to be insular and self-absorbed. But the Buddhism of Nichiren Daishonin is a Buddhism for the whole world. We must adopt a global view and recognize our membership in the family of man as we strive to become openhearted, international people, contributing to the happiness of mankind and to the creation of a worldwide human republic in the richest sense.

Now I would like to refer to the *Jigage* portion of the *Juryo* chapter of the Lotus Sutra, which we recite every morning and evening. *Ongi*

Kuden, the compilation of the oral teachings of Nichiren Daishonin on the Lotus Sutra that were delivered to his close disciples, contains an explanation of the *Jigage* passage. In this explanation, Nichiren Daishonin identifies our true selves as the free life inherent in us; this life in turn is identical with the universal life. Another part of *Ongi Kuden* tells us that universal life is manifest in us as the Buddha nature. In other words, the universe is life, its operations are the pulsating of life, and the life in each individual is equal to the immense power of universal life. This life is the Law, and the same Law permeates each of us and the whole universe.

Victor Hugo has said that the sky is vaster than the sea, but that the human heart is vaster still. Buddhism goes a step further to say that the human heart—that is, the life within the human being—is equal in vastness to the whole universe. Seen from the outside, the physical vessel of our life is an unimposing few feet high. But viewed by an inward-directed light, our life becomes apparent for what it is: something that extends beyond the realm of consciousness into the immensity of the world of the subconscious.

It is now a fact recognized by specialists that the life within the human being is one with the life of plants and other animals. Three thousand years ago, Buddhism had already penetrated to the truth that the life in man is the same life that permeates everything. The sole aim of Buddhism is for the indivual to manifest the life that he shares with the universe. I have no doubt that turning a powerful light on limitless life and thus bringing the Buddhist philosophy to true prosperity and influence is the sole way to rectify the wrongs of modern civilization and guide it to a higher plane.

Working Now for the Future

Recently I met the outstanding American biochemist and philosopher, René Dubos. We had a meaningful discussion on a number of points, including transmigration and the nature of human life. I asked Mr. Dubos what he thought would be the fate of communism, capitalism, and nationalism in the twenty-first century and which of these he thought was the ideal way to the salvation of mankind.

After saying that the question was difficult and then giving it some thought, Mr. Dubos replied that ideologies of the kind I had mentioned have already lost their creative strength. He feels that they have become too autocratic, in that they regard all things from the viewpoint of conflict and attack and treat only the economic and political aspects of human nature. He believes that it is now time to turn our attention to more basic and universal human aspirations. He then added that our task in the twenty-first century will be to re-examine mankind as the source of these basic and universal aspirations and to reorganize our social system so that it can satisfy them. When I mentioned that I have long insisted that the twenty-first century must be an age of deep respect for life, Mr. Dubos nodded his assent. He and I are in agreement that mankind must return to basic humanity as the starting point for new development.

A sincere struggle for the improvement of mankind is the movement that must open the twenty-first century. We must go about our task secure in the pride that coming generations will praise this work. Difficult times threaten the construction of a realistic society for tomorrow. But I want each of you to continue to manifest the treasure inherent in your lives through faithful chanting of Daimoku. In addition, I want each of you to make your daily life a fortress of faith and to find your way out of present difficulties by calling on the mighty power of your own life.

Nichiren Daishonin's *Sado Gosho* (Letter from Sado) says: "An arrogant man will be overcome with fear when he meets a strong enemy, just like the haughty Ashura who shrank and hid himself in a lotus flower blossoming in Munetchi Lake when reproached by Taishaku" (*Gosho Zenshu*, p. 957). This passage tells us that the proud heart, upon encountering a mighty enemy, invariably cringes and attempts to surround itself with a small wall of protection. But, when further hard times come, the wall itself collapses and falls—like the anger of Shura—into a cold lake. When this happens, a life of idle dreaming is shattered and changed into a life of misery. Only the enduringly brave man who walks the way of unshakable faith is the true human monarch. Such a monarch has no need of crown, external glory, pomp, or authority. He needs no empty theories or plans. None of these things reveals the brightness of the deepest human spirit. We all know how society can sully and ravage all forms of life. The envious jeers that bring suffering to the righteous man are not new. But no matter how dark the blackness of evil, we can dispel it with the shining mirror of the Buddhist Law. I ask that all of you live bravely with confidence in our mission of universal propagation of true Buddhism. I ask that you join with me in raising the banner of humanity and dedicate 1974 to preparing the way for a new human century.

The Future Is
Your Responsibility

Delivered at the Twenty-second General Meeting of the Youth Division of Soka Gakkai, held in Kita-kyushu, January 20, 1974.

When we are young, the years seem to fly by. From the bottom of my heart, I urge you to make the best of your youth by putting it to fruitful use in carrying our faith to all the peoples of the world. At the thirty-sixth general meeting of Soka Gakkai, held on December 16, 1973, at the Nakanoshima Central Public Hall in Osaka, I said that 1974 is to be called the Year of Society and that it will become the curtain-raising year for the full-scale spreading of our faith over the entire globe. By way of explanation of how this movement must develop, I should like to open my talk with some remarks about the overseas situation.

Struggling Together to Bring the Faith to All Men

Today, the Buddhism of Nichiren Daishonin is active in more than fifty nations, in all parts of the world, excluding the communist sphere. I am deeply aware, however, that among all of our overseas groups, the ones in the United States have the largest membership and are most joyously engaged in our religious task. Three thousand members from the United States held a convention on October 11,

1973, at the head temple, Taiseki-ji, in Shizuoka Prefecture. This convention has a very special meaning for us and for the growth of our movement.

In 1279, Nichiren Daishonin gave the world the Dai-Gohonzon to serve as the fundamental object of religious veneration for all mankind. The people who attended the October convention at the Taiseki-ji are, it is true, all citizens of one nation. But seven hundred years ago, when Nichiren Daishonin gave us the Dai-Gohonzon, the ancestors of those people inhabited many parts of Europe, Asia, and Africa. Consequently, a convention of citizens of the United States is more than a congregation of members of Nichiren Shoshu from one country. It amounts to a ceremony of praise for all mankind. And as such it is proof of the prophecy made centuries ago that the true Buddhism will spread to all parts of the world.

In *Kangyo Hachiman Sho* (Remonstration to Hachiman) and in *Kenbutsu Mirai Ki* (On the Buddha's prophecy), Nichiren Daishonin said that the true Buddhism will be propagated in a westward direction; that is, from Japan to China, then to India, and from there to the rest of the world. The outstanding flourishing of the American Nichiren Shoshu groups—located east of Japan—may seem to contradict this prediction, but I do not think that such is the case because I see a profound Buddhist meaning in this phenomenon.

In the time of Nichiren Daishonin, the American continents were unknown lands. Of course people lived there. Mongoloid peoples who crossed from Asia by way of the Bering Strait had developed high-level cultures in many parts of America. It is true that in about 1000 of the Christian era, Norsemen visited parts of the eastern coast of North America. But the existence of the inhabitants of the American continents was unknown in the European cultural sphere.

Then in 1492—roughly two hundred years after the death of Nichiren Daishonin—Columbus discovered the New World, where, from that time on, peoples from Europe, Asia, and Africa were to live and work together. Many different motives and causes took these peoples to America. Unable to tolerate the oppressive conditions prevailing in the Old World, some people went to America in search of economic or spiritual liberty. Others were taken against their wills, at the hands of wicked slave traders. No matter what took them there, however, all of these peoples lived together and, while maintaining some elements of their individual cultures, built the society and nation that is today called the United States. It is in the composite nature of this society that I find the profound Buddhist meaning I mentioned earlier.

I am convinced that the early and rapid progress Nichiren Shoshu is making in the Americas—virtually a concentrated version of the entire world, because of the eclectic nature of the people's ethnic backgrounds—proves that the Buddhism of Nichiren Daishonin—the Buddhism of the Sun—will become the heart of the faith of people everywhere and will thus grow to be the true universal religion.

In the thirty-sixth annual general meeting I announced my intention of traveling abroad as much as possible this year in the hope of encouraging our fellow Nichiren Shoshu members, stimulating cultural exchanges among peoples, and laying foundations for the further propagation of our faith. As the first step in this program, at the end of January, I intend to make a trip to Hong Kong and neighboring areas. Nichiren Shoshu is the Buddhism for the entire world, and the compassion of Nichiren Daishonin is afforded in equal measure to all peoples. We must act quickly to avoid losing time. I have responsibilities to the members of our faith everywhere. For that reason I will have to be away from Japan for a while. During my absence, I entrust the well-being of our members here to your care.

Now I should like to make a few comments about current social conditions. In matters of this kind, the essential and comprehensive teaching of Nichiren Daishonin is the *Rissho Ankoku Ron* (The security of the land through the propagation of true Buddhism), the very title of which summarizes his earnest wish that all people realize the Buddha nature inherent in their lives, that society be filled with peace, and that all lives be happy. In the opening part of that work there is a passage that says: "There was once a traveler who, staying as a guest at the house of another, spoke these words in sorrow: 'Beginning in recent years and continuing even today, we find unusual happenings in the heavens, strange occurrences on earth, famine and pestilence, all filling every corner of the empire and spreading throughout the land. Oxen and horses lie dead in the streets, the bones of the dead crowd the highways. Over half the population has already been carried off by death, and there is not a person who does not grieve for some member of his family.' "

A few months ago, when a mood of flourishing prosperity filled the air, many people probably regarded this passage as no more than a record of something that happend long ago. More recently, however, the tragedy of that distant time has been reflected in news of current events.

Inflation is an especially grave issue. An article in a recent issue of the Japanese-language newspaper, *Asahi Shimbun,* pointed out the possible cause of the trouble. The article said that the sudden runaway price increases in Japan are a kind of suicidal rioting on the part of the business corporations of the nation. The article went on to say that criticizing this or that particular party will not solve the problem, which is the outcome of devotion to nothing but the pursuit of profit. The offspring of this devotion has been panic buying by consumers and hoarding by distributers, who hope to drive prices higher still. The article concluded with a plea for consumers to unite.

No matter whose statistics we examine, it is clear that the price rises of the past few weeks are out of proportion to the shortages of materials and goods. An overlapping and intertwining of greed and selfish interest have produced the prevailing conditions, which in themselves reveal the low spiritual level of the leaders of commercial enterprises. In other words, malignant inflation is obviously related to the human spiritual condition. If greed has brought about this sad state of affairs in Japan, it is certainly at work in overseas Japanese undertakings as well. It is scarcely to be wondered that the Japanese meet with unfavorable reactions in neighboring Asian nations. Problems in relations with South America in the near future are also predicted.

This means that a spiritual reformation of our society is a matter of the utmost urgency. I have said that as part of the goal of our Year of Society, I hope to develop a worldwide spirit of friendly cooperation in an attitude of liberty and independence. I have symbolically called this mood the Forum of Mankind. The realization of this forum and of an individual human revolution must be carried out simultaneously with the spiritual reformation of society. From our standpoint, the discussion meeting is the basis on which all of our thinking and acting in connection with these goals must rest. We must strive to refine our discussion meetings further in order to make them more effective. I rely on you to do this in the spirit of engagement in a struggle of the utmost value.

The troubles facing us today—inflation, fires, traffic accidents, shortages of certain kinds of food, drought, and others—fall into the category of calamities. In his commentary on the *Rissho Ankoku Ron,* Nichikan Shonin, the twenty-sixth high priest of Nichiren Shoshu, has the following to say about the causes of calamities.

"I shall now briefly clarify the three causes of calamities according to fundamental Buddhist truth. The first is the influence of the karma of all people. That is, bad karma is born with the individual, and as an effect, this karma invites calamity. . . . The second cause is kings who reject their proper and reasonable roles. By this is meant that when kings adopt an unclear attitude and turn their backs on the teachings and on reason, heaven punishes. The punishment is calamities . . . . The third is slander of the true Law. As is said in the four sutras,* all of the people and the kings invite disasters as a consequence of this act. It is essential to realize that the bad karma of the first cause leads to slandering of the true Law. In the case of the second cause, too, turning one's back on the laws of the secular world becomes turning one's back on the Buddhist Law. Rejecting the fundamental truth of the Buddhist Law leads to slandering that Law. On the other hand, a profound knowledge of the law of the world leads to Buddhism. If one is enlightened to these three causes of calamities, all of one's troubles can be solved."

To put this in general terms, I offer the following explanation. There are three causes of calamities. One is the karma all people bring into this world from preceding existences. This necessitates human revolutions and alterations in fate in different periods of time. The second cause is rejection of their proper roles by political leaders and the resulting immoral government that is not compassionate toward the people. The third is the attempt to destroy Buddhism or the

---

*The four sutras in which the causes of calamities are explained are, in Japanese: the *Kongomyokyo,* the *Daishikkyo,* the *Ninnokyo,* and the *Yakushikyo.*

rejection of Buddhism as the highest reason and the great spiritual mainstay of each age.

The first cause of calamity is the people themselves; the second is political rulers; the third is both the people and the rulers, or the whole of society. Furthermore, the first and second causes inevitably revert to the third cause. Nichikan Shonin's commentary on the *Rissho An-koku Ron* points out the true basic cause of calamity as rejection of the true Buddhist Law.

Recently at a meeting of the Women's Division, I advised that we do all we can to avoid inviting disaster from afar.* Medical treatment of symptoms alone cannot cure an illness. Similarly, treating only the phenomena and immediate causes of disasters cannot solve the problems at hand. If we fail to find the true, profound cause of the trouble and treat only the superficial phenomena, disasters will only recur. The *Rissho Ankoku Ron* is important because it contains a prophetic warning, showing us that we must eradicate the fundamental cause of our trouble. I hope to use this opportunity to bring this vital message not only to you present today but also to the people of Japan and to all peoples everywhere. In achieving this, I shall need your help.

Materialism and Greed: The Weakness of Western Culture

In Nichikan Shonin's commentary on the *Rissho Ankoku Ron,* there occurs the following passage: "The heart of man changes with the times. According to the Thousand-character Classic, 'When one protects the truth and is resolute in the pursuit of a goal, one's intentions change. Average humanity alters according to the things it is taught. For instance, if a man encounters good, he becomes good. If he encounters evil, he becomes evil. The heart is unsettled, and its will shifts according to the thing at hand. Chuang Tzu said that the ordinary human being is physically limited yet seeks the infinite. In short, the human heart is never settled.' "

---

*This is a reference to the *Mushimochi Gosho* of Nichiren Daishonin. In this passage it is pointed out that becoming an adversary of the Lotus Sutra invites calamities from great distances.

This passage about "average humanity" teaches that human nature to a large extent depends on the influences of education, manners and mores, and the social environment. Furthermore, it suggests that it is essential for people to be educated throughout their lives according to the teachings of the good Law. Soka Gakkai is a kind of university dedicated to cultivating the good aspects of humanity. In this sense, all of us who are members and who have devoted our lives to the organization are blessed.

Property and money are needed for the support of the lives of individuals and families and for the sake of enriching society and the world. For these aspects of human life, the production, distribution, and accumulation of property and wealth are indispensable. It is a deflection from the right way, however, to become so engrossed in these things that *the true nature of the human heart* is forgotten. Since the Industrial Revolution, the culture of the West has concentrated on amplifying and elaborating the material and economic aspects of life. The refusal to see beyond these aspects has been the greatest weak point of Western culture.

A society that has sacrificed so much to material wealth that it has forgotten the human heart and the better human aspirations degenerates into something compassionless, doctrinaire, ignorant, and ultraconservative. When this happens, fundamental solutions to calamities become impossible. If we protect the truth and are resolute, we are capable of creating peace and prosperity. And the truth we must protect ought to be high and great.

Freedom from Fate

Our great truth—the thing that we must protect to the utmost—involves ethics and the best of human nature. But more basic than anything else is our duty to guard the truth of life, the truth that we and the universe are one, and that a single ordinary human thought contains the entirety of universal life. This is the great rule of the Mystic Law, and protecting it will make us resolute and will enable us to find our own meaning in life and to create a society that has a reason for existing. The *Kaimoku Sho* (The opening of the eyes) says, "At this moment I, Nichiren, am the richest man in all of Japan.

I have dedicated my life to the Lotus Sutra, and my name will be handed down in ages to come."

Most of you are still too young to have financial wealth, but you can all be absolutely certain that you are wealthy in that fate has ensured your future. You are additionally wealthy in that, as members of the family of Nichiren Daishonin, your hearts are filled with resolution. Keep this as the source of your highest pride as you strive with me to make this a year of significant reconstruction for mankind.

I should now like to say a special word to the Young Women's Division. Do not allow yourselves to become the playthings of fate. In the past—and possibly today—many young women have suffered because of fate, but the maidens of the Mystic Law have the opportunity to be liberated from the bonds of karma. Once you have been freed from those bonds, everything depends solely on your own effort and perseverance.

When karma is recognized and faced openly, it can be changed. Bottled up, however, it generates trouble. A geological peculiarity of northern countries illustrates what I mean: In the winter, in the cold plains of the north, small hillocks slowly develop in places where in warmer weather the land is flat. This dramatic topographical change—obviously an impediment to the construction of satisfactory architectural foundations—prompted geologists to investigate the nature and cause of the hills, and this is what they learned. Underground water is deprived of outlets when the surface of the ground freezes in winter. The water then moves about inside the earth until it finds weak places in the surface crust. Having found such weak spots, it collects and forces the ground upward. In this way, small hillocks form where there is level land in warm weather.

Human karma is beneath the ground layer of life, figuratively speaking. If we allow our minds and hearts to freeze and deprive this karma of an outlet, it will seek our weakest points and erupt, forming obstructions to our plans and hopes. In this way our lives are forced off their courses into paths that lead to misery instead of to happiness. These hillocks cause disturbances and undermine the bases of our mountains of happiness, which must then come toppling down.

But, as Nichiren Daishonin points out in *Tenju-Kyoju Homon* (Lessening one's karmic retribution), it is possible for us to transform our lives through Buddhist practices—that is, faith and the chanting of the Daimoku—and thus to prevent ourselves from being victims of the influence of karma.

Consequently, while you are still young, refuse to allow yourselves to give in to hardships, sufferings, or temptations. Stride boldly down the path of fate, and, for your own sakes, make your own way. The life you have in this world is precious. My deepest hope for you is that you pioneer your own way so as to make that life truly rich and blessed.

As far as activities for this year are concerned, I hope that you will widen your circle of friendships and place more emphasis on the rural and semirural regions. The time has passed when all attention and all action centered on Tokyo. From now on, the capital and the outlying districts must be treated equally. Indeed, it may be that the outlying districts ought to receive greater cultural benefits. Each of you must gain a firm and accurate understanding of the region closest to you and must attempt to develop a more effective program of activities in that district. I want you to extend your realm of friendship, strengthen bonds of mutual understanding with others, and increase the luster of your wisdom, so that you will grow into the kind of people for whom all society feels warmth and trust. I make this request of you, and I shall watch with pleasure while you fulfill it.

You belong more to the twenty-first century than to this century. In the year 2000, on the average, you will be in your fifties, an age when human beings are mature enough to act with independence and self-confidence at home and on the job. Although many of you may be facing problems now, I am certain that if you walk forward in hope, encouraged by belief in the human revolution, you will all become mature human beings in the fullest sense. In all endeavors I ask that you always bear in mind the word *perseverance*.

A person who walks the path of faith must never lose his sense of justice. According to the ways of the secular world, it may sometimes be necessary to compromise by accepting the bad with the good. But if a person does this too often and too readily, he is likely to become soiled. In the world of faith, there can be no accepting evil, even along with good, because one who loses his sense of justice becomes a powerless person of shadows and obscurity. But one who is true to his faith will inevitably become a good person. It is not enough to be good-natured. You must be tempered and disciplined in many ways. To this end, I urge you to train yourselves at home, on the job, in Soka Gakkai, and wherever you may find yourselves. Make the changes needed to train yourselves and force yourselves to carry out your plans.

Some of you may feel that this talk of tempering and disciplining sounds old-fashioned. But I disagree. Many young people today talk of freedom of life and action, but all too often this means no more than license to amuse themselves as they wish. A person who has spent a year in frivolous pursuits will have made no growth as a human being. He will have failed to expand his abilities and outlook. A person who cannot train and discipline himself labors under a handicap.

This is true in all walks of life. If self-discipline is difficult for you, find encouragement in chanting the Daimoku and persevere. I did the same thing when I was your age, and all of the senior leaders of Soka Gakkai faced similar difficulties in becoming the strong men they are today.

The principle that sorrow in life is connected through enlightenment with the human revolution and the attainment of Buddhahood indicates that we must have courage and discipline. Therefore, for your own sakes, I urge you to be courageous and to find strength in carrying out your Buddhist practices without fail. I will be chanting the Daimoku with the prayer that each of you will grow and develop to the best of his abilities. My prayer is that you will live your youth in hope and health.

Revival from Within

*Delivered at the Sixteenth General Meeting of
the Student Division of Soka Gakkai,
held at Nihon University Auditorium, Tokyo, March 3, 1974.*

In recent months and years, I have had occasion many times to point out that at present Japan and the world are confronted by a number of serious crises. Some of these crises—pollution and the depletion of our natural resources, the population explosion, and the growing spiritual vacuum—threaten the entire fate of humanity. More immediate economic crises arising from the oil shock are related in a very direct way to the fundamental crises. Somewhere in between these categories is a crisis arising from a tendency to revive fascism. At the thirty-sixth general meeting of Soka Gakkai, held in Osaka late last year, I insisted that one of the best specific courses of action we can take against creeping fascism is a campaign to protect Japan's constitution of pacificism.

What Is Fascism?

The answer to this question is not easy, because fascism includes many elements. In the case of Nazi Germany, government was controlled by one party and one all-powerful dictator; and freedom of thought, speech, and assembly was ruthlessly suppressed. This reactionary, racist society felt justified in using military power against other nations to secure its own ends. The essential principle behind these elements was the exaltation of group power at the expense of the individual human being. In German fascism, the individual was buried within the group, and his individuality was blotted out by force.

The process whereby the individual is absorbed and destroyed by the group has been explained very clearly from a psychoanalytical point of view in Erich Fromm's *Escape from Freedom,* written when Nazism was at the zenith of its development. Fromm asked why the people of Germany were willing, even happy, to accept Hitler's dictatorial rule and why, when the Weimar Constitution gave them an ideal form of democracy, they turned to a fascist system.

Fromm's answer is that the Germans were suffering from an illness arising from a spiritual void and frustration traceable to the time of the Protestant Reformation. The illness manifested itself as an urge to bow before authority and expressed itself sometimes in the form of Nazism or fascism and sometimes in the form of capitalism.

Men are psychologically prone to seek spiritual stability and fulfillment by subordinating themselves to the group. This is to some extent inevitable, because no living being—let alone man, with his highly developed spiritual functions—can exist in complete isolation. The important question is whether the identity and personality of the individual are respected or denied within the group. Does the individual exist for the sake of the group, or the group for the sake of the individual?

In the ancient periods of human civilization there was almost no recognition of personal, individual independence. The individual was part of the group, and there was no means whereby he could live separately from it. This was true not only from the materialistic and technological viewpoints but also from the spiritual viewpoint as well. The individual was submerged in a group that collectively bowed before the authority of a ruler, and everybody shared the same spiritual framework, which was sustained by myths and legends about the acts of heroic gods and goddesses.

By way of contrast, the developed religions—Christianity, Islam, and especially Buddhism—put prime emphasis on respect for the individual. Christianity and Islam proclaim eternal gods. Buddhism teaches an eternal, immutable Law, offering the individual eternal salvation from the suffering and impermanence of the here-and-now. Emphasis in these religions is necessarily on the individual, and their doctrines stress respect for individual life. Having progressed from Hinayana through Provisional Mahayana to the Mahayana of the Lotus Sutra, Buddhism makes it clear that there is a Buddha nature within all living beings. This Buddha nature is an eternal, immutable law, forming an indestructible foundation for the principle of respect for individuals. Here, Buddhism avoids the inconsistency that arises in Christianity and Islam, in which God, while said to exist inside the human spirit, is often treated as an absolute, ineffable deity, existing over and above human beings.

The respect for the individual that the developed religions strive for and have to some extent attained is anathema to fascists, according to whose lights the ancient religion apotheosized group power, which could be invested in a particular individual as an object of extreme hero worship.

In order to stir the German people to the depths of their souls and thereby gain control of them, the Nazis attempted to revive pre-Christian Germanic mythology. The people were told that they were a super-race and were encouraged to listen to the chauvinistic operas of Richard Wagner, in particular the saga of the heroic Siegfried in *The Ring of the Nibelung*. The message had strong appeal in a Germany still dazed and reeling from its defeat in World War I.

In Japan during the same period, super-patriots urged the people to return to the pre-Buddhist, native religion, Shinto, which, in its modern, state-sponsored form, considered the emperor to be the personification of godliness. The Japanese people were taught to sacrifice individualism for the sake of the nation as a whole. Similarly, in Italy, the fascists played up the heroes and gods of pre-Christian Rome to persuade individual Italians to submerge themselves in a racial group.

History has taught us the true nature of fascism, of which these iniquitous revivals of primitive religions were only one aspect. To combat fascism, we must understand the fundamental principles of the teachings of Buddhism, the loftiest and most perfect of the developed religions. Who is it that has the greatest power and responsibility to resist the threat of fascism? There is no doubt in my mind that it is you, you who have embraced the Supreme Law of the Buddha and are practicing Buddhism.

In addition to withstanding the danger of fascism and guarding against the desecration of human life, you must wage a determined battle against the weakness and spiritual emptiness that constituted the psychological mechanism of fascism in Germany, Italy, and Japan. You must direct the sense of fulfillment, the life and the wisdom that flow forth from your inner selves, into the great work of spreading Buddhism, for this is the best way to uproot the weed of fascism and prevent its growing on this earth again.

Universalism and Provincialism

A scholar whom I admire and respect once said to me that the history of Japan since the beginning of the Meiji era in 1868 has been a series of cyclical changes between world-oriented universalism and Japan-oriented provincialism. In the first two decades of the Meiji era, when the chains of seclusion that had locked the country in for two and a half centuries were being broken, there was a groping, searching movement toward universalism. The government followed a policy of cultural enlightenment; and among the people there arose a demand for democracy, symbolized by the movement for civil rights. New leaders propounded the sovereignty of the people and worked for regular elections and a unicameral parliament. Some even argued in favor of a republican body politic, rather than an imperial state.

Before long, however, those in power began to regard this movement as dangerous and set about suppressing it. The leaders of the movement compromised supinely with the authorities, and the movement was quickly broken. No doubt there were many reasons for this defeat, but one of the most important must certainly have been the movement's lack of grass-roots, popular support. The few people who participated were led by a segment of the intellectual class, and even the leaders had only a conceptual understanding of what they were aiming at. The philosophy of freedom and democracy was not deeply ingrained in them.

The imperial constitution of 1889 was established amid the ruins of the democratic movement. The constitution served as a legal foundation for an imperial state, and religious support was sought in Shinto. Education was employed to instill the system into the people of the whole nation; and an imperial rescript on education, based on conservative Confucian principles, was proclaimed. The spirit of universalism that had prevailed for a time changed quickly into nationalism backed by Shinto, in other words, into a Japanese form of provincialism.

Provincialism is a very strong force. In Japan's more distant past, it gave birth to popular beliefs of many sorts and to a culture rich in local variations. After the middle of the nineteenth century, an attempt was made to harness all the forces of provincialism behind the Japanese state and state Shinto.

Why did the people turn to Shinto in particular? Perhaps this was a peculiarly Japanese psychological reaction, involving a frenetic movement away from the noble principles of democracy and toward something that was the exact opposite. In any case, Japanese, high- and low-born alike, became united in a single spiritual force powerful enough to achieve victory in wars with China and Russia and to create at least the appearance of flourishing.

In the second decade of this century, the pendulum swung again, this time under the impetus of such events as the Russian Revolution and the victory of the democratic nations in World War I. Political parties enjoyed increased status in government, and a labor movement with overtones of socialism arose. This was the age of what was called "Taisho democracy," after the name of the reign era (Taisho— 1912–26). The word *culture* was on all lips. Comfortable houses were spoken of as "culture dwellings." Modern ways of living, new lecture societies, and even pots and pans used in modern kitchens were dubbed "cultural." Culture referred to anything modern as opposed to traditional, comfortable as opposed to Spartan. The trends of the Taisho era were perhaps superficial, but a certain inclination toward universalism was abroad. At the same time, general impotence and spiritual emptiness made it possible for militarists to turn the yearnings of the people in the direction of fascism.

Clear indications of the rise of fascism are to be seen in a number of political incidents, beginning with the assassination of Premier

Tsuyoshi Inukai on May 15, 1932, and progressing to the army revolt of February 26, 1936. Japanese militarism grew like a cancer as the Manchurian Incident escalated into the Sino-Japanese War and the Sino-Japanese War into the Pacific War. Shinto was glorified as the spiritual and philosophical backing for militarism, and the imperial rescript on education was drummed into children from the time they were able to walk. Most of the Japanese nation came to believe that militarism and fascism represented beautiful expressions of the Japanese soul—the "spirit of Yamato"—which was Japan's cultural heritage, and the nation seethed with nationalistic passion.

Defeat in World War II destroyed the myth of infallible protection by the gods. What followed was not a mere swing of the pendulum but a total turnabout. Almost instantly everyone was talking about the principles of democracy; and Japan was given a new constitution, which, unlike any other national constitution of the past, explicitly renounced war.

Japan's version of democracy permeates the educational system and the social system. The extent to which the principle of universalism has entered the hearts of individual Japanese, however, is a moot point. Indeed, the word "democratic" sometimes sounds empty today. We hear a flood of talk about dignity of life, respect for the individual, humanism, and freedom and equality, but the spirit of the pacifist constitution is often ignored. Our skies are cloudy with smog, and we are trampled on by unscrupulous businessmen. The restlessness of the time can be seen in the recent wave of panic buying and the increased public interest in fortune telling. I cannot help feeling the frustration and spiritual vacuity deep in the minds of our people.

Which way will the pendulum swing when distrust and uncertainty come to a head? Since, as I have pointed out before, Japan is still to a large degree spiritually isolated from the rest of the world, nationalism and provincialism, tied to a brainless, emotional philosophy that aims to revive the "spirit of Yamato," may again rear their heads. This could lead once more to madness and conflict.

Such a course, however, is far from inevitable. Indeed, I am confident that there is another way but that there is *only one* other way: Buddhism, the philosophy and religion absorbing the better features of provincialism into Universalism. Universalism as such is no more than a concept. In order for it to have true meaning and value, it must embrace the individualistic qualities of provincialism. Provincialism, an intrinsic, indispensable part of real life, is inherent in the everyday customs and modes that have accumulated over the centuries. A universalism that allows no place for provincialism or localism has no real roots. We must aim for a supreme fusion of the general and the particular on a new, higher level.

Today, when Japan, caught somewhere between universalism and provincialism, is once again undergoing a period of soul-searching, I propose a path for a Third Great Revival. That path is Buddhism—a Buddhism that permeates the Orient, that has survived the storms of Oriental history, that champions the true individual self and the universality of mankind, and that provides modern man with an escape from frustration and emptiness. In this Buddhism, I see a bright new future for Japan.

Enlargement of the Self

I should now like to take up the subject of enlargement of the self as it relates to Nichiren Daishonin's concept of humanity. In doing so, I shall refer to the relationship between the Sovereign of Life (Shin-O) and the Life Expressions (Shin-Ju). In simple terms, the Sovereign of Life is the principal axis of all activity—he reigns within our hearts. Life Expressions are the dynamic aspects of movement and actions. When Life Expressions function smoothly about the Sovereign of Life, men develop their strongest, most versatile potentialities.

From the historical viewpoint, Buddhism first focused its attention on the Sovereign of Life, which is the ultimate nucleus. The explanation eventually achieved was the famous T'ien-t'ai Theory of the Nine Consciousnesses. Later, however, Nichiren Daishonin showed that the Sovereign of Life resides in the Mystic Law within the Self and set forth the idea that the "Palace of the Ninth Consciousness that is the unchanging reality that reigns over all life's functions" is within the body of the person who has embraced the Gohonzon.

This idea is developed in the *Reply to Lady Nichinyo* (The real aspect of the Gohonzon), where the following statement appears: "Never seek this Gohonzon outside yourself. The Gohonzon exists only within the mortal flesh of us ordinary people who embrace the Lotus Sutra and chant Nam-myoho-renge-kyo. The body is the Palace of the Ninth Consciousness, the unchanging reality which reigns over all life's functions" (*Gosho Zenshu*, p. 1244).

In order to explain this, I must take up the Theory of the Nine Consciousnesses in connection with the philosophically perplexing entity called Self.

The word *self* often has evil connotations, as in *selfishness* and *self-seeking*. In such cases, however, *self* refers to what Buddhists regard as the minor, or smaller, self; and Buddhism teaches that there is a major, or larger, Self—the True Self—that transcends the smaller self and expands to become one with the great sea of life itself. The whole Buddhist philosophy of life is centered on the idea of breaking out of the prison of the smaller self and arriving at the infinitely expanded True Self. The Theory of the Nine Consciousnesses was developed as a means of achieving this goal. This theory is a development of the so-called "Consciousness-only" (Sanskrit: *Vijnap-ti-matrata*) principle, but it was given new meaning by Nichiren Daishonin, who saw it as an explanation of the totality of life.

Shakyamuni and other Buddhist thinkers discovered the truth that, if we examine the Self in what might be considered a vertical progression from outer surface to inner heart and thence from the conscious to the deeper levels of the subconscious, we find that the life space occupied by the Self gradually expands horizontally. In my opinion, the Theory of the Nine Consciousnesses may be regarded as a philosophy of life development precisely reasoned from this original principle.

Six Consciousnesses

At the surface of spiritual existence are sensory consciousnesses—sight, sound, smell, taste, and touch. In Buddhism these are the Five Consciousnesses. The materialistic civilization of today is directed toward building a worldwide pleasure dome in which these superficial, instinctive senses are constantly stimulated and satisfied. In terms of the Ten States of Life, these five are the consciousnesses of the Self loitering in the Six Transmigratory States—a Self whose life space is both shallow and narrowly ephemeral. Over and above the five senses, however, is such spiritual activity as that involved in thinking and forming judgments; in other words, mental processes, which in Buddhism constitute the Sixth Consciousness. By making use of the Sixth Consciousness, men are able to rise above the Six Transmigratory States and find new life in which the Self is vastly enlarged. Specifically, they can arrive at the halfway mark represented by partial enlightenment, such as Learning and Realization, the sixth and seventh of the Ten States of Life. At this stage, however, they are still beleaguered by the Six Consciousnesses; and their bliss can easily be destroyed in a storm of impulses, desires, emotions, and fateful occurrences. The Self of the Sixth Consciousness is larger and more expansive than the Self with only the Five Consciousnesses but, in comparison with the Self that includes the unconscious impulses and emotions lying beyond the Six Consciousnesses, it fails to break through the limits of the smaller self.

The Seventh Consciousness, which is found in the subconscious of the Sixth Consciousness, is called the *manas* Consciousness. This is the consciousness of thought or reflection, the consciousness of the states of perception and revelation, in which the Self attempts to find order and law within the transitory phenomena of the world. Pioneers in scholarship and art experience the awakening of this Seventh Consciousness. The intelligence generated by it becomes a driving urge to seek the laws governing society, history, and nature.

In the states of Learning and Absorption, even after having experienced the Seventh Consciousness, the Self is not free of the impulses and fateful occurrences that beset a life dominated by ego. On the contrary, in this state the Self faces the further danger of satisfaction with its condition. It not only eschews further enlargement but also may become enveloped in the darkness of a world where the body is mortified and wisdom is stultified. It is not uncommon for people in this state to destroy themselves and others as well. Those whose insight into Buddhism enables them to overcome the impulses of egoism and the machinations of fate proceed beyond the Seventh Consciousness to a profounder realm of inner life. This is the Eighth Consciousness, or *alaya,* where the Self approaches the life that is the source of all things and arrives at a state in which it is identical with the stream of life and death flowing from the infinite past to the infinite furure. It acquires a compassionate energy and a reflecting seeking-power capable of supporting all living existence. This is the Self of the bodhisattva.

The Ninth Consciousness

Even in the Eighth Consciousness, however, not only the pure elements but also the sullied elements of life remain. Together with the compassionate energy that is the essence of purity, a directly opposite egoistic impulse toward destruction of life—the antithesis of purity—persists. The conflict of these two within each individual life continues without end. The Eighth Consciousness, therefore, is not the true Sovereign of Life. The Sovereign of Life resides in the Ninth Consciousness, *amala,* which is the fundamental purity, the fusion of the generating forces of the universe, the great sea of the ultimately harmonious, true Self.

The great Chinese Buddhist scholar T'ien-t'ai experienced the existence of the Sovereign of Life from the inner viewpoint. Nichiren Daishonin, on the other hand, realized that the Sovereign of Life was identical with his inner Self and revealed to humanity a positivistic, practical way whereby all men can arrive at this sublime stage of consciousness. This is the essence of our faith.

In the two thousand years of the Former and Middle Days of the Law, Buddhism considered the Sovereign of Life from the introspective viewpoint; but the Buddhism of Nichiren Daishonin causes the light of the Sovereign of Life to spread over us entirely. The Buddhism of Nichiren Daishonin enables us to cast ourselves once again into the turbulent sea of the world's harsh realities and to fight for the sake of good. This is a religion for youth and a philosophy for the human revolution and the new social movements of our century. The way toward the Sovereign of Life is still in the realm of theoretical teachings; the way from the Sovereign of Life to reality in the universal sense is in the realm of true teaching. This is why in *Ongi Kuden* (the oral teachings of Nichiren Daishonin) the Sovereign of Life is identified with the theoretical truth, and Life Expressions with the actual truth. The same idea is conveyed in the *Reply to the Widow of*

Lord Ueno (Hell and Buddhahood) in which Nichiren Daishonin said: "The words of a wise priest, 'Base your heart on the Ninth Consciousness and your practice on the Six Consciousnesses,' are indeed well said" (*Gosho Zenshu*, p. 1506). From our viewpoint, keeping our hearts in the Ninth Consciousness is achieved by the Gongyo and the chanting of Daimoku. Performing religious practice in the Six Consciousnesses means to be active in the difficult and sorrow-laden Six Paths, where we must encounter the realities of our world. It means to polish and refine ourselves and to save others—this is the essence of our Buddhist practice. The world of reality may be a muddy torrent of instinct and egoism, but we must not waste time dreaming of a better world. We must be able to act freely in both the Ninth and the Sixth Consciousnesses, for this is the bright way toward our human revolution. Morning and evening, call forth the Sovereign of Life before the mirror of the Law, the Gohonzon, and at other times devote your youth to the bettering of the actual world. Base yourselves firmly on the ultimate religion, and with steadfast determination travel freely through all the various realms of life.

Socrates and Plato

Socrates stands out in the history of mankind as one of the giants of philosophy, but it was his disciple, Plato, who systematized Socrates's philosophy for the rest of mankind.

Socrates and Plato first met when the latter was about eighteen or twenty years old—about the age that you are now. Full of pride and confidence, the young Plato was on his way to a contest, where he intended to read a dramatic poem he had written. By chance, he encountered Socrates in front of a theater and was so moved by the philosophical ideas that the older man was propounding that he became ashamed of his own work and destroyed it. Plato studied under Socrates faithfully for about ten years thereafter. During that time, Socrates had many conversations with the young man; and, wherever the philosopher went, the disciple followed. When the Athenian authorities charged Socrates with various crimes, Plato remained faithful and, at the time of Socrates' trial, offered to guarantee the fine. In the words of one scholar, "Plato remained an unswerving follower and intimate friend until Socrates' death. Even afterward, he kept the image of his mentor in his mind's eye and composed many dialogues in which he recorded the words and deeds of Socrates for posterity."

Socrates chose to preserve his integrity by drinking poison. His death was the beginning of Plato's voyage into the inner depths of philosophy. Wherever Plato traveled, the voice of Socrates continued to ring within his heart. Eventually he succeeded in compiling Socrates's philosophy, developing it, and establishing on the basis of it one of the world's great streams of philosophic thought.

The question of the actual and the ideal—what is and what ought to be—has been a basic philosophical issue throughout the past and will no doubt remain one as long as philosophy exists. Plato became the great philosopher of the ideal—what ought to be—and Plato's follower Aristotle became the great philosopher of the actual—what is. All mankind has profited from the wisdom and virtue that grew out of the master-disciple relationship between Socrates and Plato.

Instead of writing down his ideas in detail, Socrates developed them in dialogues, which Plato recorded for future generations. Had there been no Socrates, there would have been no Plato; but, had there been no Plato, Socrates would not have survived to become the lifeblood of a whole philosophical epoch.

Similarly Christ had his Paul; Shakyamuni had his Ten Great Disciples; T'ien-t'ai had his Chang-an; Dengyo had his Gishin; and the Buddha of the Latter Day of the Law, Nichiren Daishonin, had his Nikko Shonin. In each of these instances, the spread of a great philosophy was brought about largely by disciples or followers, rather than by the original thinker.

You young people are the Platos of Soka Gakkai. In consonance with the great life that we call the Mystic Law, you who are now still tender, green sprouts will grow into great, sturdy trees. When you do, the great philosophy of true Oriental Buddhism will rise like a mountain before the adoring eyes of all humanity.

The world is now seeking a great religion that will cast an infinite light upon humanity. I am speaking not only of the members of Nichiren Shoshu but of mankind as a whole. The various intellectual leaders in the world with whom I have conversed all agree with me that there is a great need for a new religion suited to the coming century.

It is perhaps presumptuous of me, with few scholarly pretensions, to undertake to spread the message around the world, but I do this in the confidence that you, as my followers, will employ your learning and wisdom to create in the world of the future an era of true peace. You are following the way of the Bodhisattvas of the Earth, who sprang from the ground as described in the Lotus Sutra. May you become glittering stars in the heavens. The cultural heritage of mankind flows in your veins, and from that One Thought *(ichinen)* in your hearts there will develop a new world of freshness, greenness, and life. If there are bad days—days of cold winds and bitter frosts—look upon them as an opportunity for developing your sacred inner lives. Persevere in joy, be wise and brave and righteous, and you will overcome all difficulties. Though we live in a weak, anxiety-ridden age, those of you who have spirit will certainly be recognized and looked up to as the bearers of culture in the twenty-first century.

Toward the Twenty-first Century

Delivered at the University of California at Los Angeles, April 1, 1974.

The invitation extended to me by President Charles E. Young and Vice-President Norman P. Miller to speak at the University of California at Los Angeles, one of the leading intellectual institutions in the United States, gives me deep pleasure. Today I should like to talk not as a speaker from a platform but as a friend, a person who respects you and who expects much of you as the men and women responsible for the future of the United States and of the whole world in the opening years of the twenty-first century.

Arnold J. Toynbee, the famous historian and philosopher, is deeply concerned about the fate of humanity in the coming century. Over the past few years, it has been a source of great personal enrichment and intense intellectual stimulation for me to be able to engage in an extended series of dialogues with this great man. On two occasions—in May 1972 and again in May 1973—I met with Mr. Toynbee in London to discuss many important topics.When we have been unable to meet personally, we have carried on a dialogue by correspondence. We have chosen the dialogue form of examining modern civilization and the prospects for the future, because of the valuable personal contacts it affords.

Mr. Toynbee would set an excellent example of industry for you younger people. Although he is now eighty-five years old, he is up at six forty-five every morning. Most of you are still sleeping at that hour. Or perhaps you have gotten up briefly to make a trip to the toilet and are going back to sleep. But that is not the way of life of Mr. Toynbee and his wife. Working together, they make their beds and prepare their breakfast. By nine o'clock every morning, whether or not he has a specific task in hand, Mr. Toynbee is at the desk in his study, ready for work. I saw him seated at that desk, and I was struck by the beauty of his old age. Of course youth like yours is beautiful; but age can be beautiful, too. Give your parents a chance to grow old beautifully. Work hard in your studies, and do not worry your parents haggard. Take your motto from Mr. Toynbee, who took his from the Roman emperor Lucius Septimus Severus. Once not long before his death, this industrious leader, though ill and forced to carry out operations in the cold of northern England, gave his soldiers the word *laboramus,* or "let us work," as their motto for the day. Mr. Toynbee has adopted *laboramus* as his motto, and he does work very hard. This is the secret of his continuing vigor and determination to go on with his tasks. It is the lifelong battle with meaningful ideas that is the ultimate beauty of mankind. Mr. Toynbee has this kind of beauty.

Our talks ranged over an immense field of topics, including civilization, the phenomenon of life, learning, education, literature, art, natural science, international issues, social topics, humanity, the problems of modern women, and many more. Our first session of conversations lasted for over forty hours. On the occasion of our second personal meeting, by way of greeting Mr. Toynbee gave me a serious look and urged me to get down to work at once, since we would be talking for the sake of the people of the twenty-first century. Mr. Toynbee is urgently concerned with what will happen on earth after his own death. He very much wants to leave an intellectual message for those of us who are younger. His desire to do something for the future was the dominant note in our dialogues; and I hope to speak to you today with no less intense a dedication to the good of posterity than that which I recognize in Arnold J. Toynbee.

Toward the end of our discussions, when I asked for some words of advice for the people of the coming century, Mr. Toynbee said that in the twentieth century, mankind's intoxication with technology has led to the poisoning of our environment and the threat of self-destruction of all humanity. He went on to say that self-mastery is the only way to approach a solution to the current crisis. But self-mastery cannot be achieved either through extreme self-indulgence or extreme asceticism. The people of the twenty-first century must walk the middle path, the way of moderation.

I find this interpretation of the best solution to our dilemma especially congenial, because moderation and the middle way are pervasive elements in Mahayana Buddhism, which is the spiritual main current of the Orient. By moderation in this sense I mean the way of life that is a synthesis of materialism and spirituality.

The path of moderation is the only answer to the current crisis of civilization; but, to follow that path, mankind requires a reliable guide. Technological theories fail us because, as the very nature of our dilemma proves, they have no final answers. To find the kind of guide needed today, we must return to such basic issues as the nature of the human being and the meaning of living. In my talks with Mr. Toynbee, perhaps the most impressive topic was the nature of life itself. I am firmly convinced that knowledge of the nature of life is fundamental to knowledge of the human being as a manifestation of life and is therefore a basic element in the formation of cultures and civilizations. The twenty-first century will—indeed must—cast light on the fundamental nature of life and in this sense will move away from technology to create a civilization that is humane in the richest, fullest meaning of the word.

If time permitted, I should like to share with you some of the things Mr. Toynbee and I discussed in relation to such topics as the eternity of life, the death penalty, suicide, euthanasia, and many others; but I have decided to limit myself to the question of the fundamental nature of life, the crucial issue in the future of humanity.

As many of you probably know, one of the primary teachings of Buddhism is the belief that human life is an aggregate of sorrows, particularly the sorrow of birth, the sorrow of growing old, the sorrow of illness, the sorrow of the death of loved ones, and ultimately the sorrow of one's own death. These are the most basic sufferings, but there are others. Pleasant times are fleeting; we must all face the sadness of seeing them go. In society today, there are many causes for sorrow and unhappiness: for instance, national and racial discrimination and the widening gap between rich and poor.

In other words, sorrow occurs as the outcome of many different kinds of conditions. But what is the basic reason for sorrow itself? The Buddhist answer is this: nothing in the universe, no phenomenon in human life, is constant. Sorrow is the result of man's inability to understand the principle that there is no immutable constancy.

The changing nature of everything is immediately apparent. All young things must grow old. All things that have form must disintegrate. The healthy sooner or later become ill, and all living creatures must die. As the Greek philosopher Heraclitus said, all things are in a constant state of flux; nothing in the universe remains the same, but everything alters from instant to instant like the current of a mighty river. The microphones on this table and the table itself are sturdy enough; but, given time, they will be destroyed. Things are not stable, no matter what our senses suggest to our brains. And clinging fast to the deluded belief in the stability of things causes the sufferings of the human spirit. This is a basic tenet of the philosophy of Buddhism.

To hope for permanence is only human. Probably no young man troubles his head about what his girlfriend will look like after thirty or forty years, because he hopes—even believes—that she will not change much. We all want beauty and youth to last. We trust that whatever wealth we have will endure, and we work for the sake of acquiring the good things of the world. Still, we realize that, no matter how hard we work and no matter how big our bank accounts, we cannot—as the saying goes—take it with us. Nonetheless, we do work in order to enjoy the benefits of our earnings, and we want to enjoy them as long as we can. Undeniably this desire leads to suffering: we cannot keep our material things forever. The same is true of possessive relations with human beings. No matter how much one tries to keep the loved one near, someday a parting must come. And this is perhaps the cause of the greatest spiritual suffering man is called upon to endure.

Attachment to people leads to suffering. Attachment and greedy desire for things can be the cause of war and the consequent sorrow at loss that one or both of the warring parties must undergo. Incidentally, I might point out that one of the firmest stands of both Mr. Toynbee and myself is adamant opposition to war of all kinds. He has lost many people who were dear to him in the two world wars. I too have lost a close relative in war. Mr. Toynbee and I agree that there is absolutely no excuse for the wasteful taking of life and destruction of property caused by war. Attachment to one's own life, too, sometimes causes people to sink into a morass of worry and fear. Most of us do not worry ourselves constantly about the imminence of death. On the contrary, we carry out the affairs of our daily lives more or less convinced that we will live forever. There are people, however, who are unable to assume this blindly optimistic view. They are led into worry and sorrow by the fear of death, aging, and illness, and a frantic desire to stay alive as long as they can.

In spite of all our efforts, human life is constantly changing and therefore is sorrowful. Our own bodies, a physical manifestation of the changes of the universe, must someday die. To live our lives meaningfully and sanely, we must face fate coolly and fearlessly. Buddhism teaches that the way to do this is to accept the fact of constant universal change. Such acceptance opens the path to enlightenment.

But it would be wrong to dismiss entirely the value of concern about the changing nature of all things. As long as we are alive and human, we strive to preserve life, to value the love of others, and to enjoy material benefits. This is entirely natural.

In the past, Buddhist teachings have been understood as directed toward the severance of all connection with the passions and desires of the world and as opposed to—according to some interpretations, a hindrance to—the advancement of civilization. It is unfortunately a fact that today many of the parts of the world where Buddhism is the heart of civilization are retarded in terms of scientific technology. If Japan is an exception to this statement, it is not because she has adopted Buddhist principles as a fundamental philosophy, but because she has concentrated on incorporating the framework of the Western technological revolution. It may be that the backwardness of these nations can be attributed in part to the Buddhist doctrine of transience. But this doctrine is only one aspect, not all, of Buddhism.

The true Buddhist teaching is not severance from the desires of the world or isolation from all attachments. It is neither resignation nor nihilism. The true Buddhist teaching is the immutable Law, the essential life, that underlies all the transience of actuality, that unifies and gives rhythm to all things, and that generates the desires and attachments of human life.

Each of us can be analyzed into a lesser self and a greater self. To be blinded by transient phenomena and tortured by desires is to exist for no more than the lesser self. To live for the larger self means to be enlightened to the universal principle behind all things and to employ this enlightenment to rise above the transience of the phenomena of the world.

What is the larger self? It is the basic principle of the whole universe. At the same time, it is the Law—the reality—that generates the many manifestations and activities that make up human life. Arnold Toynbee describes the greater self as the ultimate reality behind the universe and considers the Buddhist concept of a universal Law closer to the truth than notions of anthropomorphic gods.

To live for the greater self does not mean abandoning the lesser self. The lesser self is only able to act because of the existence of the greater self. Desires and attachments experienced by all of us as smaller selves have stimulated the advancement of civilization. If man had not been attracted to wealth, economic growth would not have taken place. If man had not struggled to overcome the natural elements and provide relief from such things as cold, the natural sciences would not have flourished. Without the mutual attachment and conflicts of the sexes, literature would have been deprived of one of its most famous and enduring fields of expression.

Although some branches of Buddhism have taught that man must try to free himself from desires and have even gone so far as to condone self-immolation as one way of escape from this life, such an approach is not representative of the highest Buddhist thought. Desire and sorrow are basic parts of life; they cannot be eliminated. Desire and all it implies constitute a generative, moving force in life. But they and the smaller self that they affect most directly must be correctly oriented. True Buddhist teaching strives to discover the greater self and, instead of suppressing or eliminating the smaller self, to control it and direct it so that it can contribute to the growth of a better world civilization through its relation with the greater self.

Buddhism teaches the transience of all things and the need to face death with open eyes in order to demonstrate the existence of the immutable Law behind impermanence. The Buddha was not a prophet of resignation, but a man who had attained enlightenment to the Law of the impermanence of things. He taught the need to face death and the transience of phenomena without fear, because he knew that the immutable Law behind all things is the source of life and of value. None of us can escape death, but Buddhism shows that behind death is the eternal, unchanging, greater life that is the Law. Secure in the absolute faith that this is the truth, we can face both death and the impermanence of all worldly things bravely.

The Buddhist Law means that, since life itself is eternal and universal, life and death are merely two aspects of the same thing. Neither aspect is in any way subordinate to the other. The ultimate, eternal life governing individual lives and deaths must be understood in terms of the concept of *ku,* which transcends our understanding of space and time. In effect, *ku* is limitless potentiality; it is the essence from which all things are made manifest and to which all things return. It surpasses the space-time framework, because it is eternal, ultimate, and all-pervasive. In our many discussions of the issue of eternity, Mr. Toynbee said that he felt the idea of *ku* approximates what he calls the ultimate spiritual reality.

It is impossible to explain in detail the nature of *ku* in a short time, but I should like to try to make a few points in connection with this concept. First of all, *ku* is not nonexistence. It is neither existence nor nonexistence. These two terms represent human interpretations based on the space-time scale by which we ordinarily gauge our experiences and environments. *Ku* is more essential; it is a fundamental reality.

Perhaps I can illustrate the nature of *ku* by referring to an experience that all human beings have. The physical and psychological changes the individual undergoes from infancy to maturity are so great that the entire person seems to alter drastically. Yet throughout all the changes there is a persistent self uniting both the mind and the body and remaining relatively constant. We are not always aware of this self, which is manifest on both the physical and the mental planes, but it is the basic reality that lies beyond the realm of existence and nonexistence.

Buddhism interprets this consistent self as directly connected with the greater universal life and as capable of operating eternally—now in the life phase and now in the death phase. This is why Buddhism interprets life and death as one. The lesser self of each of us includes the greater self. Therefore each of us breathes with the immutable universal life while living in the world of transience and change.

It makes me unhappy to have to say that the civilization of the world today is swayed almost completely by the desires of the lesser selves of mankind. Human greed has produced an immense, sophisticated, technological society, but only at the cost of polluting the environment and threatening to exhaust the natural resources of the planet. Attachment to things and desires and passions have led to the creation of huge buildings, sprawling express transportation networks, and ominous weaponry. If the developments and attitudes that have produced these things proceed unchecked, the self-destruction of mankind seems inevitable. I am convinced that the current worldwide tendency to reflect on the nature of modern society and to turn again toward humane values is a sign that at last man is striving to discover his own nature as a human being.

No matter how lofty a man's intellectual abilities, he is no more than an animal if he is subordinated entirely to passions and the pursuit of the impermanent things of the world. It is now time for all men to turn their eyes to the permanent aspects of life and in this way to live so as to manifest their true value. How can we do this and how will the people of the twenty-first century be able to do it? Once again, Arnold J. Toynbee has provided us with an excellent suggestion. He calls the greed and desires of the lesser self the diabolic desire and the will to become one with the greater self the loving desire. He insists that man can control the diabolic desire and give full rein to the loving desire only if he exercises constant vigilance and self-control. In the next century, I hope that human civilization will break away from bondage to the lesser self and will move forward to progress based on an understanding of the greater self, the permanent entity underlying worldly transience. This is the only way for man to be worthy of his humanity and for civilization to become truly humane. Believing that the permanent Law behind the universe is life itself, I insist that the twenty-first must be a century devoted to respect for life in the widest sense.

The basis on which mankind chooses to operate will determine the success or failure of future civilization. Will man elect to founder in the mire of selfish desires and greed? Or will he walk safely on the firm ground of enlightenment in the greater self? Whether the coming century will be a realization of the dreams of well-being and happiness of all humanity depends entirely on whether mankind is willing to concentrate on the immutable, unchanging, powerful reality that is the Law and the greater life. We have arrived at the turning point where this decision must be made.

Our time is a transition from one century to the next. But it is more: it is a time in which man must decide whether to become human in a rich, full sense. Though my words may sound extreme, it seems to me that in the past, man has rarely advanced beyond the stage of an intelligent animal. Seven hundred years ago, Nichiren Daishonin, the founder of the religious group of which I am a member, wrote of the "talented animal." As I observe the actions of man in the modern world, these words assume increasing significance. It is my belief that mankind must become more than an intelligent or talented animal. I believe that it is time for man to become active in the spiritual sense and in relation to knowledge of the greater self and of universal life.

Each individual human being must find his own way. I have found mine in Buddhism; and with faith in its teachings, I have embarked upon the journey of life. You young people are capable of pioneering and building much for the good of mankind. You stand at this important turning point of the age. Today I have offered some fragments of the wisdom of Buddhism. I shall be very happy if what I have said can be of any assistance in helping you choose your path to the future.

Creative Lives

Delivered at the Fourth Entrance Ceremony of Soka University, held in Hachioji, Tokyo, April 18, 1974.

Knowledge and learning do not of themselves produce good or bad results. After you have spent four years studying at this institute of higher learning, you may go out into society and become smart operators, or you may become public-minded citizens. It is up to each of you to decide the way you will go. It is my fervent hope that during your four years as college students you will conduct yourselves conscientiously and with rectitude.

I have just returned from a trip undertaken to promote international good will and cultural exchange. I left on March seventh and returned on April thirteenth, and in that interval of roughly forty days visited numerous places in North, Central, and South America. Invited by the heads of a number of universities, as the founder of Soka University, I held many discussions concerning the changes that are needed in our concept of education to meet the challenges of contemporary civilization.

Mission of the University

The first place I visited was the Berkeley campus of the University of

126

California, where I enjoyed a dialogue with Chancellor Albert H. Bowker. The University of California has ten Nobel Prize winners on its faculty, and I told Chancellor Bowker that I would like to invite these splendid scholars to lecture or hold seminars at Soka University. In addition, I urged the chancellor and his wife to visit Japan.

Next I went to the University of New Orleans, where I talked with Chancellor Homer L. Hitt on such subjects as the setting up of an International Organization for Educational Cooperation and the creation of international assemblies for the establishment of such an organization. The assemblies would include an International Conference of University Presidents, to maintain liaison among educational institutions, and a World Federation of Student Associations, to bring students of the various nations together. I am happy to say that Chancellor Hitt was in agreement with me. The subject of the International Organization for Educational Cooperation came up again later, during my talks with Vice-Chancellor Norman P. Miller of the University of California at Los Angeles. Vice-Chancellor Miller and I thoroughly agreed that we should make educational exchange a focal point in our efforts toward world peace. While at UCLA, I delivered a lecture entitled "Toward the Twenty-first Century."

In addition to schools in the United States, I also visited the University of Panama and San Marcos University, in Peru, where I talked with people about student and professor exchange. It will take some time before our goals in this field can be accomplished, but we agreed on the basic principles. Rector Guevara of San Marcos University gave me a message for the students of Soka University. I am turning the message over to President Kazuo Takamatsu, with the request that he transmit it to you.

Not long before I went to the Americas, I visited the Chinese University of Hong Kong and made similar proposals there, as I had already done last year at various universities in Great Britain and France. I am confident that our program to have more and more students and professors from other countries visit this university is now on a firm working basis, and I suspect that there will come a day when we will want some of you to go abroad as well. The exchange program will keep us busy, but we are going about it with great enthusiasm.

It is my firm resolve to undertake any task that may be necessary for your well-being, and I want desperately to open a way for you into a new world. I traveled to talk with various educators throughout the world primarily with you, who are an important object of faith and trust for me, in mind. I have drawn a few points in time and space. I ask you to connect the points into lines and create a three-dimensional structure of peace.

Today, political efforts to achieve peace often seem futile. An International Organization for Educational Cooperation is our last and strongest trump card, our surest way of achieving true world peace. For the purpose of setting the stage for an International Organization for Educational Cooperation, I proposed an International Conference of University Presidents; and to enable you and other students to participate in the peace movement, I proposed a World Federation of Student Associations. I cannot bring these organizations into being by myself, nor am I qualified to do so. I do, however, ask you to work toward the realization of my proposals.

Gradually, the world will come to look upon Soka University as a birthplace of new ideas; and it behooves you to acquire the world stature to meet the needs of that day. Create a powerful movement for the promotion of mutual world trust and a vital program of international exchange among peoples.

At San Marcos University, more than twenty professors attended my conference with the rector. Each of them wrote down his motto for life. All these men, who were among the top-ranking educators in Peru, expressed interesting ideas, but I was especially impressed by one who wrote: "Professors and students alike must work with the masses. Together they must overcome all difficulties until we reach the goal of wisdom and peace and happiness for mankind."

Students to Play a Leading Role

Most intellectuals today habitually try to avoid the problems and difficulties of society. This is not right. To justify its existence, a university must work with the masses of humankind to overcome difficulties and arrive at a higher level of life. I contend that this is, always has been, and always will be the mission of a university.

I am sure that if the teachers and students of Soka University and the other universities of the world work together with the common people, we can arrive at the goal of peace for mankind. It is because of this belief that I visited various universities and made the proposals I have mentioned. Now, more than anything else, I want you, who are the builders of this university's scholarly vision, to take over this worthy cause.

On the occasion of last year's entrance ceremony, I talked briefly about the origin and development of universities. At that time, I stressed the fact that a university is not the result of a system or a building program, but a product of the determination and passion of young people seeking new knowledge and wisdom. First of all, determined young people must aspire to make truth their own. To help fulfill such aspirations, teachers and instructors will be found; and, through the cooperative effort of students and instructors, universities will evolve. Fundamentally, the university begins with a thirst for knowledge and a love of truth on the part of the students. The atmosphere of such thirst and love must prevail. A university without eager students is a university without life, a university in which the main purpose has been forgotten. Unfortunately, Japanese universities today suffer from stagnation and loss of direction. The time has come to return to the true origins of university education. You who are entering the university today must regard yourselves, no less than me, as founders and creators of this university. Not only while you are in school, but throughout yonr lives as well, you must join together to go on building Soka University.

During a discussion of the gap between professors and students, a leading professor at San Marcos University brought up two interesting points. First, he said that the dialogue between students and professors must always continue. Second, he said that the university must always permit students to take a responsible part in general affairs and activities. In his search for the proper direction in which to lead his university, he perceived the importance of giving students the leading role, and he was trying to find new solutions suited to the trends of our time. Here at Soka University, you must not wait passively for the university to do something for you but must join proudly, bravely, actively, passionately in making this university a new light of hope. Dialogue must continue, but it must be useful and profitable and based on reponsibility and trust, not irresponsible arguments. This is your university. You are responsible for it. Remember that we are all united in wanting to make Soka University a springboard for the advancement of human culture. If you remember these things, your dialogues will be fruitful.We must create at this university a magnificent community of human beings joined together in a common cause.

I want to talk to you about the special nature of private universities. Fundamentally, the purpose of private universities is to create an opportunity for free, spontaneous pursuit of knowledge, unhampered by government controls. In a free university, it is possible to develop human beings who are capable of considering the future of mankind as a whole and of maintaining a universal viewpoint. It is the special function of a private university to send out into the world young people who are free of narrow nationalism or racial contentiousness, who can think broadly enough to act on a world-encompassing stage and who can work for a revolution in our troubled and hectic society.

Like all other institutions of higher learning, private universities must be devoted to scholarship and research; but a private university should always have a liberal, lively atmosphere, completely free from the clannishness of scholarly cliques. The special mission of the private university is to maintain conditions under which there is always absolute freedom of thought, freedom of study, and freedom of publication. An institute of learning founded on such freedoms will invariably foster independent research and yield scholars rich in individuality and creativeness. It is the duty of a private university to avoid being caught up in evanescent trends and to sponsor long-range research of the widest possible scope.

The type of education and research of which I have been speaking have been the true goals of the university system ever since the first such institution was founded. Unfortunately, for all their undeniable good features, government universities can never ignore the demands or limitations imposed on them from above.

While meeting the needs of its own country or that country's people, the private university is free to look beyond to the needs of the world in general. The private university must be a stronghold, resisting interference from government authorities and offering firm protection to true learning and culture.

Since the late nineteenth century, it has been the custom in our country to regard government schools, and particularly national or prefectural universities, as the main sources of education and cultural enlightenment for youth. Not only among educators but among many other people as well, government universities are thought to represent the mainstream of education. As I consider the future of Japan and the rest of the world, however, it seems to me that, if the spirit of the university is to be a living force in society, we must reverse this situation and find the mainstream of education in private universities.

Today we need bright young people who have studied at private universities to acquire not only knowledge and wisdom but also freedom and independence of thought. When such young prople travel about the world, working or relaxing with the masses of humanity, we will begin to have a new kind of cultural exchange and fusion among individuals and peoples. We will, in short, have cultural interchange at the grass-roots level, instead of only among diplomats and the elite. The day will come when cultural bridges will link the peoples of the earth, when friendships will stretch across all national barriers, when people's hearts will respond joyfully to a birth peal of a new global culture and a new civilization for all mankind. You must become the envoys and the builders of the bridges of culture and peace connecting the peoples of the world. It is you who must toll the great bell announcing to future generations the birth of a new global culture. The reverberations of that bell will echo the yearnings of multitudes of people in all nations.

"Power" and "Wisdom"

Recently the French social scientist Georges Friedmann, who is noted for his research on labor movements, published a book called *La Puissance et la Sagesse* (The power and the wisdom). Some of you may have read it in a Japanese translation. The word "power" in the title refers to human power to control the environment by scientific or technological means. "Widsom" means to him the intelligence to harness this and use it creatively for the welfare of humanity. Though I do not intend to explain the contents of Friedmann's book, I should like to make use of his distinction between power and wisdom.

From the late nineteenth and early twentieth centuries until the end of World War II, Japanese education, and particularly college education, was all too strongly oriented toward acquisition of power. Its purpose was to absorb knowledge, master various techniques, and bring Japan up to the same level of power as the nations of Europe and America. After long years of seclusion, Japan was far behind the Western nations in science; and there was a real fear that, without power, acquired as quickly as possible, it might be colonized and trampled upon by other countries. By virtue of the so-called "rich country, strong army" policy, Japan did manage to maintain her independence, while other countries of Asia were, one by one, being deprived of theirs. In the long run, however, excessive emphasis on power and continued pursuit of the "rich country, strong army" policy resulted in an unprecedented defeat in war.

Regarded as a means to the attainment of power, prewar education lacked the respect for human beings that is ultimately the lifeblood of learning and failed to inculcate in young people a sense of the dignity of human life. Instead, it strove to produce people who were valuable to the nation or industry, people who were mere cogs in government or industrial organizations. Education was the means whereby this end product was achieved.

It is important to acquire power, but the acquisition of power must always be accompanied by the development of wisdom. Wisdom is rooted in the souls of human beings. The way to acquire it is to follow the simple advice of Socrates: "Know thyself." This is the starting point for the establishment of a sense of human dignity, preventing the degradation of human beings into anonymous, interchangeable cogs in a machine. The essence of true knowledge is self-knowledge. This is the ideal of education and learning at Soka University. There are countless splendid universities and research institutions in the world that can give power. But what have they done for humanity? The cruel emptiness and frustration of contemporary civilization are the outcomes of their kind of education.

Your mission is to acquire the wisdom that will enable you to use all power for the sake of the happiness and peace of mankind. Know yourselves and, armed with that knowledge, study. Think of things in relation to yourselves as human beings, re-examine the meaning of knowledge, science, and art to humanity, for such inquiry can lead to a new revival of mankind. I pray for your personal growth and development. I am certain that if we accumulate both power and wisdom, eventually a great Renaissance will take place in human culture.

The French art historian René Huyghe gave a lecture at Tokyo University entitled "Forme et Force" (Form and strength), as related to nature and art. At one point he said: "The crisis of our times is a crisis of civilization, the danger of materialism carried too far. The failing of our culture is compartmentalization of everything and failure to keep sight of whole. I believe that human civilization is a single, indivisible entity and that intellectuals must use their knowledge and power on behalf of civilization. The crisis we face today is not merely a social or political crisis, but a fundamental crisis of civilization."

Open the Door

Last year when I spoke to the entering freshmen of this university, I asked them to strive to be creative human beings. Today I should like to elaborate on what we mean by a creative life. I am not about to launch forth upon a difficult philosophical disquisition or try to give you a definitive explanation of life. I only want to urge you to become cheerful travelers on life's long road. Let me suggest something from my own experience that may help bring honor and glory to your future.

I feel most deeply that I have done something creative when I have thrown myself wholeheartedly into a task and fought it through unstintingly to its conclusion and thus have won in the struggle to enlarge myself. It is a matter of sweat and tears. The creative life demands constant effort to improve one's thoughts and actions. Perhaps the dynamism involved in effort is the important thing.

You will pass through storms, and you may suffer defeat. The essence of the creative life, however, is to persevere in the face of defeat and to follow the rainbow within your heart. Indulgence and indolence are not creative. Complaints and evasions are cowardly, and they corrupt life's natural tendency toward creation. The person who gives up the fight for creativeness is headed ultimately for the hell that destroys all life.

You must never slacken in your efforts to build new lives for yourselves. Creativeness means pushing open the heavy door to life. This is not an easy struggle. Indeed, it may be the hardest task in the world. For opening the door to your own life is more difficult than opening the doors to the mysteries of the universe.

But the act of opening your door vindicates your existence as a human being and makes life worth living. No one is lonelier or unhappier than the person who does not know the pure joy of creating a life for himself. To be human is not merely to stand erect and manifest reason and intellect: to be human in the full sense of the word is to lead a creative life.

The fight to create a new life is a truly wonderful thing, revealing radiant wisdom, the light of intuition that leads to an understanding of the universe, the strong will of justice and a determination to challenge all attacking evils, the compassion that enables you to take upon yourself the sorrows of others, and a sense of union with the energy of compassion gushing forth from the cosmic source of life and creating an ecstatic rhythm in the lives of all men. As you challenge adversity and polish the jewel that is life, you will learn to walk the supreme pathway of true humanity. He who leads a creative life from the present into the future will stand in the vanguard of history. I think of this flowering of the creative life as the human revolution that is your mission now and throughout your lives.

The nineteenth-century French poet and writer Péguy said: "The crisis of education is not a crisis of education, but a crisis of life." The crisis we face today strikes at the very roots of education and learning. And yet it is in education and learning that we will find the doorway to the future. And that is why I put so much faith in Soka University.

Daisaku Ikeda with Dr. Aurelio Peccei, president of the Club of Rome, in Paris, May 1975.

With André Malraux in Paris, May 1975.

With Arnold J. Toynbee in London, May 1972.

With Kurt Waldheim at the United Nations in New York, January 1975.

*With Dr. Arquitecto Enrique Zambrano, chancellor,
at Guadalajara University, Mexico, March 1981.*

At the ruins of India's Nalanda University, the great Buddhist center of learning in the fourth to the twelfth century, February 1979.

Opposite left: *Mr. and Mrs. Ikeda visiting the Sorbonne in Paris, May 1973.*

Opposite right: *With university officials at Oxford, May 1972.*

Speaking at the second Takiyama Festival at Soka University, Tokyo, July 1973.

Playing ping-pong with students of Soka Junior and Senior High School, Tokyo, December 1971.

With Deng Yingchao, widow of Zhou Enlai, at her Beijing residence, April 1980.

With the late Alexei N. Kosygin and an interpreter in Moscow, September 1974.

With Henry Kissinger in Washington, January 1975.

With the late Zhou Enlai in Beijing, December 1974.

*With Peruvian children in the garden of the Nichiren Shoshu
community center in Lima, March 1974.*

Protecting Human Life

Delivered at the Thirty-seventh General Meeting of
Soka Gakkai, held in Nagoya, November 17, 1974.

November is an important month for Soka Gakkai. It was on November 18, 1930, that founding president Tsunesaburo Makiguchi's *System of Value-Creating Pedagogy* was published, marking the real beginning of Soka Gakkai. It was on November 18, 1944, just thirty years ago tomorrow, that President Makiguchi, having so valiantly opposed the oppression of the militaristic government of that time, died in the prison into which that government had thrown him. On the eve of the anniversary of this historic date, this meeting has been convened to set our guidelines for 1975; and I want at this time to reaffirm our future course in the propagation of the faith.

Soka Gakkai was born of the people and has grown by the spontaneous will of the people. I want solemnly to declare, here at this meeting, that Soka Gakkai will forever stand on the side of the people and will under no circumstances take the part of the authorities. In the past, a number of other organizations and movements have espoused the cause of peace but have fallen by the wayside. When this has happened, it has usually been because the organization has become too closely associated with the ruling powers and has been utilized by them. Soka Gakkai will not make this tragic mistake.

In the movement for peace, nothing provides a stronger stimulus than religion. At the same time, there are occasions when nothing in the whole of society is weaker than religion. What is it that makes religions oscillate between strength and weakness? Religions are made strong by the tenacity of the human spirit. On the other hand, human beings are only human; and it is easy for them to become indolent and forget the right things to do.

It is the purpose of Soka Gakkai to cast the light of the life philosophy of Buddhism on human beings, to lead them toward a human revolution in which men work together to strengthen each other and to side with the people in the effort to rid the world of war.

The year 1975 will be the fiftieth year of Showa, the era coinciding with the reign of the present emperor. This name was decided upon on December 25, 1926, when the present emperor succeeded his father, Emperor Taisho. It was inspired by a passage on the legendary Emperor Yao in the *Book of History* that says, "The people were enlightened and happy, and all the countries cooperated in peace." The characters meaning "enlightened" and "peace" were used together to make the name Showa in the hope that the reign of the present emperor would indeed be one in which the people would prosper and the world would be at peace.

In fact, however, owing to the rise of ultranationalism during the first twenty years of Showa, the people were oppressed both materially and spiritually. It was an age enveloped in dark clouds. And, far from "cooperating in peace" with all nations, Japan's militarists led the country into a war against nearly all of them, including the United States, China, the Soviet Union, and Great Britain.

Defeat in World War II brought about the collapse of nationalism and military control. A new constitution was adopted, and a great shift took place in popular thought patterns. Various democratic movements were inaugurated; and, even amid the hardships of the postwar period, a breath of fresh air blew throughout the land.

Still, today, as I look back over the past thirty years, I wonder whether Japan has really been democratized, whether the changes in our system of government and in outward appearances are genuine. It seems to me that we are suffering from social unrest not unlike that of the early Showa period and that there is a serious danger of a revival of fascism.

Soka Gakkai was created by former presidents Tsunesaburo Makiguchi and Josei Toda to counter the mounting confusion of the early Showa period, and today we must once again take up our original mission. In those days, our organization was much too small to guard the welfare of the people and lead the nation in the right direction. Instead it was crushed by militaristic authority. Now, however, we make up more than one-tenth of the Japanese populace; and, if we stand, uniting our voices with the strength and the people's demands for justice, we can do much to prevent Japan from once again choosing the wrong path. This is our mission, and we must carry it out. It is my firm belief that we must be leaders in the movement for world peace. We must show the way.

Satan's Handiwork—Nuclear Armaments

I should now like to discuss nuclear weapons, an issue connected with the mission of Japan and particularly with our own mission. Nuclear armaments continue to proliferate. In a recent United Nations report, it was recorded that the United States alone has the equivalent of 610,000 bombs of the size dropped on Hiroshima. Since one bomb killed 100,000 people in Hiroshima, this means that the United States has enough bombs to kill 61 billion people. In other words, the United States could kill everybody on the planet sixteen times with the nuclear armaments it now possesses.

The Soviet Union has about an equivalent stockpile of nuclear devices; and, though the scale is smaller, England, France, China, and India all now belong to the so-called nuclear club. Other countries are making efforts to join; and even Japan, though refusing to manufacture nuclear weapons of its own, relies for its security on being under the American nuclear umbrella.

Why are these weapons necessary? The answer we are usually given is the nonsensical one that they are a deterrent to war. That is like saying that when two people are holding each other at dagger's point, they are in no danger.

As many public-minded people have warned, there is an ever-present danger that sometime, somewhere, one of these fearsome weapons will be detonated by accident, by miscalculation, or by the hand of a madman, and that such an explosion could start a war that would destroy mankind.

What would happen, for instance, if a nuclear weapon were stolen? This is by no means idle speculation; many authorities have pointed out that nuclear stockpiles have grown beyond the limits within which effective control can be exercised. This is no time to be talking about the "balance of nuclear power." It is too easy to imagine an incident that would strike terror in the hearts of people everywhere.

Man must give up the foolish, essentially barbarian notion that peace can be achieved through armament. We must be civilized and realize that peace is to be achieved only by discarding weapons. We must put behind us the idea of preventing war by means of fear and work to achieve true peace through mutual trust and understanding. In short, we must change our fundamental way of thinking about war and peace.

The first step is to prohibit the manufacture, testing, and stock-piling of nuclear weapons in any country. The second is to do away with the weapons already in existence. I insist that this is the goal toward which we must exert all our efforts.

Seventeen years ago, on September 8, 1957, our teacher, former President Toda, announced as the first article of his will a plea for the abolition of atomic and hydrogen bombs. Our attitude has not changed in the slightest in the intervening period. And to keep President Toda's statement alive, enthusiastic members of our Young Men's Division have carried out a nationwide campaign to collect ten million signatures on a petition urging the abolition of nuclear armaments. On behalf of the signers, I want to issue a call to the United Nations and to the leaders of the countries of the world.

As I have pointed out in my novel, *The Human Revolution,* nearly twenty nations have the capacity to produce nuclear bombs. The time has come to hold a world conference in which all nations, whether or not they have nuclear arms, will be represented by their most responsible leaders. This conference should wholeheartedly set about the task of ridding the world of nuclear arms and should remain in session until a solution has been found, even if it takes months or years. At this summit meeting, I trust that serious attention would be paid to the opinions of the Japanese people, who are the only people ever to have suffered an atomic attack.

The bombings of Hiroshima and Nagasaki were not merely tragic experiences for Japan but also lessons for all humanity. Having undergone this ordeal by fire, Japan must exert its utmost energies for the abolition of nuclear armament, moving forward with renewed confidence and faith toward this goal. This is Japan's historic mission and the greatest contribution that Japan can make to the future.

As a second step, I think that the Secretary General of the United Nations should take the initiative in the antinuclear movement and should be given the authority not only to preside over the international conference but also to supervise the actual disposition of weapons. The United Nations should have the power to enforce decisions relating to nuclear disarmament.

As a prerequisite, the peoples and leaders of all nations must discard the idea that possession of nuclear weapons increases national prestige. We must inculcate in ourselves recognition of nuclear weapons as the handiwork of Satan, capable of bringing nothing but misery to humanity.

We must mobilize the strength of peoples all over the world who hope and pray for peace. The combined wisdom of these citizens of the world could restrain large nations, should they threaten to violate the principles of nuclear disarmament.

In May of this year, when I had a series of talks with André Malraux, he voiced the opinion that the United Nations was no more than a ghost. Vice Premier Li Xiannian of China dismissed the organization as a mere rostrum, with much talk but little action. Unfortunately, they are right, so far as the present United Nations is concerned. I think, however, that it is too early to conclude that the organization cannot be revived.

What has deprived the United Nations of real strength? More than anything else, it is the nationalistic egoism of the big nations, sustained by feelings on the part of their peoples.

Such nations feel able to walk roughshod over the United Nations, which lacks commensurate support from the citizens of the world. To mobilize and solidify such support is the way to give life to the ghost of the United Nations and make it a powerful, effective, international organ.

It is not possible for the multitudes of people desiring peace to sweep these terrible nuclear weapons off the face of the earth? From the technical point of view, it should certainly be possible; politics, not science, stands in the way of eliminating nuclear weapons. If we employed the full resources of our scientists, it should be possible to disassemble all such weapons and to use the nuclear power they represent for the benefit of mankind.

After this has been done, the United Nations should be given supervisory powers over nuclear installations, to make sure that nuclear energy is being used solely for peaceful purposes. In view of the world's future needs for increased energy, we should establish a world conference of scientists, who must represent the interests of no particular nations but must work for the benefit of the whole world. In this connection, I believe that the scientists of the world should forthwith and without exception abandon all research on nuclear weapons and refuse ever to have any part in it again.

Next year it will have been thirty full years since the atomic bombs were dropped on Japan; and, in 1977, it will have been twenty full years since President Toda asked us to work for nuclear disarmament. I think we should regard this three-year interval from 1975 to 1977 as the Years of the Peace Wave, and that we should make a special effort during these years to promote the world movement toward peace. I expect the Young Men's Division, the Young Women's Division, and the Students Division to play active roles in this project.

We must persevere until our movement becomes worldwide and sufficiently strong to destroy not only the nuclear weapons now in existence but also the principles upon which nuclear armament is founded. Never before have I felt so strongly the need to honor President Toda's will.

The Food Problem

Along with nuclear weapons, another global problem that must be solved quickly if humanity is to survive is the growing worldwide shortage of food.

I am sure you have seen on television or read in the newspapers that, because of repeated floods and droughts, India, Bangladesh, and countries in Africa are suffering from severe famines. The number of people who have died in those places from starvation staggers the imagination. As a fellow human being and as a Buddhist believer, I am shocked and horrified by this situation.

From November 5 to November 17, 1974, a world conference was held in Rome to consider means of averting a threatened world food crisis. I followed this meeting with great interest, because of its great significance as the first such conference attended by cabinet-level representatives. It seems to me that all the people concerned are to be praised; but at the same time I was disappointed to see that, even in the face of such a serious and urgent problem, nations continued to bicker with each other and jockey for settlements favorable to themselves. There were even times when I felt that the food crisis was being used as a weapon in an international political and economic struggle. Terms like "food strategy" were bandied about shamelessly; and I was reminded of warfare in the past, when besieging armies starved their enemies into surrendering. This idea that the world's food supply, which is necessary to the survival of humanity, can be used as a strategic weapon is itself a creation of Satan. This is no time for "food strategies." Nations adopting such policies will eventually find themselves destroyed by them.

According to data prepared for this world conference, in 1985, just ten years from now, about eight hundred million people, or about one-fifth of the world's population, will be faced with malnutrition. Even if we assume this to be an exaggeration, it is imperative that we realize the seriousness of our present situation. Not even the industrialized nations can afford to be optimistic at this point. We have reached a stage where man must cease wasting his intelligence and his resources on the development of nuclear weapons or on other preparations for war. We must now focus our attention on the problem of producing enough food to keep mankind alive.

Watching this recent food conference, I felt that many of the discussions and debates completely missed the basic point. The conferees showed little concern for the sufferings of people in famine-stricken countries who might die today or tomorrow. They seemed to be more concerned with the advantages or disadvantages of a given policy for their own countries.

While this meeting was proceeding, television was showing documentaries on the horrible conditions in Biafra, where fifty thousand people had already starved to death. In Rome, a multitude of inter-related national interests were being discussed; while, in Biafra, tens of thousands of people died for lack of the very food the conferees were bargaining over.

Some time ago, Jean-Paul Sartre asked what literature could do for those who are starving in Africa. Today it appears that not only the writers but also the world's political leaders, the rich, and the participants in the food conference are helpless to devise quick, effective means to save famine victims.

For this reason, I should like to consider the basic approach that future discussions of the food problem should adopt and the principles that the peoples of the world must uphold. In the first place, each country should start by asking itself not what it can receive, but what it can give. Nothing constructive will be accomplished as long as nations haggle with each other over the advantages each is to receive in the ultimate agreement. They should be talking about what each of them can contribute. If they did this, we would find a solution not only for the immediate food problem but also for problems that may arise in the future. Furthermore, the next international food conference should be held in one of the countries actually suffering from famine, so that the delegates can witness the horror for themselves.

The basic approach to foreign aid should be similar to the one I have proposed for the food conference. Until now, when advanced nations have given aid to developing nations, almost invariably strings have been attached, and aiding nations have in the long run profited from the deal in one way or another. This is called "give and take," but in less polite terms it might be described as "capitalistic invasion." Often, for example, the ulterior motive in advancing economic aid has been to secure military bases or ports of call for ships laden with nuclear weapons. I think we must admit that, if this sort of thing continues, we will face destruction. Such "give and take" must be done away with completely.

As a major economic power, Japan must now ask what it can contribute to the world. I would like to suggest several things that need to be done. In the first place, Japan is in a position to offer valuable technical aid to many countries in the field of agriculture. The fundamental solution to the food problem is to create a situation in which the developing nations can support themselves. Conditions in many of the countries threatened by famine are similar to those in Japan, and there is little doubt that Japanese technical aid and advice would help greatly. Twenty years ago, President Toda proposed that Japan make a valuable contribution to the world by sending agricultural technicians to live in some of the less highly developed nations. Today, Japanese agricultural methods are even more advanced; and it is high time we devoted ourselves wholeheartedly to helping developing countries learn how to produce more food.

In the second place—and this is very basic—we must recognize that one cause of the world food shortage is Japan's domestic agricultural policy. We supply all too few of our own food needs. Japan's reliance on imports for foodstuffs is said to be higher than that of any other nation. It is true, of course, that Japan is poor in natural resources and must import a great deal of its necessities. At the same time, it seems anomalous that, because of rice surpluses, the Japanese government continues to reduce the area of land under cultivation and to minimize the agricultural population. Our country is wide open to the criticism that it has used the money gained from industrial development to deprive other needy countries of the food that otherwise would rightfully belong to them. It is Japan's responsibility to the world to review its attitude toward agriculture and to attempt to become more self-sufficient where food is concerned.

In the third place, I think that we Japanese should pay more attention to food problems in other countries. Until now, we have been all too inclined to dismiss overseas difficulties as someone else's worry. But what is happening now to others could easily happen to us tomorrow. As good Buddhists, we must extend a helping hand to the troubled areas of the world. Many countries are suffering from famine because they lack funds to purchase agricultural surpluses from the larger countries. We ought to do something about this; and I want to ask our Young Men's Division, Young Women's Division, and Students Division to consider this matter thoroughly and take appropriate action.

If things go on as they are, one day our supply of imported grain may be cut off; and we will face famines more severe than those now raging in the developing countries. For the sake of our own future, we must devise forward-looking, effective ways to contribute to the welfare of the rest of the world.

A strong international organization, continually reminding nations of their obligation to give what they can for the good of the world as a whole, is urgently needed. I have in mind a world food bank of the kind that, I am happy to say, came up for discussion at the recent conference. Such an organization might function as a world distribution center that could take concrete, immediate steps to assure a balanced supply of food throughout the world. At the moment, of course, its first task would be to move foodstuffs into famine-stricken areas.

The bank could buy up agricultural surpluses from various countries, providing long-term, low-interest financing when necessary. Since the long-range solution of the problem lies in making the developing countries self-reliant, the bank could take a leading role in encouraging improvement of agricultural methods. This bank has been a pet project of mine for some time, and I have talked to quite a few world leaders and prominent intellectuals about it. I am glad that the world now seems to be moving toward a solution of this sort.

I will leave it to the experts to decide how the bank could be set up and operated; but, if it is to work, it must be based on the compassion of the Bodhisattva, who devoted his life to relieving others of suffering and giving them happiness. The bank must not be regarded as a means of making profits for particular countries, but must devote itself altruistically to the recovery of basic human rights for all mankind.

And when I speak of "relieving others of suffering," I am talking, not about temporary relief, but about excision of the fundamental causes of suffering. What this amounts to is enabling each individual to stand on his own two feet. And what is true of individuals is true of societies, too. When a society is sick, the solution is to attack the fundamental causes of the sickness. When I speak of providing happiness, I do not mean momentary pleasure. I mean the abiding happiness that comes from having the necessary life and fundamental strength to forge continually and steadfastly into the future.

When foreign aid is given, the recipient nation's standpoint should always be respected. Policies must be formed in such a way as to be suited to the prevailing natural conditions and cultural traditions of the recipient nation. Obviously, much thought and wisdom must be exercised by the leaders of the recipient nations.

Even if a world food bank is established, it will not work effectively unless leaders in both the advanced and the developing countries are able to forget selfish national interests and take the sufferings of the weak upon their own shoulders. Leaders who accept the sufferings of the starving as their own hardship will know what to do in all situations.

If we put the total wisdom of mankind—in which I firmly believe—to work on increasing the food supply, expanding the area of land under cultivation, improving agricultural methods, and reducing population growth rates, we shall certainly find solutions. What we need now is a global viewpoint: we must forget about national pride and work together for the preservation of humanity as a whole.

I have made several proposals concerning the abolition of nuclear weapons and the food problem; but, no matter what specific measures are taken, a sense of oneness on the part of all peoples is the thing most urgently needed today. We must have the strength to replace distrust with trust, disunity with mutual understanding. The weakest point in international relations thus far has been lack of this kind of strength.

If we consider world conditions profoundly, from the Buddhist viewpoint, we must conclude that the fundamental cause of human suffering lies within human beings themselves. This fundamental cause is nothing other than a lack of compassion. I cannot help being reminded of the profound words of Nichiren Daishonin, the Buddha of the Latter Day, who said, "Unless there be compassion, heaven will not protect this country; if we hold wicked views, we will be deserted by the Three Treasures" (*Gosho Zenshu,* p. 1552).

The cause of all suffering is lack of compassion, coupled with wicked, egocentric views. As I look forward into the future, I am convinced that we have arrived at a point where, if we do not adopt compassion as the basic element of our thought, our whole world is destined to go up in smoke. It is to prevent this that Soka Gakkai exists. We must hold to the Buddhist faith as the force that can bring about world peace.

The Open Home

Next I would like to discuss the Year of the Family, which is our designation for the coming year.

Since the development of human culture, the family has always been the foundation for life and the basic unit of society. We have chosen to call next year the Year of the Family, because the family is the setting in which we will find the human revival that is vitally needed today. Here I should like to stress the need for the family to be an open, outgoing institution.

When we speak of the importance of the home and the family, we do not mean the feudalistic family of the sort that developed from the traditional Japanese system. This feudalistic home was not a happy collection of individual human beings, but an authoritarian force, taking precedence over individuals. Inhumane and oppressive, it had to be done away with.

The kind of family that we are striving for is one in which each member develops his own potentialities, while at the same time respecting the rights and needs of the other members. The feudalistic family was closed; in it, individuals were subordinated to the group and forced to preserve unity, no matter what their personal wishes might be. Today we need open families, which can serve as environments for the development of individual humans.

An open family has no room for narrow selfishness. It is not a refuge from society, but a miniature version of society. In an open family, what one does, what one learns, what one experiences all help one to become prepared for life in the larger society.

A home should be a place of rest, a place where one replenishes energy, both spiritual and physical. It should not be a place for blowing off steam about things that go wrong in the outside world. Nor should it be a place where a tyrant reigns, utilizing the sacrifices of his family in order to be active elsewhere. From the humanistic viewpoint, a man who enslaves his family, even when his domestic arrangements look ideal to outsiders, is ugly and cowardly. The home should be the foundation for human life and the source of the energy that human beings need to create values in society. In a deeper sense, for most people, a happy home is the prerequisite to a happy life.

Postwar Japan has put economic development before home life. We have become an economic power through industrialization and urbanization, but the cost has been great. We are experiencing a chronic housing shortage and a proliferation of small families in which both husband and wife work. Happy family life has been sacrificed to increase the gross national product. We have achieved national prosperity only by ignoring, or even sacrificing, the home life most people require for true happiness.

Such being the case, if ordinary people are going to resist the economic juggernaut and seek happiness for themselves, their first step must be to recover the blessing of a happy home life. This is important not only for the happiness of the individual but also for the sake of society, since happy homes create happy societies, in which there is warmth and room for individual growth. In my opinion, the creation of happy homes should be considered a part of the people's tenacious struggle for peace.

Beginning with the oil crisis of late 1973, we have experienced a year of almost terrifying price rises. Rice is much more expensive; utilities are much more costly; everything is much higher. At the same time, industrial activity is so stagnant that numerous small and medium-sized business enterprises have been forced into bankruptcy; and even a number of big business concerns are threatened.

Presumably on the theory that there will be a depression, many people in government and business have begun to talk about holding down wage increases in the coming year. In other words, the livelihoods of the great majority of the people are being squeezed between the rise in prices on the one hand and a recession on the other. Apparently this is the inevitable result of a dog-eat-dog, laissez-faire economy, but the point is that the ordinary people—the little people—

are the ones who suffer the greatest damage. In these social circumstances, how is the home to be protected? The most direct method is to avoid all forms of waste.

The economic growth we have experienced during the past two decades has to a large degree been achieved by encouraging people to consume, to buy things they do not need, or to invest needlessly. This being the nature of our society, the best way for ordinary people to hold their losses to a minimum is to plan household budgets to avoid wasting money.

It is difficult not to be rankled by government attitudes. Until now, the consumer has been king, but suddenly the virtues of thrift are being touted abroad. Nonetheless, we must protect our homes. This means that housewives will have to keep a close eye on budgets and try somehow to weather these evil times. The ordinary people must create a solid front of such great strength that big business and those in the government who support it will be deterred from ignoring the general welfare.

There has been so much talk about high prices that people seem to have forgotten about the problem of pollution, in spite of the outcry it caused a few years ago. Whether we are combating high prices or protecting ourselves from pollution, however, we, the common people, must stick together. This is the way to protect ourselves and guard our livelihood. We must put up a united front, one which we must work steadfastly to broaden.

Inflation

Directly related to our home lives, the inflation of the past few years is by no means confined to Japan. All of the advanced nations are caught in a rising wage-cost spiral of such proportions that, even when there is a surplus of commodities, prices do not fall. Some predict that we are plummeting helplessly toward a worldwide depression of the sort that we experienced in the 1930s.

As direct causes of inflation, we can point to the Vietnam War, during which dollars expended for American military needs were scattered over the earth, and to the oil crisis that began with the war in the Middle East last year. In only one year, the price of oil increased fourfold, causing steep increases in all other prices.

The present inflation is unlike previous inflations, in that it reveals basic flaws in the world's economic structure. To make matters worse, no one seems to know how to deal with the situation. The Keynesian economic approach is no longer convincing, and economists in general have trouble concealing their inability to cope with the complicated economic patterns that have come into existence. The world has come to an economic turning point. Natural resources are clearly limited and are rapidly being exhausted by continued high economic growth rates. Man's very existence is in jeopardy.

Japan is experiencing a rate of inflation higher than almost anywhere else, not only because the country is poor in resources but also because the rapid postwar economic expansion, which on the one hand encouraged big business and on the other created a complicated distribution system, has proven singularly ineffective against rising prices.

I see personal thrift as the most effective means whereby the people can protect themselves in the event that a big-business-oriented government policy should lead to widespread unemployment. I fear that a situation requiring the people to bear the burden of economic adjustment may arise.

Thrift on the national level, especially with respect to military expenditures like those called for by the Japanese government's Fourth Defense Program, is the more pressing need.

All over the world, too much money is being spent for military purposes. By eliminating only a portion of these expenditures, the world would be well on its way to solutions for such problems as pollution, excess population growth, food shortages, and depletion of our energy resources. We will find no basic solutions to our problems until we are willing to shift from a consumer-oriented philosophy to a self-regenerating civilization. We must change from a civilization with ever-expanding desires to one in which desires are suitably modulated. If government leaders in power continue to protect big business alone, sooner or later the people will rise up against them. A hardhearted policy of favoring the strong over the weak cannot be allowed to continue. Today many small and medium-sized businesses are going bankrupt, and social unrest is continually increasing. Our government representatives must protect the ordinary little people and take immediate steps to aid the small businessmen. If they cannot, they are unqualified to govern.

Lifelong Education

Character building is the most important phase of child training in the home. And the actual conduct of parents invariably serves as a model for child behavior. This means that, to educate children, parents must not rely on verbal instructions, but must strive constantly to raise their own educational levels. In short, they must educate their children by educating themselves. Children are much smarter and more observant than many adults think. They distrust people who do not practice what they preach. One of the worst things a child can be told is, "Do as I say, not as I do." Parents must constantly study to keep up with the demands made on them by their children's training.

Adult self-education is important in childless households, too. The mutual respect binding husband and wife together grows stronger, the more educated each member of the couple becomes. Married people who are always learning steadily refresh the atmospheres of their homes, and this in turn keeps love from going stale.

Our age makes ever-increasing demands for new knowledge and new abilities. A person who fails to train himself in adult life and to be always on the lookout for new knowledge will soon find that the times have passed him by, leaving him stranded and dependent. Unflagging pursuit of new knowledge is essential today, if a person is to hold his own in relation to society and our age.

The passage in the sutras that says, "at the start I pledged to make all people perfectly equal to me, without any distinction between us," means that the Buddha intends for all sentient beings to manifest the Buddhahood within them and to enter a state of equality and identity with him. No statement could be more pertinent to education. Educating means recognizing the fundamental equality of people and adopting this as the supreme value to develop well-rounded human beings. Education must stimulate the manifestation of inner potentialities and thus enable human beings to acquire the knowledge and the technical skills that will glow like gems in their lives.

The Japanese word *doshi* (the guiding teacher, or master), when applied to the Buddha, suggests no condescension toward mortals, no attempt to regard ordinary people as subordinates. It merely means that the Buddha tries to guide each person to exercise his own abilities to the utmost. In this respect, in both principle and practice, Buddhism represents the quintessence of education.

As Buddhist believers, we enjoy the philosophical ground and the faith in practical application that are best suited to lifelong self-education. Our human revolution is lifelong education under a different name, and our duty is to work to educate ourselves as long as we live, while, in our practical activites, making contributions to all of society.

The Gosho *Movement*

Since the time of Nikko Shonin, the second high priest, and Nichikan Shonin, the twenty-sixth high priest, the fundamental Nichiren Shoshu tradition has been to regard the *Gosho* as the actual words of the true Buddha and as the supreme teaching for the Latter Day of the Law. Tsunesaburo Makiguchi, founder of Soka Gakkai, and Josei Toda, his successor, insisted that the *Gosho* is the origin of everything and the sole source of guidance in the propagation of our faith. I insist today that Soka Gakkai remain forever faithful to this principle.

The attitude of Nichiren Daishonin to the sutras, particularly the Lotus Sutra of Shakyamuni, the Buddha of the Former Day of the Law, can be found in *Ongi Kuden* (Oral teachings), where he trains the light of his wisdom on each word and phrase, explains their deepest meanings, and brilliantly and lucidly reveals the significance he attributes to them.

The *Gosho* quotes T'ien-t'ai's explanation of the Lotus Sutra: "Every single word is itself the true Buddha" (*Gosho Zenshu*, p. 1484). Taking this phrase to heart, Nichiren Daishonin sought the meaning of every character in the Lotus Sutra in relation to himself. With resolute practice of his faith, he manifestly demonstrated the truth of every word. Because of his valiant struggle, at a time when it was in danger of being robbed of its meaning by formalistic interpretations, the Lotus Sutra was reborn, like a great phoenix, and made to live vibrantly again. The teaching for our age is the *Gosho,* and we must approach it the way that Nichiren Daishonin approached the Lotus Sutra. My own master, Josei Toda, claimed that we should study the *Gosho* with the same kind of strict discipline a master swordsman forces himself to undergo; that is, we must face all rigors and difficulties. The *Gosho* of Nichiren Daishonin is part of us. Engraving it on our hearts, we must live it with all our beings.

A passage in *Ongi Kuden* says, "*Nam* is a Sanskrit word meaning being devoted to or returning to. Both Person and Law are included in the implications of this meaning. To return to the Person means to devote oneself to Shakyamuni. To return to the Law means to devote oneself to the Lotus Sutra" (*Gosho Zenshu,* p. 708). This statement reveals what we should entrust (or return) our lives to. In other words, the Dai-Gohonzon of the Three Great Secret Laws, which is at the same time a manifestation of both the Person and the Law, is the ultimate thing to which we must entrust ourselves.

In our time, devotion to the Law means devotion to the Gohonzon. What then, does devotion to the Person mean? Of course, it means devotion to Nichiren Daishonin, the Buddha of the Latter Day of the Law, the Mentor and Parent. But I should like to stress an important point. In practical terms, the devotion to the Person to which *Ongi Kuden* refers is nothing other than devotion to Nichiren Daishonin's teachings; that is, devotion to the *Gosho.* The *Gosho* is Nichiren Daishonin's life. It is the record of the principles he verified in his life.

A man with an immortal guiding principle is a happy man. Today, too many people lack such a principle and live meaninglessly, day in day out, with nothing to rely on or believe in. Dark, gloomy twilight awaits them, for futile living cannot lead to true, lasting happiness. But we have the *Gosho,* with its truths as pure and enduring as gold. It is our inevitable destiny to employ the *Gosho* to illumine our times. In *Shoho Jisso-sho* (The true entity of life), Nichiren Daishonin wrote: "No matter what, maintain your faith as a votary of the Lotus Sutra and forever exert yourself as Nichiren's disciple. You are of the same mind as Nichiren, you must be a Bodhisattva of the Earth. And since you are a Bodhisattva of the Earth, there is not the slightest doubt that you have been a disciple of the Buddha from the remotest past" (*Gosho Zenshu*, p. 1360).

In this passage, "maintain your faith as a votary of the Lotus Sutra" refers to devotion to the Law and means accepting the Mystic Law as your basis and performing spontaneous good works in you rown society. "Forever exert yourself as Nichiren's disciple" means devotion to the Person and remaining within the solidarity of our comradeship, which is cemented by eternal oneness of heart. Obviously, the source of our unity is Nichiren Daishonin himself.

Being of the same mind as Nichiren means adopting Nichiren Daishonin's heart and spirit as your own and accepting him as your fundamental master in a condition where master and disciple are one. In this condition, outwardly, you will be a Bodhisattva of the Earth; and inwardly, a disciple of the Buddha from the remotest past, or a disciple of the eternal Original Buddha.

Buddhahood is not otherworldly; it is manifest in your own heart when you practice the faith of a Bodhisattva of the Earth and spread the Mystic Law in the corrupt world of the Latter Day.

Briefly, a Bodhisattva of the Earth performs acts of great compassion, and the Buddhism of Nichiren Daishonin finds in the universal life called Nam-myoho-renge-kyo the power to take great compassion and its refreshing goodness to all parts of the world.

Ongi Kuden says, "The spirit with which Nichiren and his disciples chant Nam-myoho-renge-kyo is the spirit of supreme mercy" and "The Nirvana Sutra says, 'All the sufferings of mankind are without exception the sufferings of the Tathagata.' I Nichiren hereby declare that all the sufferings felt in common by mankind are without exception the sufferings of Nichiren himself" (both quotations from *Gosho Zenshu*, p. 758). Once Josei Toda said to some of his youthful followers, "It is a struggle in which you must love all people. But how can young people love all other people, when many of them do not even love their parents? The way to achieve such love is the human revolution, which enables you to rise above compassionless self and to enter the sphere of the Buddha's compassion."

Today, in a hardhearted society wherein conniving people seek only selfish profit, we must radiate the light of mercy. To do this, we must accomplish our own human revolutions, which will permit us to manifest true compassion. Our human revolutions are eternal and continuous and must be carried out together with the people.

In concluding, let me express my hope that your lives will be filled with glory, happiness, joy, and peace and offer you this short poem:

> May radiance grow
> On your soaring wings
> Till you reach the
> Rainbow of
> Faith worldwide!

A Global Society of Equality
and Mutual Respect

Delivered to The Japan Society,
New York, January 10, 1975.

First, I should like to offer my gratitude to Mr. Shapiro, your President; to his wife; to Mr. MacEachron, your Executive Director; and to all of you members for the warm, sincere greeting you have extended to us today. Although brevity is generally considered a merit on occasions of this kind, for the sake of continued amicable relations between the United States and Japan, I ask you to be forbearing if my speech is somewhat long.

I want to express my deep respect for the efforts of your society in gradually advancing American-Japanese friendship and for your achievements in that cause. Because of the visit of President Gerald Ford to Japan, last year was epoch-making in the relations between our two countries. At present, close ties between the United States and Japan exist not only in the realms of culture and economics but also in a wider area, including the life styles of our peoples. The fields of endeavor of those responsible for the continued development of these relations will expand in the future. In these activities, your society, which already has a distinguished history in such work, will be expected to do still more.

Now I should like to say a few words about Soka Gakkai in connection with a number of problems that have concerned me deeply in the past and that will continue to be a source of great concern.

The Global Crisis

It is beyond dispute that, during the remaining twenty-five years before the beginning of the twenty-first century, we will face an age of unprecedented difficulties on a global scale. I have just come from a visit to the United Nations, where I met with Secretary General Waldheim. In our talk, I became deeply aware that he and I share the same opinion on this subject. Though approaches and viewpoints may vary, in guiding the world toward the next century and in ensuring the continued survival of the human race, we all have parts that we must play sincerely and with a sense of responsibility. It is as if we were on a ship sailing by a nautical chart leading to the future of humanity. In your navigation, I hope that you will keep your compasses set on an accurate course to a luminous, lasting peace.

I have many friends throughout the world. As one human being traveling among other human beings, I have heard a swelling hymn to life that has awakened a response in my own heart. I have seen human happiness and the lofty peaks of peace. I have also seen human beings in poverty, misery, and futility. Such sights are burned indelibly on my mind. As we sit here, enjoying a pleasant time together, somewhere in the world people are starving or are fleeing from the fires of war. I cannot forget this, and the lamentations and cries of the masses of humanity sweep through my heart like a storm.

What is the cause of human suffering? Undeniably, the causes differ with time and place. Whereas, in some regions, people suffer because they do not have food for tomorrow, in others, even in materially blessed conditions, people must endure spiritual starvation. No matter what the difference in material well-being, however, people everywhere want a society in which they can live in a truly human fashion.

The current age is characterized by an awareness of the oneness of all mankind. This awareness has been dramatically intensified by mutual exchanges, made possible by sophisticated means of travel and communication. In the past, humanity has gone through many periods of crisis, but never before has awareness of such crisis reached all the ends of the earth as it does today.

What is the nature of the crisis? Inflation, economic recessions, and problems of energy sources have partly paralyzed the world. But the true nature of the problem cannot be analyzed in these terms alone. A vague feeling of insecurity fills the hearts of men today. Concepts like growth and progress, which once seemed to promise wealth and happiness, have turned out to be two-edged swords, posing grave threats.

The crises accompanying scientific progress have already been pointed out by many other people. Aurelio Peccei, the leader of the Club of Rome, which is attempting to work out definite programs for dealing with some of these crises, has commented: "The limits of material growth are not far off, but there is vast room still for growth in the human spirit. It is here that we will find the key to the survival of mankind. . . . We need now as never before a new humanism, a renaissance of the human mind." The suggestion is an excellent one; but, at present, we are still groping in the dark for a concrete way of achieving a human spiritual renaissance. The major problem facing us today is the lack of an ideal that can make it possible for mankind to live the remaining quarter of this century in peace and happiness.

Intellectuals point out many problem points. For instance, in the extended dialogues and correspondence focused on basic issues of humanity and life that were conducted between the British philosopher-historian Arnold J. Toynbee and myself, Mr. Toynbee said that, in the twentieth century, man has been intoxicated by technological power and that this has damaged the environment and invited the destruction of humanity. He added that man must examine himself and attempt to acquire the wisdom to control himself.

The Buddhist Viewpoint

The origin of Buddhism was an attempt to find how to deal with human suffering, the causes of which were identified as birth, aging, illness, and death. This is a problem related to very nature of life itself, and the perspicacity of Buddhist wisdom is seen in the way in which it revealed the nature of life, the element in which suffering must take place.

I believe that the twenty-first century will be essentially a time in which light is shed on the fundamental nature of life. Against the light that Buddhist philosophy will shed on humanity in that age, Soka Gakkai will provide impetus for union among the hearts and minds of all men and for a human revolutionary movement. Soka Gakkai is an organization devoted to constant work for peace from the standpoint of human concerns. In the final analysis, greed and egoism are the driving powers behind all of the major problems facing man today, including nuclear weapons and environmental pollution. In short, these problems are caused by human lack of self-control.

But such a cut-and-dried interpretation cannot exhaustively explain the basic nature of man. To illuminate that nature, Buddhist philosophy provides wisdom and the earnest effort to learn what man truly is. It is an immense human philosophy, elucidated in the dimension of life. More than a way to alter ways of thinking and living, Buddhist philosophy is a practical method for a universal human revolution.

Last year in Japan a book called *The Great Prophecies of Nostradamus* became a best seller. The Buddhist way of living and the Buddhist attitude toward the future are not limited to the kinds of simple prophecies found in that book. Instead, from an elevated viewpoint, Buddhism emphasizes what we must do about the future. A term often used in Buddhist philosophy is *issai shujo,* which means all sentient beings but which implies compassion, a profound will to assist others, and a sense of mercy and responsibility to try to take action to make things better. Soka Gakkai is an organization based on and firmly rooted in a sense of mission of this kind.

The Direction Mankind Should Follow

Basing my thoughts on these Buddhist ideals, I believe that the following points sum up the new direction that man must adopt: First, in the latter part of the twentieth century, mankind must cease limiting his views to given societies or national states and must adopt a total, global standpoint. Second, man must come to realize that his nature as a life entity is an absolute fact, transcending matters of society, state, and race. Human beings as social entities vary in nature, according to historical periods, races, or nations. For people to live as they should, they must firmly grasp the knowledge that their most basic point of origin is as a life entity, not a social entity. In other words, we must realize that, in the figuratively vertical direction, our origin is to be found in our nature as life entities and that, in the figuratively horizontal direction, we share this nature as a life entity with all other human beings on the globe, with whom we form a universal union. One of the main goals of our life-oriented humanism movement is the elimination of war and the building of a society of peace and mutual respect and understanding as the outcome of developing universal union among all peoples in such fields as politics, economics, and culture. Sir Thomas More once said something to this effect: War would seem suitable to the beasts, yet none of the beasts wars as much as man. The only path for man now is to cease being a beast endowed with reason and to live in a fashion worthy of his humanity.

Undeniably, the trend of the historical current is toward world unification and a global community. Just as undeniably, however, narrow nationalism, racial and cultural prejudices, and ideological conflicts stand in the way of such unification. There is still a wide gap between the ideal and strict reality.

For some time, I have advocated the establishment of what I tentatively call a United Nations of Education. I have taken this stand because I feel a need to reinforce such international organizations as the United Nations in the fields of politics and culture and to further the strengthening of international cooperation. In addition, I am motivated by a need to plan and put into operation an enlightened system of education that will allow the awareness of the oneness of mankind—a oneness subsuming all politics and economics—to take still deeper root. The sponsoring of an education that can bring about a revolution in awareness and of philosophical enlightenment is in line with the Soka Gakkai movement for mankind.

I hope that all nations—including, of course, Japan—will act as banner bearers in the establishment of the United Nations of Education. This is one of the goals of our movement. But, for the sake of lasting peace for the global family and for an international society of all nations in the coming century, each country must assume the responsibility of setting up an educational and social society based on common respect for the personality—on a deeper level, for the life—of each individual. The fundamental life, which deserves the highest respect, transcends race and nations.

In the light of the severe ideological struggles and egoistical national behavior of our times, many people may consider my proposal too idealistic. Nonetheless, I intend to pursue this "impossible dream" for the rest of my life. As history shows, ideas that revolutionize thinking and assume leadership in their time always break with accepted common sense and look so far ahead that they are at first misunderstood.

Mankind will have to face many severe winters yet. But the bright spring will never come unless we all work together in a spirit of indomitable faith and courage to build peace for the world. It is my sincere wish that during this year all people will join hands and work even more resolutely toward this goal.

The Middle Way
as a Foundation for Peace

Delivered at the first IBL (International Buddhist League)
World Peace Conference, held in Guam, January 26, 1975.

Perhaps the meeting is a small one. Perhaps not all nations are represented today. But centuries from now, this conference will remain glowing bright in history. The names of all of you will be splendidly engraved in the history of mankind and in the history of the propagation of Buddhist philosophy.

The world today is operated on the basis of arms, politics, economics, and personal gain, all of which hinder the achievement of peace and create a dangerous condition of constant tension. What can make it possible to break out of this dilemma? In my opinion, a higher religion. Not a religion involving ideas only, but a higher religion, capable of opening the long way to peace in practical terms.

In the *Gosho* occurs the famous passage, "If *itai doshin* (many in body, one in mind) prevails among the people, they will achieve all their goals" (*Gosho Zenshu*, p. 1463). Many interpretations have been made of this text. I think it means that only when all nations and all peoples come together in deep faith in the Mystic Law and are one in spirit, though different in other respects, and move forward in mutual assistance, will lasting peace be possible.

Of course, as practical issues, politics and economics are important.

But, unless the peoples of all nations are harmoniously united in faith in the life philosophy—the basis of which is Buddhism—peace will be unattainable. This truth is the essence of Nichiren Daishonin's message.

The British philosopher-historian Arnold J. Toynbee has devoted time and effort to the question of how to create a global state or federation for a world whose history to date might be equated with a history of warfare. In discussing higher religions, he has said that, first, a world federation must be set up. Then a religion will spread through the world, and an ideal society can be achieved.

During the ten days of discussions between Mr. Toynbee and me, I clearly disagreed with him on this point only. My feeling is that the world state or federation and the ideal human society can come about only after the worldwide spreading of a higher religion. During the course of our talks, Mr. Toynbee, a great, though modest, scholar, revised his thinking and, afterward, came to agree that the dissemination of a worldwide religion could become the spiritual basis on which to create an ideal world state. On the final day of our talks, I asked him if he had any opinions to state about Nichiren Shoshu Soka Gakkai. With a wave of his hand, he said no. He added that he is a scholar and not a man of practical affairs. Though Soka Gakkai may have been criticized by many people, it has continued steadily to struggle for lasting peace. In the light of this, Mr. Toynbee requested that we go on bravely with our task of carrying the Buddhist doctrine of the Middle Way to the people of the whole world.

A few days ago, I took part in a meeting with the Secretary General of the United Nations, Kurt Waldheim, a man who is deeply serious and concerned about the peace of the world. At the conclusion of our meeting, he said—perhaps by way of encouragement—that he would like to know more about the principles of our movement and to use the knowledge gained from them in a reconsideration of the management of the United Nations as a substantial organ for peace. We must respond to his request.

The sun of Nichiren Daishonin's Buddhism is beginning to rise over the distant horizon; the time for the intital phase of the worldwide propagation of the true Buddhism has arrived. I hope you do not seek after your own praise or glory, but instead dedicate your whole lives to sowing the seeds of the Mystic Law for the sake of the peace of the whole world. I shall do the same thing. Sometimes, I shall be in the vanguard leading. At other times, I shall be either beside you or in the rear, observing and supporting you with all my being. Become disciples of Nichiren Daishonin, filled with courage and compassion and burning with justice. Make your lives periods of sunlight devoted to your nation, the common people, and priceless humanity.

A New Road to East-West Cultural Exchanges

Delivered at Moscow M. V. Lomonsov State University, May 27, 1975.

Nearly eight months have passed since I visited Moscow in the golden autumn of September 1974; and, as I returned to this country, it was with eagerness to see the unforgettable friends that I made here on my previous visit. When people have directly and candidly exchanged opinions and, through such exchanges, have become friends, the passage of time cannot alter their relations. Such friendship surpasses social systems and evokes undying warmth. Today I should like to comment on some of the warm feelings inspired in me by thoughts of the Soviet people, by their culture, and particularly by their literature.

The indomitable will of the Russian people turned a new page in the history of human liberation when, like the tender grasses of spring rising through the frosts of Siberia, it broke from the long bondage imposed by an oppressive social system. It is a great source of pride for the people of this nation that the Russian land nurtured and protected this will, which I believe to be the most salient feature of the Russian national character and the force that has enabled the Russian people to create a great popular cultural tradition. Russian literature symbolizes the essence of this tradition in the eyes of the whole world.

It may seem presumptuous of me to discuss Russian literature in front of a group of students and teachers of the University of Moscow. But I ask that you listen to my words and accept them as the frank opinions of a friend from another country. In my interpretation, the leading characteristic of Russian literature is its constant concern with the role of literary art in the happiness, freedom, and peace of the people. Assisting the people to enjoy these blessings has been the goal held high before all Russian literary artists.

Literature is not the exclusive property of any privileged class. It cannot exist if it ignores the ordinary people, who suffer in oppression, hunger, and poverty and who, time and time again, become the victims of war. The literature of many European nations has tended to serve art for its own sake and to be limited to a few specific genres. In contrast to this, almost all Russian literature has demonstrated keen interest in social problems. It has always reflected a profound sense of oneness in fate, sorrow, and happiness with the common people.

In the play *Lower Depths,* which made an indelible impression on me when I read it for the first time shortly after the end of World War II, Maxim Gorki has Satin, one of the characters living in a world of decadence and degradation, say, "What a proud and resounding thing is the word *chelovek* (man)." When I read the play, I was at the impressionable age of seventeen or eighteen. I was living in a nation that had just suffered defeat in war and that had lost all sense of values. Though we were hungry, my friends and I gathered together what few books had escaped the fires of war and read constantly in the search for a ray of hope for the future. This line from *Lower Depths* provided that ray, which has remained with me ever since. Indeed, in the word *chelovek* I sense a concentrated expression of the characteristic Russian view of humanity. The word itself resembles a call to all peoples, a call rising upward from suffering and desolation. I feel closer to Lenin, the great revolutionary, when I realize that he and Maxim Gorki were friendly.

One of the reasons for the great sympathy I feel with Russian literature is its concern with the indomitable will of the ordinary people. The great Russian writers have always shed light on the persistent hope and faith in the future that the people of Russia have preserved, even under unspeakable oppression and enforced conditions of bitter submission. The starting point and the ultimate destination of the social movement of Soka Gakkai, the organization I head, is the welfare of the ordinary people. We hope to bring about an autonomous union of the wills of the people and to direct the energies of the people toward peace.

Pushkin, the great poet of the Russian people, has said that political freedom in his time was inseparable from the liberation of the serfs. Throughout their lives, Gorki, Nekrasov, Turgenev, Tolstoy, Chekhov, and other great Russian literary figures were friends of the common people. Even though they may have had European educations and may have depicted the way of life of the aristocratic classes, they were never able to limit themselves to such a framework, but invariably produced pictures of human beings that are reflections of a purely Russian image of mankind. This can be said of characters as apparently different as Tatyana in Pushkin's *Eugene Onegin* and Platon Karataev in Tolstoy's *War and Peace*.

But what did the great writers have in mind when they created characters of this kind? I suspect that they were looking beyond the culture of Europe, which, by the nineteenth century, had already entered a phase of overripeness, to express a hope—even a prayer— for the full flowering and the liberty of mankind in our time. It may be this kind of foresight that caused such European writers as André Gide to voice amazement at the range of towering peaks of achievement that constitutes Russian literature.

Characteristic Russian concern with humanity is not limited to the field of literature. It found expression in the uprisings of Stenka Razin, of folk-song fame; Pugachev; and the Dekabristy and Narodniki movements of the nineteenth century. Indeed, the victory of the people in the Soviet Revolution would have been impossible without an accumulation of energy directed toward human liberation. I trust and believe that the same devotion to the people and their freedom continues to flourish not only in Soviet literature but in all other phases of Soviet culture as well.

Though these comments are somewhat off the main theme of my talk, I think they might interest you. Once in a discussion with young friends who love Russian literature, my conversation partners and I began to think of words that symbolize the characteristic traits of different nationalities. For the French we selected *esprit* and for the English, *humor*. For the Russians, one of the young people present suggested that the word *posledovatel'nost'* would be most apt. I do not speak Russian, and I find long words like this one difficult to pronounce, but I am told that this word means consistency or thoroughness, the refusal to be satisfied with anything less than completion, a stubbornness to achieve a goal.

The People, the True Soil of Russian Literature

I agreed with the suggestion that such a trait might be said to characterize the Russian people. Undeniably, this concept fits the basic nature of their literature. Given literary expression, this idea transcends barriers of race, nationality, and language to produce such deeply moving outbursts as the word *chelovek* in the line I quoted from Gorki.

A tradition of this kind cannot be created overnight. Its history is long, and its earliest buddings may be traced to ancient oral traditional literature and songs. As is widely known, no people has as rich a treasure of folk songs and proverbs as the Russians. Most of these are the products of the people's oral traditions; and in many cases, the story or song tells of a hero who challenges and overcomes evil. A large number of the stories tell tales of how the peasantry rose up against cruel and oppressive landlords. These stories, which are strongly satirical, reveal both the nature of the soil in which the Russian literary tradition is rooted and the powerful spirit of resistance that enabled the Russian people to topple the tsarist regime and to repel such invaders as Napoleon and Hitler.

Something similar can be said about the folk songs that people in all parts of your land enjoy singing. We Japanese, too, know many of these songs. In those of the Cossacks and in the famous "Song of the Volga Boatmen" can be heard more than desperation and the misery of submission. Though in the depths of suffering, the people symbolized by these songs do not lose hope for happiness. The songs themselves are a protest against unreasonable sorrow. The "Song of the Volga Boatmen," like *Steel* by Ostrovski, reveals the truth that the deeper the suffering, the greater the spiritual drive to survive the trial. Without the deep soil that is the Russian people and their love of songs, folk-tale gatherings, culture, and art, the brilliant literary achievements of nineteenth-century Russia would not have been possible. In the light of this background, it is not surprising that the great Russian writers of the nineteenth century observed the suffering of the people with a keen eye and were filled with a deep need to seek the true meaning of literature. The examples set by these men inspire in me a sense of sympathy with Russian literature. But they do more. They become one of the driving forces leading me to determine to devote my life to the creation of the lyric poem of peace and cultural creativity.

A French philosopher has posed this question: What can literature do to help starving children? In asking it, he was questioning the value of the kind of literature that demonstrates no concern with social inequalities in a world where man's very existence is threatened. This criticism sharply reveals the failure of the literatures of advanced European nations, literatures that tend to shut themselves away in enclosed worlds of their own.

Russian literature has already surpassed the question itself. Writing and the other arts in Russia have developed together with the communal desire for happiness, freedom, and peace of the people. This tradition leaves no room for questions of the kind asked by the French philosopher. I am convinced that the profound Russian understanding of human nature, as reflected in the writings of leading Russian literary artists, is deeply rooted in the Russian people themselves, for it is they who have served as the womb in which the national and racial personality has grown. For this reason, Russian literature could have created nothing apart from the people.

In the fields of culture and art, individuality need not necessarily conflict with universality. On the contrary, it is possible to be universal in validity precisely because of the possession of individuality. In times like these, when the unification of mankind is an urgent need, the spirit of Russian culture and its deep understanding of humanity must inevitably become an inspirational force for all peoples and must make great contributions to cultural exchanges in the twenty-first century. If I may presume to say so, it is in this connection that you young people will find your missions and your responsibilities.

Now I should like to turn to my major theme of the day: A New Road to East-West Cultural Exchanges. I dare say that the very topic wakens thoughts of the Silk Road that served as a connection between East and West in the distant past. Passing between two continental routes of oases and steppes, the Silk Road and its many branch routes were a major thoroughfare for trade between the Orient and the Occident. But, in addition, they were the route for cultural exchange between the two spheres. Iranian and Scythian culture contributed much to the civilizations of later times. Buddhism passed from India to almost all of Asia. Christianity and Islam, too, exerted great influence on the art, architecture, music, and general culture of much of the world. All of these phenomena were assisted by the Silk Road. The cultural traditions of Eurasia traveled this route and ultimately reached the Japanese islands.

Adjacent to the compound of a large temple called Todai-ji in the city of Nara, long ago the capital of Japan, is a building called the Shoso-in, which is a repository housing a wide variety of objects dating from twelve to thirteen centuries ago and constituting a collection of immense historical interest. One of the most unusual of the articles in the Shoso-in is a five-stringed lute decorated with inlaid flowers made of amber, tortoise shell, and mother-of-pearl. In addition to these flowers, the skillful craftsman, who must have spent a great deal of time on this elegant piece, has depicted boulders and some birds flying among the branches of tropical trees. The viewer of the lute is inevitably moved by the artistic skill and talent of the artisan who made it.

Four-stringed lutes are said to have orginated in Persia. The five-stringed lute, however, originated in India and passed through Central Asia to the Chinese kingdom of the Northern Wei dynasty. It is said to have been perfected during the Chinese T'ang dynasty. The example of this kind of instrument in the Shoso-in is clearly Sassanid Persian in design. Its history, therefore, suggests the way in which both Persian and Indian culture traveled along the Silk Road to come into contact with China and finally cross the seas to reach Japan. The Silk Road, in other words, prompted blendings of different cultural elements and stimulated the development of new cultures.

Among its many treasures, in addition to this lute, the Shoso-in houses a harp from Mesopotamia, a decorated wooden box from

Egypt, and glass from the Eastern Roman Empire. It is true that articles stored in the Nara building were the exclusive property of the privileged class and that they do not represent a conflux of mass popular culture. Nonetheless, they are an example of the way in which cultural exchanges—even if only for the privileged—took place in the past.

Turning Suspicion into Trust and Hostility into Understanding

What was the cause for the wide cultural diffusion and propagation that occurred on the Silk Road in the past? Trade and expeditions of conquest certainly provided openings, but I do not believe this completely explains the phenomenon. The very nature of culture is to stimulate exchange. In other words, essentially, culture is universal in nature; it is the breath that enlivens the activities of human life. Joy strikes a sympathetic chord in the hearts of all peoples and causes harmonious reverberations. In a similar manner, culture is a fundamental human undertaking that conquers all distance to stir the hearts of peoples everywhere. I believe that this kind of sympathy among human hearts is the point of origin of cultural exchanges. Consequently, accord and harmony are the fundamental nature of culture based on such sympathy. This kind of culture is diametrically opposed to the force of arms. In contrast to military power, which threatens humanity and tries to exert control from without, culture arises within the human mind as a liberating force. Furthermore, armed might is pervaded with the philosophy of power, which infers that militarily and economically strong nations will invade smaller and weaker nations. Cultural exchanges, on the other hand, are based on the idea of intake and must adopt independence of the receiving party as an initial premise. Finally, destruction is the basis of military power, whereas culture must rest on the concept of creativity.

In brief, culture is an enduring product of human life and rests on a framework of harmony, independence, and creativity. Cultural flowering is the one way to liberation and to resistance against military power and privilege. I am convinced that the path Russian literature has followed provides reliable suggestions for cultural growth in the future.

Ties To Unite Human Hearts

During the eighth century, the Silk Road, which had done much to promote East-West cultural exchanges and which had stimulated cultural development in the lands of Central Asia, began to be abandoned. Today, it is no longer used. The rise and fall of the Saracen empire and, somewhat later, the ravages committed by the Mongols on the oasis cities along the way are given as major causes in the decline of the Silk Road. The destructive influence of military power on cultural undertakings is awesome. Some people argue that military expeditions stimulate cultural growth and exchange. But, as armed power increases and becomes more destructive, it can strike the death blow to culture, as people living today well understand. In our age, war not only has a destructive effect on culture, it also threatens to obliterate civilization itself.

As the Silk Road became more difficult to travel, Europeans began to seek a sea route to the Far East. Assisted by modern science, the Portuguese and the Spanish succeeded in opening routes eastward around the Cape of Good Hope at the tip of Africa. This deprived the overland route across Central Asia of its practical value; and the Silk Road, which had been a priceless connection between East and West, fell into disuse.

In the twentieth century, developments in means of transport and communications have made it possible to travel from one place to another very distant one at great speeds. An incident that occurs in a remote country is known to all parts of the earth on the very day of its occurrence, thanks to modern communications media. And thanks to scientific skill, the volume of exchange between the East and the West is today incomparably greater than it was in the heyday of the Silk Road. Nonetheless, I am always amazed to think that, in spite of the figurative shrinkage of distance caused by improved means of transportation, vast distances still separate the hearts of men. Though efficient exchanges of things and information take place on a large scale, exchanges on the personal, human level among the peoples of the world remain rare.

Intelligent thinkers with a worldwide view of the human condition now insist that cultural exchanges on a broad basis including both the West and the East are the way that we must follow to unite the minds of human beings everywhere. The friends I have made in many lands and the national leaders with whom I have discussed the matter are united in hoping for the earliest possible realization of this ideal. The desire for East-West cultural exchanges is being voiced by people all over the world. At no time in history has there been so great a need as there is now for a spiritual Silk Road, extending through all the cultural spheres of the globe, transcending national and ideological barriers, and binding together all peoples at the basic level. Cultural exchanges that are the spontaneous manifestations of the wills of the common peoples can turn suspicion into trust, can convert hostility into understanding, and can lead the world away from war and in the direction of lasting peace. Too often in the history of mankind we have witnessed the overnight dissolutions of agreements made solely on the governmental level and the tragic clashes of arms that failures in politics have brought. But we must not let this phenomenon repeat itself.

There are some people who sincerely believe in national hostilities cultivated throughout history, but I regard this kind of thing as a phantom. I recently read of the interesting experiences of an internationally famous Greek actress who from childhood had considered the Turks enemies. When she traveled to Nicosia, on the island of Cyprus, to work on location for a film, she found the city divided into Turkish and Greek quarters with checkpoints between the two. Because she was able to travel back and forth, she was frequently entrusted with messages or small gifts from Greeks for Turks on the other side of the boundary. As time passed, she found herself asked by Turkish people to perform similar errands and to take letters and other things to their Greek friends in the Greek zone. Reflecting on this situation, she said to herself, "These two peoples can be friends. Governments find it convenient to stir up hostility between them; but, if they were left to themselves, the Turks and the Greeks could live together in perfect peace."

No matter how difficult it may seem to break away from one's historical background, people living today have absolutely no responsibility to burden themselves with the animosities of peoples of the past. When one person recognizes the humanity of another, walls that may have been separating them crumble at once. I am talking to all of you at this moment; we are engaging in an exchange. I believe that you are all friends who share my desire for peace. Am I correct in assuming this?

I am convinced that even difficult, apparently unsolvable problems, if illuminated on the human level, can be solved peacefully, without recourse to arms. No person, however high his position, has the right to inflame people against each other or to cause the shedding of human blood. To repeat myself with greater emphasis, the word *chelovek* (man), as employed in the quotation I cited from Gorki, must find sublimation in a cry of peace for the unification of all mankind. To unite the world and to build lasting peace, I wish to proclaim the pressing need for a spiritual Silk Road to bind together the hearts of the peoples of the East and the West.

Mutual Equality as the Lifeline of Exchange

Now I should like to discuss actual ways of promoting exchange. In the world today, in addition to the so-called advanced industrialized nations, a large number of other nations are at various stages of development. The issue to be faced is determining ways to stimulate fruitful relations between these two groups. Generally, scholars examine the situation from the standpoint of what is known as the North-South problem; that is, the difference between the "have" nations of the North and the "have-not" nations of the South. Of course, each nation regards the issue from its own viewpoint.

In the preceding part of this talk, I have spoken of East-West relations. By these terms, I do not mean relations between communist and capitalist societies; I am talking about exchanges between the cultures of the Orient and the Occident. In connection with the North-South issue as well, I am not examining social systems. Unless this point is clarified in discussing the needed relations between the two zones, not only will wholesome exchanges be impossible, but also the danger exists that the basic natures of the cultures of the North and the South could be misunderstood.

The distinction between the "have" North and the "have-not"

South is based entirely on economic development. But economic success does not prove the excellence of a culture. On the contrary, economically developing countries frequently are culturally as advanced as nations who outstrip them in wealth and power. For this reason, it is desirable to use standards other than economics alone in evaluating the achievements of a people. For instance, what revelations would we experience if we examined the nations of the world in terms of musical achievements? Undoubtedly, in terms of other aspects of human culture, economically advanced nations might appear much less advanced than other nations that are usually regarded as only developing. Our green planet, the home of four billion human beings, would present a more varied picture if it were examined in the light of the art, religion, traditions, life styles, and psychology of its inhabitants. In all probability, under such examination, the present distinction between advanced and developing nations would disappear. The relations between the nations of the North and South today do not deserve the designation *exchange*. Too often they are unilateral from North to South, and sometimes they deserve the criticism of being economic or cultural incursions.

Spiritual Silk Road Connecting the Nations of the World

Cultural exchanges can bring together peoples everywhere. They can become a lute string striking harmonious vibrations in the hearts of all men. But to this end, complete mutual equality must be maintained at all times. Unilateral cultural incursions plant the dangerous seed of pride in the people on the transmitting end of the operation and fill the hearts of the receivers with a sense of inferiority or even hatred. For this reason I insist on complete mutual equality among all parties and respect and admiration for other peoples and their cultures. When this attitude is firmly established, we will have plotted a new spiritual Silk Road to bind together not only the East and the West but also the North and South.

I am making these comments today because, in the Soviet Union, I find a valuable and instructive example of the way in which to build a bridge between the cultures of the East and West and to stimulate wholesome exchanges between the North and the South. The distinctive and profound Russian interpretation of human nature is one of the things leading me to say this. Other important indications of the role you and your nation will play in the future are the geographical location of the Soviet Union—a vast junction point between the East and the West—and the valuable experiment made in bringing together fifteen different nations of various levels of economic development in a single republic representing cultural exchanges between the North and the South. Indeed, the 126 peoples—including Russians and Ukrainians as well as Mongoloid people resembling the Japanese—make of the Soviet Union a great melting pot in which various cultures and races have been harmoniously combined in a distinctive blend.

The situation today differs sharply from that prevailing under the tsarist government, which tended to stir up discord among the peoples of the nation for the sake of political expediency. One of the first steps taken by the Soviet government after the revolution was the proclamation of equal rights for all the peoples of the union, regardless of race or economic level. At the time of the founding of the Soviet nation, Lenin said that he hoped for a federation of nations based on free volition, on complete trust, and on a clear awareness of brotherhood and spontaneous agreement. Even in the nineteenth century, however, the peoples of Russia were aware of the unity of Eastern and Western cultural spheres. For instance, under the tsars, the scholarly study of Eastern matters was highly advanced. Very shortly after the revolution, the complete works of the Indian sage Rabindranath Tagore were published in this country. Indeed, the very opposition between the Westernizers and the Slavophiles may have taken its beginnings in the awareness of the union of the two realms. The Soviet Union, then, is capable of understanding the feelings of both Asia and Europe, of both the developed Northern and the developing Southern nations. For this reason, I am convinced that the responsibility of the Soviet Union in promoting cultural exchanges is very great.

I place maximum expectations in the desire for peace of the Russian people, who have cultivated an undying spirit of resistance against oppression. This spirit helped them withstand the Tartar yoke imposed on them for almost two hundred years beginning in the thirteenth century, the invasions of the Teutonic Knights and the Swedes, Napoleon's invasion in the nineteenth century, and the ravages wrought by the Nazi armies of Hitler in the twentieth century. The spirit of resistance has had the effect of planting in the Russian heart a pure longing for peace, which I have sensed even more strongly this time than on my previous visit.

I place my hopes in you, who will bear the Soviet Union's responsibility for creating a brilliant spiritual Silk Road to connect the minds and hearts of the peoples of the world. I feel certain that you will make full use of the profound, pacific tradition of the Russian people in your efforts to bring about lasting peace. Speaking for Soka Gakkai and for myself, I promise that we will do our parts in encouraging cultural exchanges on the private level. I am determined to devote the rest of my life to traveling throughout the world for the sake of such exchanges; and, with the certainty that our joint efforts in this direction will bring us together again someday, I conclude this talk with my thanks to all of you.

The Spirit of Aloha

*Delivered at the Twelfth General Meeting of NSA
(Nichiren Shoshu Soka Gakkai of America),
held in Hawaii, July 26, 1975.*

Fifteen years ago, here in Hawaii, I started the first of my missions of peace throughout the world. I am a Buddhist. I am a believer in the absolute respect for life and the rejection of all violence. It is an article of faith with me to try to establish friendly relations with all people and all nations. As a group, basing our thought and action on Buddhism, we are striving to advance the cause of peace and culture. I have consistently maintained and have attempted to show in all my actions a belief that the way to establish peace in the world today is to strive to create among all peoples a concord transcending barriers of race, nation, and ideology. For the sake of the establishment of world peace, I have already visited thirty-seven nations.

Truly strong, deep peace relies not only on agreements among nations but also on amity and harmony among peoples and individual human beings. In other words, a personal peace based on the individual human being is the only indestructible peace.

I find this personal peace realized here in the beautiful Hawaiian Islands. I sense the flame of determination and mission in your choice of Hawaii—a place deeply significant as a crystallization of many dif-

177

ferent races in one locality—as the stage for a convention devoted to the journey along the road to the peace of all mankind.

What is it that has made possible the harmonious coexistence of peoples of different life styles and customs on these islands? I suggest that it is the spirit of aloha, born of the wisdom of the people of Hawaii. The word *aloha,* used at both meetings and partings, is an emotionally warm expression of profound good will. I believe that this kind of good will has much in common with the compassion and generosity taught by Buddhism and rooted in absolute respect for life. Furthermore, it is an expression of the spirit that can inspire mutual respect and peaceful coexistence among the peoples of all lands.

Absolute respect for life lies at the basis of Buddhist compassion and generosity. Life is a treasure richer than all others. Respect for life must have first precedence. Everything else is only a means or a method for the sake of maximum precedence to respect for life. I maintain that truly lasting peace can be attained only when this attitude toward life is firmly established everywhere.

I hope that all of you, who stand firm in the philosophy of respect for life, will put your beliefs into practice in such a way as to combine the proud, enthusiastic American frontier spirit with the aloha spirit of friendship and harmony and thus make of the United States a great, forward-looking power in the drive for peace, which is the heartfelt desire of all mankind.

The time has come in which the current of the age must flow in the direction of friendship and harmony. The recent docking of the American spaceship Apollo with the Soviet spaceship Soyuz symbolizes the beginning of a future of amity and cooperation.

Intelligence, Emotion, and Will

Delivered at an Education Division Meeting of
Soka Gakkai, held in Tokyo, August 12, 1975.

This assembly of educators at Soka University during our Year of Education is greatly significant, and it is fitting to declare this day Educational Revolution Day and to observe it yearly from now on. Thirty years ago, at the end of World War II, the people of Japan, in spite of the ruins that lay about them and the shortages of material goods that faced them, turned their enthusiastic efforts toward the achievement of the democratic idea. Now that our economy has recovered and we have grown accustomed to abundance, however, our spiritual yearning for democracy seems to have lost strength.

This spiritual debility is evident in the field of education. Before the war, military needs came first, the people second. Today, in much the same way, the economy takes first place; and the people are still second. We must reverse this situation, and the only place where a breakthrough is possible is in education—the work of cultivating human beings.

Bringing up young people is a sacred enterprise. Manufacturers of machinery or producers of food respond to present needs, but educators respond to the needs of the future. I have always regarded education as man's most important task and as my own personal main purpose. To discover the kind of education needed for the future, I have visited many of the world's leading universities, and today I should like to share with you something that Chancellor Dupront of the Sorbonne told me last May. Replying to a question about the gap between teachers and students, Chancellor Dupront resolutely declared: "People talk a good deal about the rift between students and teachers, but I think it would be more accurate to call this a lack of contact. The first need is for educators to recognize their personal responsibility to make contact with students. The most important thing in education is to listen. Instead of concerning themselves about guiding students, teachers should listen to what students have to say and give ample consideration to their opinions. They should not listen just to be able to attack students for their viewpoints."

In 1968, the Sorbonne was the scene of the so-called May Revolution that sparked a series of student revolts in universities all over the world. As the chancellor of such an institution, Monsieur Dupront has gained deep insight into the student problem. By "listening," I think he meant encouraging students to speak what they have in mind. Today it is more important than ever for educators to listen to students and to try to hear the pulsing spirit behind their words.

In order to listen properly, educators must have a deep sense of understanding and sympathy. In order to hear the pulse of the spirit, one requires love as deep as the ocean. Just as a large battery can store up a lot of electricity, so a teacher with love and sympathy can absorb and understand a great deal about his students' inner feeling. We need teachers who have this capacity to receive and who can, without speaking a word, serve as both light and strength for their students.

By being good listeners, you can be good at imparting knowledge. Educators need a sense of togetherness with their students. In this connection, I am reminded of the experience of Johann Pestalozzi, who throughout his life was the paragon of the sympathetic teacher. Writing about the time when he ran an orphanage, he said, "I cried with the children, and I laughed with them. They were together with me, and I was together with them. I was with them in sickness and health."

This captures the basic spirit of education. In ordinary schools, of course, it is impossible for teachers to live together with their students, but they should never lose their passion for education. The human approach to education is especially necessary today, when more and more young people violently disregard human life and adults increasingly ignore social injustices.

Ideally, education rounds out and balances intelligence, emotion, and will to achieve a state of harmony among the three. Intelligence, the power to learn, involves both intuition and reason. Though it is sadly lacking in many cases today, intelligence—thinking ability or intellect—is the faculty that enables us to perform the essential act of sifting the plethora of information presented to us by means of modern communications media and to arrive at a sound understanding of all the facts at our disposal. Emotion—whether in the narrow sense of pleasing or unpleasing sensations or in the wider sense, including moods, sentiments, and passions—is traditionally viewed as man's most sensitive psychological aspect. Will, the driving power propelling us to seek certain goals, is a matter of neither instincts nor natural desires. It is the conscious process of making decisions, the volition we arrive at after due consideration of the issue at hand.

Intelligence, emotion, and will are sustained by personal need for self-improvement and perfection and by the spirit of compassion for others. Without these, intelligence, emotion, and will are only concepts; and the energy we require to live our lives and create a positive social environment disappears. All that remains is sophistry, logic-chopping, and meaningless play with ideas.

Since ancient times, religion has sought the life-giving support needed by intelligence, emotion, and will. But perfect union between the need for self-perfection and the need for compassion toward others has not been achieved by religions of the past. When the need for self-perfection is overstressed, it results in egocentrism; when the need for compassion toward others is overstressed, it causes self-sacrifice and self-deception. To date, religions have oscillated between these two extremes.

The philosophy of the Lotus Sutra and the Buddhism of Nichiren Daishonin open the way for perfect harmony between self-perfection and universal compassion. When the Mystic Law is accepted as a fundamental principle of life, bodhisattva actions—that is, compassion for others—stimulate self-improvement and self-perfection. In *Ongi Kuden*, in discussing the meaning of happiness, Nichiren Daishonin said, "Happiness is to rejoice together with others. . . . Happiness is the state of sharing wisdom and compassion with others" (*Gosho Zenshu*, p. 761). This idea, which runs through all of Nichiren Daishonin's writings, is the perfect foundation for human education. It shows how to round out and complete intelligence, emotion, and will.

All of you educators who have made the philosophy of the Mystic Law integral to your lives are now working hard to put it into practice in each of your daily activities. To create the axis for a new age, we have no alternative but to rely on a new force. Some may say that it is difficult to develop the youthful strength needed for achievement in this new age—trying to reach the stars with a pole—and this is perfectly true. That is precisely why I beg you to undertake this magnificent work. I urge all of you in the Education Division to keep the passionate fire of educational revolution alive to shed abundant light on the society of the future. I ask you to take this great task as your mission, and I entreat you to carry it valiantly.

Cultural Creativity

*Delivered at a Culture Department Meeting of
Soka Gakkai, held in Tokyo, August 13, 1975.*

In the *Gosho* of Nichiren Daishonin, there is a passage that says:
"One character of the Lotus Sutra is like the earth: it produces all
things; one character is like the sea: it contains all currents; one
character is like the sun and moon: it enlightens the Four Continents."
(*Gosho Zenshu*, p. 1263).

"One character" refers to the Dai-Gohonzon, the object of veneration of all believers in Nichiren Shoshu. "Produces all things"
means that everything in the universe comes into existence through
the Mystic Law. This includes art, science, and literature, which,
when lacking the Mystic Law, are like flowers cut from their stalks
and separated from the earth. "One character is like the sea" means
that, like the ocean, the Mystic Law is broad and all-encompassing.
It is expressed in the great compassion capable of saving all men. "One
character is like the sun and moon" means that the person who has
the Mystic Law has the mission and obligation to provide leadership
for our society and the world.

It is for this reason that I ask you, who are pioneers of the culture
in which the Mystic Law is inherent, to be like the earth, the sea, the

183

sun, and the moon. I consider this the lifeline of the Culture Department.

Professor Arnold J. Toynbee has said, "Culture is a movement, not a state; it is a voyage, not a port." I agree with this entirely, but the question is where to seek the generating power for this movement. The generating power is none other than our dynamic life force; and the Mystic Law, which is the source of our life, is the wellspring for all cultural energies.

I think there is an important lesson to be learned from the history of postwar Okinawa, where the Ocean Exposition is now being held. As a battlefield of World War II, Okinawa suffered a "hurricane of steel," in which plants and trees were burned and even the topography was altered. Standing in the midst of desolate mountains and rivers, the Okinawans sought spiritual sustenance more than anything else. Where do you think they found it? Interestingly enough, in the fragments of the folk art that lay, like bits of their old culture, in the rubble around them. The people vied with each other in seeking out these broken relics, and then set up a hut in which to display them.

In the desolation that followed defeat, the Okinawans stood before the remains of their cultural heritage and cried tears of joy, because in that heritage they found new strength with which to face life. As long as their culture existed, as long as they could continue to build upon their tradition and cause it to thrive again, they felt confident that they could once again live in a peaceful Okinawa.

After the end of the war, the people of Okinawa experienced keenly the vigor and spirit that enabled their ancestors to create this tradition, and this gave them the energy to create a new Okinawan culture.

The path that Japan should follow is implicit in the Okinawa experience. In 1945, Japan set out to become a cultural nation. Now, thirty years later, though a great economic power, Japan is very different from the nation of culture that we imagined earlier. In the name of economic prosperity, we are in danger of allowing those few relics of our ancient culture that survived the war to atrophy and vanish. Personal profit, adopted as the supreme goal, is once again isolating Japan spiritually from the rest of international society.

Perhaps our new culture is no more than a means toward economic prosperity. In our current sad condition, economic priorities dominate science, art, education, and all our other cultural activities. This trend must be reversed; we must build a culture richer in purely human qualities.

Culture is born when, in the quest for truth, human lives work energetically to create values of beauty and goodness. Today, the task that faces us is to abandon a culture that has become merely the handmaiden to economic profit. The human revolution movement, with its search for truth and value, makes it possible for us to live like true human beings. The heart that seeks truth draws close to and becomes one with the eternal Law, which transcends limitations of time and space. The person with the will to create values of beauty and goodness devotes himself to the betterment of human existence. Such action accords with the way a religious man must follow. The creation of true culture frees human lives from bonds of desire. It begins with one man's struggle to elevate his personal principles through his own will. This is the practical application of the human revolution that Buddhism teaches.

To awaken the wisdom underlying our intelligence and our sense perceptions, in the depths of life itself, Buddhist thought posits Five Eyes, indicating various powers to perceive phenomena. They are the Physical Eye (*nikugen*), the Heavenly Eye (*tengen*), the Eye of Wisdom (*egen*), the Eye of Law (*hogen*), and the Eye of Buddha (*butsugen*). The person who chants Daimoku and strives faithfully will find his own life to be a mirror in which all things are reflected. Observing them in the mirror of his life, he can grasp the reality and source of cosmic life's dynamic rhythm and come to understand all things.

I ask you to express your creative spirit freely and create works that appeal to the hearts of others. Create things that give hope and courage. This will not be easy. You will encounter many difficulties and hardships on the way, but remember the words of Aeschylus, who said: "Learning is born of suffering," and accumulate learning through your experiences.

Since the practical achievements of the Culture Department are an invaluable phase of the Soka Gakkai movement, I have great hope for you in the future and earnestly request you to carry on your cultural efforts enthusiastically and vigorously.

Obligation and Responsibility

Delivered at a Tokyo Headquarters Leaders' Meeting
of Soka Gakkai, held in Tokyo, August 15, 1975.

August fifteenth is a day that cannot be forgotten by the Japanese, or, for that matter, by any who aspire for peace. Just thirty years ago, on this day, World War II came to its tragic end. Only last month, the world's attention was drawn to the docking of the space crafts Apollo and Soyuz. Listening to the news, I recalled something Valentina Tereshkova, the first woman cosmonaut, mentioned during our conversation in Moscow this past May. Reminiscing on her trip in space, she said: "I cannot describe the joy I felt when I saw the earth from space. Our planet was exquisite. Each continent and ocean had a beauty all its own. Whether one stays in space for a long time or not, just to see the earth once like that is enough to make anyone feel deep respect for our cradle of life."

As I listened to Tereshkova, I thought how good it would be if all the world's war advocates were awakened from their nightmares of belligerence by a trip into outer space, from which the earth itself looks like a great spaceship with all mankind on board. Space explorations show us that the world is one and make men aware of the whole globe. The harsh reality on earth itself, however, is one of complex, diverse struggling. Caught between knowledge of global unity and

186

the harsh reality of frequent conflicts on earth, mankind can only go on trying, through trial-and-error methods, to work out solutions.

On this thirtieth anniversary of the conclusion of World War II, I want to examine the directions that our own organization and all of Japan must follow in the future. Though only a limited human being, I continue to exert all my efforts to ensure that Japan and the world are never again subjected to the ravages of war. In the hope of achieving my goal, I should like to ask what kind of attitude we Japanese people must assume if peace is to be preserved and war prevented.

In any war, it is the nameless people who must undergo the most terrible suffering. When society becomes distorted, it is the powerless people, lacking in either political or economic influence, who must bear the brunt of social injustice. Why did the Japanese let themselves swept up in war? Unless this basic question and the problem underlying it are solved, there is no guarantee that another such tragedy can be prevented.

It seems clear that a major cause of Japanese willingness to condone war was the miserable situation of the people at the time. Unable to say what they should have said, they were further unable to do what needed to be done. Ordinary social rights and obligations were distorted: the administrators held all the rights, and the common people bore all the obligations.

The points of origin of a democracy are the guarantee of the fundamental rights of the individual human being and the recognition of the rights that are attached to various social obligations. In other words, rights and obligations are neither separable nor arbitrarily apportionable. Those who hold certain rights are responsible for the obligations they entail, and those on whom obligations are imposed are entitled to the specific rights their obligations demand. We must recognize this intrinsic inseparability, realize its import, and take the action that it requires of us.

When Japan was reborn a democracy after World War II, it adopted a fundamental dedication to peace. To give democracy a firm foundation and make it a reality, however, the populace in general and each individual citizen must clearly understand the nature of rights and obligations and must act in accordance with that understanding.

It is vital that the common people recognize their natural right to enjoy peace and their responsibility for achieving it. We must realize that the course of history is never separated from the people's will. Each person bears a central role in the evolution of history. The primary key to historical reformation is awareness that each person plays a leading character, whether on the stage or behind the scenes. There is no other way to protect human dignity or secure peace for our country and the world. To be successful, action must be unpretentious. Out of simple, steady action comes the most precious victory of all. Removed from our daily life, action sooner or later proves to be no more substantial than mist.

Only with day-to-day chanting of Daimoku, continuing efforts to create harmonious families and expand the circles of friends in our neighborhoods, and daily fostering of trust and respect in our places of work, can we truly begin to gain in life. Actions that place common sense first and foremost accord with Buddhism and harmonize with Soka Gakkai in its striving for *kosen-rufu* and its determination to be a movement for peace and for the human revolution that evokes and brings to fruition the wisdom and energy of the ordinary people. Nichiren Daishonin's *Reply to Toki Nyudo* contains this statement: "Life has an end. Yet you should not be grudging with it. Your ultimate objective should be the Buddha land" (*Gosho Zenshu,* p. 955). *Ongi Kuden* says that " . . . 'ultimate' indicates the attainment of *kosen-rufu"* (*Gosho Zenshu,* p. 772). These words show us clearly that our movement is a mainstay of Japan and a sun shining brightly for the whole world. No matter who may criticize us, we must cherish Nichiren Daishonin's golden words and move proudly and steadily forward on our way.

Women as a Force for Peace

Delivered at a Women's Division Meeting of
Soka Gakkai, held in Tokyo, August 17, 1975.

The future of mankind cannot be guaranteed by talking. We need more than words. We desperately require a strong, tenacious force for global, unbreakable peace; and this force must take the form of an active movement. I am convinced that Soka Gakkai can and must be the nucleus of such a movement. Buddhism opposes all kinds of violence; and, as the heart of Buddhism, Soka Gakkai must make peace its sacred mission.

Apart from squabbles in the home, women do not start wars. Men are almost always the instigators. Accounting for more than half the population of the world, women must band together as a great force for peace. When they do, we will have gone a long way to preventing all future wars.

Discovering the true nature of war requires deep delving into human psychology. A look at world leaders at the times of the two world wars of this century illustrates this need. These men twisted the truth that right makes might and clung stubbornly to the idea that might makes right. Ironically, however, few of them were in favor of war. They spoke out against it and in favor of pacific solutions to world problems. But, at the mercy of some diabolical inner notion, they could not bring themselves to renounce belligerence absolutely. Torn between two poles, they clearly represent moral and psychological schizophrenia of a kind that can only be cured by the same Buddhist philosophy of the indivisible oneness of mind and body (*shikishin funi*) that we require today if we are to cultivate leaders who can prevent war.

The men who led the world into war twice in the twentieth century lacked compassion. The whole of civilization suffers from the same lack, but doctors and psychiatrists are impotent to cure the condition. We have assumed the responsibility for dealing with this problem, and we will spread the faith in Buddhism to inspire people with the spirit to abandon war.

One great leader, Josei Toda, arose from the destruction of World War II. He pleaded for mankind to renounce the idea that one people has the right to sacrifice another people and said, "Send, not the moonlight, but the light of the sun to the peoples of Asia and the world."

Three decades have gone by for the world, Japan, Soka Gakkai, and each of you since the end of World War II and since Mr. Toda issued thisc all. We are now about to launch on another three decades, the final in this century, which will be a time demanding deep thought on all your parts. In the coming thirty years, the world must eliminate low-level, national squabblings and devote its attention fully to blazing a path to greater happiness and peace for everyone. To do this, we must wisely and heroically engage in as many dialogues with as many peoples as possible.

The *Ongi Kuden* commentary on the *Juryo* chapter of the Lotus Sutra says: "The 'land where this chapter will be propagated' indicates Japan and in general the entire word; the 'converts' indicates all the people in Japan; 'practice' is to attain pure, doubt-free belief; and those 'doing the conferring' means the Bodhisattvas of the Earth." Specifically, this passage refers to Japan; on the broader plane, it refers to the whole world. The general implication is that if Japan stands firm for the cause of peace, so will the world. Consequently, for stability in Japan, and for peace everywhere, we must propagate the true Buddhism.

I am happy that you women have been able to get away from your workaday duties and come to hear a few serious words on some vital topics. Although the daily life of a housewife is not spectacular, it offers the chance to do something of tremendous importance: to remain steadfast in the building of fine homes and good lives. I hope that, for you and all of yours, the next thirty years will be a time of happiness, longevity, and bright personal triumph.

Pillars of Strength for Society

Delivered at a Men's Division Meeting of Soka Gakkai, held in Tokyo, August 18, 1975.

As we observe the thirtieth anniversary of the end of World War II, my heart goes out to the many among you who actually had to fight in that conflict. Looking back over the history of the postwar years, I cannot avoid the feeling that the world as a community faces one very serious crisis: lack of nations that are capable of leadership in solving global problems. The countries now classed as first-rate have more military strength than could have been imagined in past decades, but they are curiously impotent when it comes to leading the world out of its economic difficulties. None of them seems to have a comprehensive policy about distribution and pricing of the world's resources. To make matters worse, we have entered a stage in which the industrialized countries have all the products they need; whereas the developing nations, though sorely in need of such products, lack funds to pay for them. The effect is that people cannot sell what they make.

In our own country, ninety percent of the population already has television sets, refrigerators, and the like; and, though the percentage of distribution is lower for automobiles, we certainly have all the cars we need. Manufacturers of these products, then, can sell no more new products than are required to replace old ones.

True, we need more and better housing, as well as greater welfare benefits for our old people; but at this point the country does not have the economic strength to provide them. The Japanese economy, therefore, has reached a state of high-class bankruptcy, and other countries of the world are apparently headed in the same direction. Our experts call this "stagflation," by which is meant economic stagnation in the midst of inflation.

As a Buddhist, I cannot help worrying about the global calamities confronting us. In Japan, too, I suspect that there will be hard times for several years to come and that we will be forced little by little to give up much that we have accumulated. I hope that you members of the Men's Division will recognize this trend of the times and will fight to protect your lives against the raging waves of society.

A superficial look at the experience of Soka Gakkai to date suggests that among the young people, the Young Men's Division has taken the lead, and the Young Women's Division has followed. The Men's Division has undertaken the most difficult job of all: carrying the whole organization—women and young people included—on its shoulders. If this were not the case, Soka Gakkai would not be where it is today. Our tremendous development has been make possible because you of the Men's Division—you who must attend both to the affairs of this world and to those of Buddhism—have implanted yourselves firmly in the Buddha's teachings and have worked with all your might.

There are, however, situations in which even this is not enough. A passage in *Ongi Kuden* concerning the chapter of the Lotus Sutra called *Yujutsu* refers to "the ultimate depths of life, that which is the absolute reality." Nichiren Daishonin is saying that the Bodhisattvas of the Earth spring valiantly forth from the soil of life, which is the ultimate reality. "The ultimate depths of life" is Nam-myoho-renge-kyo. "The absolute reality" means the fundamental source of all thought, philosophy, and religion—this, too, is Nam-myoho-renge-kyo. As the true entity of Nam-myoho-renge-kyo, we must work even harder to support the Youth Division and the Women's Division, for the sake of propagating the faith and saving the people of the world. We are all comrades, friends, and brothers of the same family. More, we are men working together, united in spirit, dedication, and fervor, laboring to make Soka Gakkai the most beautiful organization in the world.

In *Reply to Myoshin Ama,* there is a statement that says, "The character *myo* is the moon, the sun, and the stars. It is a mirror, clothing, food, and flowers. It is the earth, the great oceans—the crystallization of all blessings and the jewel capable of granting every wish" (*Gosho Zenshu,* p. 1484). The enlightening rays of the character *myo* are like those of the sun, the moon, or the stars. This single character is the mirror in which to see our true selves. It clothes us, feeds us, provides us with beauty as do the flowers, and supports us as does the good earth. It is the sea around us and the sum total of all the blessings in the universe. It enables us to create all treasures at will.

And this *myo,* which makes all things possible, is identical with the Gohonzon bestowed upon us by Nichiren Daishonin. We have the Gohonzon; everything else is up to our faith. Nam-myoho-renge-kyo is the source of all things, the Mystic Law from which the whole of creation emerges. The fundamental energy of the cosmos pulses within the Mystic Law and flows infinitely, making all things possible. Therefore, we are able to change our destiny. Any difficulties confronting the society around us, the country we live in, or the world as a whole can be prevented or overcome.

We must establish union with this infinite source of strength and unite with the universal rhythm. Then we will find happiness in life and be filled with pure, invincible life. Some of you might think this entails staying up all night chanting Daimoku, but there is no need for that. We are ordinary men, with ordinary bodies. When it is time to rest, we must rest. We must find the proper rhythm for our lives. We must not overstrain or attempt the impossible.

As is written in the *Ichinen Sanzen Homon*: "If the votaries of the Lotus Sutra practice in accord with its teachings, they will all achieve Buddhahood within their lifetime. Rice seedlings are planted in spring or summer, and though some varieties ripen faster than others, all will still be harvested within the year. In the same way, the votaries of the Lotus Sutra may differ in capability, but they will all attain enlightenment in their lifetime" (*Gosho Zenshu,* p. 416). Those who practice true Buddhism according to guidance from Soka Gakkai will achieve Buddhahood. The good we accomplish will benefit our families, our children, and our grandchildren into future generations.

Implicit in the quoted passage from the *Gosho* is Nichiren Daishonin's deep conviction that, if we cherish the Gohonzon of the Three Great Secret Laws and diligently carry out our faith, practice, and study, our unflagging efforts toward the human revolution will, without fail, exert great influence on our lives and the society around us. And we will be able to live a life in which all desires are fulfilled.

I pray that, as the central force of Soka Gakkai, you will fully develop your potential and, in the fleeting time allowed us, become pillars of strength and trust in society. May you work even harder to propagate true Buddhism to the entire world, maintaining perfect harmony between the priesthood and our lay organization.

Take care of your health, so that you will live to see the twenty-first century. If you should die before you accomplish all you have set out to do, pass your work on to your children, and always endeavor to show kind and loving care toward your wives.

Buddhist Humanism and
the Human Revolution

Delivered at a Men's Division Meeting of Soka
Gakkai, held in Tokyo, August 20, 1975.

Many centuries ago, Nichiren Daishonin gathered more than one hundred disciples to live together at the foot of Mount Minobu, where he continually taught them the meaning of the Lotus Sutra. Preaching and study, he said, are "the most important Buddhist functions in the world." Today, when most people are escaping the heat in vacations in the mountains or at the sea, you are here trying to fathom the Daishonin's eternal wisdom as recorded in the *Gosho*. Your effort may seem small and insignificant, but it is truly a magnificent undertaking. In the words of Nichiren Daishonin, it is "the most important Buddhist function in the world." Be confident that you are doing something vitally important as you follow the Buddhist way of self-improvement and self-perfection.

Let me remind you that our entire struggle and our entire effort are directed toward establishing a firm foundation for the next thousands of years in the Latter Day of the Law. Let me reaffirm that our struggle embraces all peoples of the world, at any place and at any time.

Life Fulfillment

In the chapter of the Lotus Sutra called *Hoben* we find this passage: "That old vow of mine has now been fulfilled." In *Ongi Kuden*, Nichiren Daishonin commented on this passage: "Belief in the Nammyoho-renge-kyo that Nichiren teaches will raise all people of the ten thousand years of the Latter Day to Buddhahood. Does this not mean that my vows have already been fulfilled? When I say 'already,' I mean that I chanted the Daimoku for the first time on the twenty-eighth day of the fourth month in the fifth year of Kencho (1253). It is certain beyond doubt that the Mystic Law will heal the great illness of ignorance among men. With this conviction my vows are fulfilled, and fulfillment is Buddhahood" (*Gosho Zenshu*, p. 720).

Indeed, for the Original Buddha Nichiren Daishonin to have established Nam-myoho-renge-kyo, the summation of the Three Great Secret Laws, was the fulfillment of all vows, for it meant that all sentient beings throughout the ten thousand years of the Latter Day, and into eternity, could be saved. It is thrilling to think of the Original Buddha's magnificent insight into the future.

Nichiren Daishonin's life was a continual struggle to embrace all people throughout the ten thousand years of the Latter Day. In a cry from his heart, the heart of the Original Buddha, he said that "each torment of every individual" and the "common suffering of all" were his own suffering.

Since the Buddhism of Nichiren Daishonin exists to save all people living in the ten thousand years of the Latter Day, propagation of the faith by Soka Gakkai must extend over many future generations and encompass all human beings everywhere. Soka Gakkai wants to reach all people. Radical or conservative, leftist or rightist, all are human. That is what matters. The *Sokanmon Sho* states that "one person has attained Buddhahood, and then following him, all people equally can attain Buddahood" (*Gosho Zenshu*, p. 564). Our ultimate wish is to bring the human revolution to the individual, so that all people alike will be saved. It is what I call Buddhist Humanism. No matter how intricate or divergent the period in which we live, no matter that society is torn by ideologies and systems, our philosophy, our ideals, and our movement for humanity are focused solely upon man. As Nichiren Daishonin taught, in our struggle we are fighting against the "great illness of ignorance" plaguing mankind; and the only course open to us is the absolute truth of the Mystic Law.

Ignorance is darkness. Confronted with darkness, people are lost. Without Buddhist wisdom, neither scholars nor leaders, neither the powerful nor the rich know anything about life. The basic principle by which human life can be reformed is the Mystic Law, and our struggle, born of that fundamental principle, is a movement toward a human revolution in which each person must challenge the darkness in his life.

The word "fulfillment" in the passage I quoted has a wealth of meanings. There is both personal fulfillment and the more sacred fulfillment shared with others. Again, there is material fulfillment, and there is spiritual fulfillment. But what we must aim for is "life fulfillment," which is more basic still. Material fulfillment is derived from satisfaction at obtaining something desired to satisfaction of power or fame. It is temporary and vain. Spiritual fulfillment is the satisfaction scholars and artists feel when pleased with work they know is good. Though deeper and more lasting than material gratification, this, too, is less than true fulfillment.

Life fulfillment comes when life itself is in dynamic movement, when it is one with the fundamental law of life, welling up from the inner source of life that is the Mystic Law. It is life fulfillment of which Nichiren Daishonin spoke. We can find it in the true joy of doing the work of the Bodhisattvas of the Earth—in the true joy coming from upholding the eternal and omnipresent Mystic Law and from carrying out the most sacred task in life, the propagation of our faith.

Coexisting

I would now like to say a few words to you about problems of a more social and political nature. Until now, coexistence between religion and Marxism has been considered impossible. As a Buddhist, however, I feel it necessary to determine whether that is really true or not, or whether there is some way for religion and Marxism to exist together in peace. I have long wanted to discuss this question with people of the Marxist persuasion.

In my own view, socialism is a philosophy built on the goal of saving the oppressed. It is true that in the history of revolutionary socialism, there have been a number of unfortunate chapters, but in my visits to the Soviet Union and China, I have seen how the people are trying to implement the basically good intention of bringing about happiness and healthy development in society. I have tried to find in socialism the more humanistic direction that I believe underlies that effort. My expectation comes from looking at things as a Buddhist, always trying to see the good in human nature. My views are based upon my belief that, as long as we all exist in a human society, we must try to overcome differences in political or ideological standpoints for the sake of the good of that society.

Religion can develop more freely as an open and dynamic force in the free world than in the socialist nations. Buddhism does not, of course, decree that we must choose a particular type of society or system of government; but one cannot help asking why religion is unable to realize its true strength and its appeal in socialist countries. I think that, as the followers of Marx and Lenin continue the attempt to put their ideas into operation, they will eventually find it necessary to give more respect to the civil liberties, especially the freedom of thought and religion. Having to deal with this problem will, I think, open up new prospects for the development of a humanistic type of socialism.

Today, Japan is seriously disturbed by conflicts in values. The many different views now current lack common ground. I fear that the whole country may become inextricably mired down in mutual distrust and implacable disagreement. In order to build a stable, peaceful society, even twenty or thirty years from now, we must all engage in dialogue with one another and try, in spite of differences in ideology, to find a strong, common basis for mutually peaceful coexistence.

Buddhist Humanism

In the past few years, I have visited many countries, including the United States, the Soviet Union, and China, and as a result of these visits, I feel more keenly than ever the danger underlying the perilous

200 · HUMANISM AND THE HUMAN REVOLUTION

international situation. At the same time, in meeting and talking with people in many different countries, I have felt strongly that deep inside they are aware of the dangers and wish for peace. The time has come when countries must cease their continual wrangling and start talking with each other about how to enable the human race to survive. As things stand now, mankind has been led to the brink of disaster not only by the nuclear arms race in the past three decades but also by environmental pollution, population explosion, depletion of natural resources, the energy crisis, dwindling food supplies, and now by a worldwide recession. Any one of these problems threatens man's very existence; none can be solved unless all nations join forces. We will get nowhere as long as we stick to the old ideas of a dualism in which democracy and socialism oppose each other.

But the nations of the world have begun to seek a new path, and we hear more today about "detente" and peaceful coexistence. People have begun to realize that, unless they find ways to cooperate and understand each other, their own existences are in jeopardy. Nations are becoming more internationally minded, and Japan must not be the lone exception. Surrounded by complicated and radical change in the international situation, our nation must face facts and decide which path to follow. I have urged people to think about this whenever I could.

I have visited many countries, talking with intellectual, cultural, and political leaders and with ordinary people, for the simple reason that dialogue is the first step in creating mutual trust. Talking does not necessarily lead to agreement. Often it underscores differences of opinion. But no matter: the important thing is to keep moving, keep meeting, keep talking. Ralph Waldo Emerson expressed what I feel very well when he said, "Everyone I meet is superior to me in some respect, and I can learn something from each person."

Without mutual understanding, sparks of suspicion and mistrust can quickly ignite flames of fear and hatred. As Buddhists, governed by the spirit of compassion, we have a mission to find ways of snuffing out such sparks.

Ultimately, the crisis of contemporary civilization begins deep inside us. One can cite all kinds of political and social reasons for the development of extremist movements—fascism, for example—but, in the final analysis, fascism is a manifestation of unfettered desire, which is the demon within the lives of people who are controlled by ego and pride. The mission of the Buddhist believer is to overcome this demon and to bring about a human revolution within each individual life.

The theme of my novel *The Human Revolution* is the Buddhist belief that a true human revolution in a single individual can change the destiny of a nation and eventually of all mankind. That is my unchanging creed. Basically, the crisis of modern civilization comes from the violation of the sanctity of the individual; each person is attacked from within and from without. It is often said that the life of one human being is more important than the whole earth; and this indeed is the view of Buddhism, particularly the Buddhism of Nichiren Daishonin, which offers the deepest possible insight into the sanctity of life and the dignity of the individual. Accordingly, we hold that the true source of pacifism is the individual awakening in the depth of life when a person comes into contact with goodness and wisdom.

Our movement therefore puts supreme value on the single individual—not man in the abstract, but each actual living person—and the locus of our movement is everyday life: the home, the community, the workplace.

Because the foundation for our activity is in everyday life, our movement is both gradual and peaceful. In revolutionary movements of the past, the people have been led by small groups of avant-garde professionals who, divorced from the lives of the people, were often carried away by their own ideals. Some of them grew so dogmatic that their do-or-die determination led to bloodshed and sacrifice. But our movement is different—it is gradual, peaceful, and cultural, led by the people themselves. It is the diametric opposite of traditional revolution. We have resolved never to sanction war or other forms of violence and always to use peaceful means, no matter how important the task. A great thinker of our time has said, "A revolution should never kill; it should liberate people to let them live fully." This is exactly the spirit in which we reject violent methods of any kind. In short, the principle underlying all our activity is to establish the human revolution as a never-failing flow of strength, nourishing the growth of education, culture, and peace. This is Buddhist humanism, the path of the Golden Mean; it is the way of Soka Gakkai.

In closing, let me quote a passage from the *Precepts Bequeathed by Nikko* which says: "The benevolent sun of true Buddhism through the Latter Day lightens the darkness of evil slander. The Mystic Wind of the Lotus Sutra that reveals the eternity of life blows away the provisional teachings. Ah! How rare is our meeting with true Buddhism! . . . And yet through the generosity of our destiny, we had the fortune to encounter this sutra" (*Gosho Zenshu,* p. 1617).

The first sentence likens Buddhism to the sun, which, no matter how dark the times, drives away gloom and gives enlightenment throughout the Latter Day. This is absolute compassion. The second sentence means that Nichiren Daishonin's Buddhism enables us to overcome the provisional teachings that life is transient and impermanent and to embrace eternal life and happiness.

These are the words of the second high priest Nikko, closest disciple of Nichiren Daishonin and great leader in the propagation of the true faith. I hope that you will take them as a source of faith and guidance throughout your lives.

Health and Youthfulness

Delivered at the Thirty-eighth General Meeting of Soka Gakkai, held at Hiroshima Municipal Gymnasium, Hiroshima, November 9, 1975.

The decision to hold this meeting in Hiroshima reflects our determination to do all within our power to prevent the recurrence of the tragedy of nuclear attacks of the kind that destroyed this city and Nagasaki in World War II. For the next hour, I ask you to permit me to make an analysis of the outlook for the future. My approach is based on a determination to prevent future nuclear warfare.

The Executive Director's Committee has already decided to name next year the Year of Health and Youthfulness. These two blessings are irreplaceable treasures for peoples everywhere. Yet the great interest currently being shown in health regimens and health foods reflects the insecurity that all people entertain in connection with physical well-being and youthfulness. Deep in the hearts of all human beings are wishes to be strong, hale, and vigorous throughout life.

But the society in which we live is a very sick one. Because of our desire to keep hope bright through our course of life in this society, we have chosen Health and Youthfulness as the motto for the coming year. I believe that the health and youthfulness of each member of Soka Gakkai will be the source of strength we need for our mission of revolutionizing society.

203

Buddhism has always devoted great attention to human sickness and has consistently advanced its own characteristic ways of dealing with the ailments of the mind and the body. Let me quote the causes of illness as stated in the *Mo-ho-chih-kuan* of T'ien-t'ai and discussed in the *Gosho* of Nichiren Daishonin. "There are six causes of illness: (1) disharmony of the four elements; (2) immoderate eating or drinking; (3) poor posture; (4) an attack by demons from without; (5) the work of devils from within; and (6) the effects of karma" (*Curing Karmic Disease, Gosho Zenshu,* p. 1009).

According to Oriental philosophy, the world and everything in it, including mankind, is composed of four major elements: earth, water, fire, and air. Disturbances in these elements—such as disorder in the climate—can have serious effects on human health and can cause various grave illnesses. Such disturbances are referred to as "disharmony of the four elements" in the passage I quoted.

The next two causes concern irregularities in the way a person lives. When the rhythm of daily life is broken, the human being is likely to eat irregularly and to exercise and sleep insufficiently. These things are related to sickness of the internal organs, nervous system, and musculature.

The demons that attack the body from without may be bacteria or viruses, but they may also be emotional or psychological stresses. Devils that cause illness may also arise from within the individual; in this case they may be interpreted as the impulses, drives, and desires that upset the ordinary balance of life. Finally, karma is also one of the causes of sickness, resulting from distortions and tendencies in basic life itself.

In most instances, several of these causes operating together bring about the actual sickness. For example, a cold may be apparently caused by a virus, which is the demon at work. But, in order for this demon to have found an opportunity to go into action, a combination of other causes must have been present. There may have been disturbances in the climate. The afflicted person's irregular way of living may have weakened his body to such an extent that the virus met with no resistance. It is often true that devils interfering with the Buddhist disciplines necessary to the well-being of the individual cause colds.

Finally, a person who is born with a constitutional susceptibility to colds is strongly affected by karma when he falls victim to one.

In order to avoid illness, one must devise a health regimen that meets several requirements. First, it must involve an approach to daily living that takes into consideration changes in the climate. In other words, the individual's clothing and dwelling must conform to the natural rhythm. He must eat and drink in moderation and must get sufficient sleep and exercise. An orderly, well-regulated way of life strengthens the powers of resistance of both the mind and the body. Medical science is effective in helping the human being adjust his habits to an orderly rhythm while strengthening the power of life to conform to conditions and to resist attack. Further, medical science can clarify the nature of demons (viruses, bacteria, and so on) and can devise optimum ways of dealing with them.

Medical science cannot, however, deal with sicknesses caused by the action of deep-rooted devils (desires and impulses). In the case of illness resulting from karma, Buddhism alone can help. When the affliction is brought on by irregular diet or living habits, the individual himself can restore order to his life and improve his condition. When the cause is bacteria or viruses, medical science can track them down and eliminate them. But, for conditions arising from deeper causes, even after medical science and self-control have done their parts to remove superficial causes, only the power of deep Buddhist faith can destroy the devils, change bad karma to good, and restore health.

Health cannot be defined merely as the absence of sickness, however. Nor is it a matter of good physical condition alone, since the health of the mind must not be overlooked. The truly healthy person is able to live vigorously and creatively. He can overcome all hardships and can turn even the worst environmental conditions into sources of strength. The true nature of health is the constant renewal of life. The Buddhist Law finds the source of power to effect this renewal in the Buddha World—Buddhahood—within the human being. I believe that Buddhism has clarified the best health regimen for mankind more clearly than anything else has ever done.

Life is the basic essence of youth. Though young people are incomplete, because they are still forming, they possess passionately glowing life. Youth is colored richly with willingness to challenge the unknown, energy for vigorous reformations, a sense of justice, and passionate emotions. With the passing of time, as age and the corruptions of society take their toll, the ever-flowing, brilliant colors of youth lost their luster. Only a way of life rooted in the Buddha nature, which is the ultimate source of justice, courage, and compassion, can enable the sense of mission of youth to remain alive and strong in this world of the Five Pollutions. Health and vigor shine in a life that is filled with the faith of youth until the time of death. The great reformers in the history of Buddhism have preserved youthful vigor to the end. The Buddhist classics reveal that Shakyamuni himself taught people until immediately before he entered the state of Nirvana. Nichiren Daishonin continued writing and devoting his energy to the guidance of his disciples until shortly before his death in 1282. As you know, Tsunesaburo Makiguchi, the founder of Soka Gakkai, continued to teach—though imprisoned at the time—until his death. And Josei Toda exerted his best efforts for the sake of the propagation of the true Buddhism and for the sake of the training of his disciples until immediately before he died. From the ways of living of these great leaders we can draw an ideal pattern of a life in constant and brilliant exchange with the great universal life. We must all try to follow their examples and maintain youth and vigor throughout our lives.

In the *Gosho*, Nichiren Daishonin quotes a passage from a work called *Hung-chieh* by Miao-lo, in which it is said that the human body imitates the world of nature. According to this text, the head is like the heavens, the feet are like the earth, and the cavities of the body are like the great void. The warmth of the belly corresponds to spring and summer, and the rigidity of the back to autumn and winter. The 4 limbs correspond to the 4 seasons, the 12 great joints to the 12 months, and the 360 small joints to the 360 days of the year. Nasal breathing is like the winds in the mountains and valleys; oral breathing is like the wind in the void. The eyes are like the sun and the moon, and their openings and closings are like day and night. The hair of the head is like a constellation, and the eyebrows are like the Big Dipper. The arteries and veins are like rivers, and the bones like jade. The flesh is like the earth, and the body hair like shrubbery.

I have made extended reference to this passage, in the hope of using it to explain the Oriental philosophy of the relation between human life and all nature. Buddhist thought and the ancient Chinese philosophy of opposed forces (*yang* and *yin*) and the theory of five basic elements all argue that humanity, all of nature, and the entire universe exist together in a state of intense mutual relation. No human being can separate himself from the world of nature. All of us carry out our individual lives within the rhythm of the universe. Indeed, all things in the universe are subject to the same rhythm and to the constant flow of life and death. If nature, which gives birth to and rears all things, is called the universal life, it is no exaggeration to say that the individual human life, moving inevitably through its course toward death, is a concentration and intensification of universal harmony, a microcosm. The passage quoted from Miao-lo directly examines human life and the universe and explains the mutual relations between them.

Modern science finds shortcomings in the *yang* and *yin* theory and in the idea of the five basic elements that are the background against which the quoted passage was written. There are still many things about the nature of the universe that man does not understand. Nonetheless, the broad, inclusive Oriental interpretation of the relations between man and the universe contains much that deserves close examination, especially since modern Western learning has tended to run too much along analytical lines and therefore to lose sight of the overall picture. Miao-lo employed traditional Chinese thought while examining the situation from a Buddhist standpoint in order to put human life in its proper place in the great universal rhythm.

Examples from his text show that our breathing may be compared to the winds of the world of natural phenomena and that our inhalation and exhalation resemble different kinds of air currents. The gentle breezes flowing through mountains and valleys are the respiration of the world of nature. In the human microcosm, the phenomenon of normal breathing is similar to these breezes. Raging winds blowing through the atmosphere upset the operations of all living things. In the human microcosm, such a phenomenon might be compared to faulty respiratory conditions like those produced by asthma. The streams and rivers of the natural world are comparable to the circulatory system of the body. In nature, the flowing waters of the streams and rivers nurture life wherever they flow. In the body, nourishing blood supports metabolism in the cells and tissues. The damage caused by flooding and overflowing rivers is comparable to that caused in the body by cerebral hemorrhage.

The rivers, winds, and earth of the world of nature are eternally changing and producing such pageants of alteration as the four seasons of the year. The world of nature is a single great life entity. The Buddhism of Nichiren Daishonin teaches that Nam-myoho-renge-kyo is the basic source of the great rhythm that keeps all of Nature operating in harmony. In other words, the one Law—Buddha Life—is the fundamental that brings into being, supports, and permeates all life in the universe, including the lives of human beings. When this life of the Buddha nature weakens and when the total rhythm is thereby upset, both nature and humanity lose power to exist as a single life entity and move in the direction of destruction. Disturbance and destruction in the universe are connected with destruction of human life. Conversely, human life, imbued with the power of Buddhahood and mentally and physically vigorous, brings greater luster and added brilliance to the coloration of the universe.

This Oriental philosophy teaches how to live in harmony with the universal rhythm. The Buddhism of Nichiren Daishonin is not a negative way of life. Instead, it shows how an active human life can extend as a reforming energy into the whole universe. This is the greatness of his Buddhism. Indeed, the basic religious significance of Buddhism is to invigorate and illuminate society and the nation.

Our religious practices are the ones advocated by the teachings of Nichiren Daishonin. They include an unfailing guarantee of a life filled with health and youthfulness. In other words, they are of unquestionable value. We must be firmly convinced that the significance of a life of health, vigor, and youthfulness does not stop with the individual living it but is related directly to the revival of society and the nation. My deep hope is that all of you will live lives of health and vigor; that you will, in the words of the *Gosho,* grow stronger and more blessed as you grow older; and that, in this way, you will become the sun of hope of society.

The Basic Spirit of Soka Gakkai

To use a geometrical metaphor, in our new phase of development to-ward *kosen-rufu,* we have moved from a realm of lines to one of planes. In the future, as our activities become more diverse and mul-tilevel, we will pass further into a world of solid figures. But we must never forget that our basic goal is the propagation of the Three Great Secret Laws of the Buddhism of Nichiren Daishonin. As is said in the *Gosho,* "At the time of *kosen-rufu,* the entire Japanese nation will chant Nam-myoho-renge-kyo, as surely as an arrow aimed at the earth cannot miss the target" (*Gosho Zenshu,* p. 1360). The second high priest of Nichiren Shoshu, Nikko Shonin, left these words: "You must abandon your own self and strive with all your might until *kosen-rufu* is attained." The attitude in these two admonitions is the spirit that must always be the base of our progress.

It goes without saying that persistence in *shakubuku* and individual activities on the part of all members are the propelling forces leading to the realization of *kosen-rufu.* This is the essence of the practice of the Buddhist faith in the age of the Latter Day of the Law; and it is our duty and mission as disciples of Nichiren Daishonin, the Buddha of this age, and as Bodhisattvas of the Earth. No matter where you find yourself in the future, and no matter how your activities may diversify, you must always adhere to this belief. I need not say that the drive for the spreading of faith in true Buddhism and for the achievement of *kosen-rufu* is a battle for the fundamental restoration of humanity and of respect for the dignity of life. As members of an organization devoted to the creation of a society based on Buddhism, we of Soka Gakkai are reponsible for achieving the goal of producing a prosperous culture, the main support of which is respect for life. As individual members of that organization, we must contribute to society by attempting to make the areas in which we live and work harmonious and humane. In the past, Soka Gakkai has engaged in many kinds of cultural activities and has tried to appeal to society in the name of world peace. In the future, as our role in society becomes greater and as we come to enjoy increasing trust and understanding, I hope that we will continue such activities that must be of a kind suitable to believers in the true Buddhism.

The achievement of *kosen-rufu* and the building of a peaceful and harmonious civilization are related in the spirit of Buddhism, which is the salvation of all living beings. Indeed, the two are basically manifestations of one thing. *Kosen-rufu* and *shakubuku* are ways to salvation by means of the power generated by a revolution within the individual. Prosperous civilization based on respect for life is a way to salvation effected from without by means of the environment.

The *Rissho Ankoku Ron* of Nichiren Daishonin includes the following passage, which shows us that the achievement of lasting peace on earth is one of our goals: "If the nation is destroyed and families are wiped out, then where can one flee for safety? If you care anything about your personal security, you should first of all pray for order and tranquility throughout the four quarters of the land, should you not?" (*Gosho Zenshu*, p. 31).

Solving the Nuclear-Arms Problem

Now, turning to the question of Japan and current world conditions and of the role of Soka Gakkai in society, I should like to speak on the nuclear-arms issue, which is of maximum importance in connection with the promotion of respect for life. Thirty years have passed since the United States exploded the first atomic bomb in history, on July 16, 1945, and since the first atomic attack was made on this city on the unforgettable day, August 6, of that same year. The attack on Hiroshima was followed by another on Nagasaki. Later, atomic bombs were exploded on Bikini atoll. The scars of nuclear damage grew deeper and deeper in the minds of the people of Japan in the succeeding years. After the war, a strong cry that such a tragedy must never be allowed to recur rose from Hiroshima and gradually echoed throughout the country. It is largely owing to the passionate desire for peace that has arisen from Hiroshima that mankind has not been seduced into using nuclear weapons in any of the wars that have taken place in the past three decades: the war in Korea, the war in the Middle East, or the war in Vietnam. For this reason, we can call Hiroshima a holy place of peace and the point of origin of the movement to prohibit nuclear arms.

I insist that, since they know the horrors of nuclear destruction better than anyone else, the people of Japan have the qualification, the right, and the duty to make these horrors known to peoples everywhere. Last year, at the thirty-seventh general meeting, I made several proposals for abolishing nuclear weapons. In January of this year, the signatures of eleven million people opposing nuclear weapons, collected by our Youth Division, were presented by me to Kurt Waldheim, Secretary-General of the United Nations. Today, at this meeting, held in historic Hiroshima, I should like to make a few further comments on the issue.

First, I should like to call on all of you to reconfirm your determination to persevere unflaggingly until no nation on earth produces, experiments with, stores, or uses nuclear weapons and until all existing nuclear weapons have been destroyed. I issued a call of this kind at the general meeting last year. I intend to repeat it as often as may be necessary. From our standpoint as Buddhists who respect life, nuclear weapons are demons threatening destruction.

Today there are enough nuclear weapons on earth to destroy all living things on the planet. Furthermore, both their number and the number of nations holding them are increasing. The theory of arms limitation is meaningless in the attempt to halt the further spread of weapons of this kind and to prevent experimentation on them. But simply insisting that the theory is meaningless is not enough. The way to create an undercurrent of public opinion that can ultimately bring about the destruction of nuclear weapons is to make known to all peoples everywhere the truth—in the words of Josei Toda—that these weapons are in the deepest sense the products of devils and that people who would use them are devils engaged in demonic work.

Last year at the general meeting I announced that 1975 would be a year for spreading peace. As a step in this direction, I want the Youth and Students divisions to renew their vows to oppose nuclear weapons and to undertake a wide campaign for the sake of peace.

Now I should like to suggest a few concrete measures that ought to be taken to eliminate nuclear weapons. First, I believe that research, debate, and proposals at the level of private individuals on reduction of nuclear arms are essential. The Nuclear Arms Reduction Committee of the United Nations—Japan has been a member of the committee for the past five years—continues to debate the issue with no sign of progress. There may be many reasons for this failure, but the most important cause is the lack of reflection, in its meetings, of the rising universal plea for the elimination of nuclear weaponry. If this plea still fails to be entirely convincing, it is because awareness of the gravity of the threat and a thorough investigation of its nature are still wanting. Consequently, it is extremely important to conduct accurate, detailed research on the actual nature of nuclear energy, its fearsomeness, and the influences it has on human life. I insist that organizations for the conducting of such research be established at once in Hiroshima and in Nagasaki.

I have long advocated a meeting of the leaders of all nations to reach a definite plan for the abolition of nuclear arms. I realize that, at the present time, such a meeting would be difficult to arrange. But, as a first step toward arranging it, I suggest that specialists, scientists, and philosophers from all countries who realize the horrors of nuclear weapons and who are dedicated to their elimination confer together as private-level representatives. It makes no difference whether the nations from which these people come possess or do not possess nuclear weapons. I believe that the meeting should continue until debate, investigation, and discussion have led to the development of a concrete process for the reduction of these arms.

In addition to the elimination of nuclear arms, I feel that the following two points must be given precedence in the discussions at a conference of the kind I have been describing. All of the nations that possess nuclear arms must publicly declare that they will never initiate their use. Furthermore, all nations possessing nuclear weapons must swear never to use them against nations that do not possess them. Of course these two steps in themselves are insufficient, but they concern issues on which it should be easy to come to an agreement; and, if put into effect, they would contribute to the ultimate elimination of nuclear weapons. Participants in such conferences would both be giving warning to the world of the dangers involved in nuclear weapons and be serving as forerunners in the preparation of a world conference of national leaders. Even such a conference would be meaningless, however, if its participants were concerned with nothing but the welfare and safety of their own peoples. They must instead confer in a spirit of awareness of the fate of all mankind. I propose that the first conference for world peace be held in Hiroshima.

Some people may criticize my idea as too idealistic. Certainly, in not a single one of the conferences on arms reduction that have taken place in the three decades since the conclusion of World War II has a nation possessing nuclear weapons taken the initiative in abolishing them. On the contrary, most of the nations have increased the sizes of their nuclear arsenals. If the immense amounts of money now being poured into defense budgets were diverted from a war economy to an economic structure devoted to industries of peace and prosperity, the transition from arms reduction to complete abolition of nuclear weapons would come to seem much more practical. Of course, a change in philosophy as drastic as the one required to work this economic alteration demands courageous determination. But if that determination proves capable of blazing a trail for the people of the twenty-first century, historians of mankind will praise our time as a great turning point in human destiny.

Safety in the control of what is called peaceful uses of nuclear energy is a matter of major concern today. A book by John McPhee entitled *The Curve of Binding Energy,* originally published in the United States and recently translated into Japanese, has shocked the public mind, because it shows that, by using the products of the increasingly expanding nuclear industries, anyone could produce his own nuclear weapon. The control of small nuclear weapons is a pressing issue. If something like the highjacking of nuclear weapons, which I mentioned last year at the general meeting, were to become possible, it would produce mass panic.

In Japan, large quantities of nuclear-fission by-products result from the increasing use of nuclear power to generate electricity. This involves the extensive storing of plutonium, the basic material of the bomb that was dropped on Nagasaki. It is because of stockpiles of such materials that Japan is now regarded as a potential nuclear power. Since even minute amounts of plutonium are considered highly poisonous, we the people of Japan must be fully cognizant of the danger incurred in keeping them in massive quantities. I am not a specialist in these matters—and even the specialists are divided on whether nuclear energy will be the major industrial force of the twenty-first century—but, because it can destroy all kinds of life and because it is a threat to the continued existence of the human race, nuclear energy and all of its applications must be strictly controlled.

Religion and the Outlook for Humanity

An English scholar named Ronald Higgins recently published in *The Observer* an article entitled "The Seventh Enemy." The gist of what he had to say is as follows. Mankind is now faced by six threats: population explosion, shortage of food, exhaustion of natural resources, pollution of the environment, mistaken use of nuclear energy, and unbridled technology. Since all of these issues are interrelated, attempts to solve questions connected with them on an individual or a national basis make solutions impossible and merely serve to aggravate the situation. The only solution is to pool the wisdom of all mankind and to approach the problem on a plane that extends throughout humanity and into the twenty-first century. The seventh enemy to which the author refers in the title of his article is the one that prevents mankind from assuming the necessary approach to the issue. The author separates this enemy into two aspects: human moral delusions and common evils in national and international political structures. The former aspect is an internal threat; the latter an external one.

The history of modern civilization presents a picture of a constant outward flow—from individual, to society, to nature—in the search for materials to gratify desire. But in the present twilight of modern material civilization, humanity, having followed the path of the outward threat, must now turn its attention to the inner threat. Contrary to the hopes of many of us, an understanding of this inner threat is only to be found in the deep mists of insecurity and confusion. Sending a shaft of light into these mists is the greatest reason for the existence of religion. Because it shows all people how to deal with the inner threat by breaking with the fundamental blindness in human life, the Buddhism of Nichiren Daishonin is the most outstanding religion for mankind today.

For those of us who adhere to the philosophy of a reformation of life, education is of the greatest importance. As is often said, education is the act of bringing to light things that are latent or hidden. In other words, education is the process of devising ways to manifest the possiblities and creative abilities inherent in life. An especially important aspect of education is self-education. Education that overlooks this aspect can lead to authoritarianism and can thus lose sight of the true goal. Socrates, one of the greatest teachers in the history of man, said that the electric ray fish can shock others because they shock themselves, thus implying that one can teach others only what one knows or has taught oneself.

Those of us for whom the human revolution is the primary article of faith are in a position to know the basic meaning of education. Our very conversation is in itself education. Person-to-person awakening to the meaning of life will pulse outward until it is related to the way of life of all humanity. In this sense, Soka Gakkai might be called the epitome of an educational society devoted to stimulating people to an awareness of the meaning of life. The outward pulse from a human revolution to an educational revolution will continue until it becomes a political revolution and an economic revolution. Ultimately it will conquer the enemies threatening man from without and will come to occupy a definite place in the overall panorama of human wisdom. We must go on insisting that we have the key to enable us basically to alter the current of modern civilization, which has until now pursued a violent and ever-outward course, ignoring the sanctity of human life. I ask your assistance in this great task. Further, on the basis of true Buddhism, we must assume our place in a culture devoted to the goals of Soka Gakkai and, in this way, do all that we can to bring peace to humanity and to society as a whole. In this, too, I ask your cooperation and assistance.

The Economic Crisis

One of the major trials facing Japan today is the current economic slump, which affects the daily lives of many of us. Small and medium-sized enterprises have been especially hard hit. It deeply grieves me to know that many such firms have foundered on unforeseen difficulties of unemployment and bankruptcy. The present economic crisis differs from the cyclical depressions of the past. Today economists are pointing out the imperative need to take into consideration national and international economic structures and the entire human way of life. I am not a specialist in this field; but, if I may be allowed an opinion, I should like to say that I feel that, in attempting to deal with the economic crisis, the government must give first priority to saving the weak. In addition, instead of pursuing the dream of Japan as an economically mighty nation, we ought to attempt to contribute to mankind through culture and allow our nation to become a cultural storehouse. The distinctive Japanese civilization is rich enough and deep enough to allow us to do this. I am convinced that the development of a culture-oriented nation is both the surest guarantee for the safety of Japan and the way in which Japan can make its maximum contribution to the world.

The best way for Japanese enterprises to ensure their continued survival on the international market is for all of them to devote care to making products that are creative and highly distinctive. In the past, Japanese businesses have had the bad reputation of taking foreign ideas and getting rich by mass-producing articles and materials based on them. This kind of thing will not do in the future. Japan has its own traditional sense of beauty in design, and things created in accordance with that sense of beauty have charm for the peoples of other lands. Even though it may mean that economic growth is on a low level or that operations proceed on a moderate scale in the future, the way to remain economically alive is to produce commodities that are individual and irreplaceable and to cling firmly to the idea of distinctive production.

Nor is this true only of commerical enterprises; it is the only way open for relations among nations and cultures. The Buddhist theory of self-manifestation (*jitai-kensho*) is the most fundamental and inclusive way for human beings to achieve an ideal way of life and to fully develop their individual traits.

The Role of Soka Gakkai in Society

Today, a large part of the Japanese population consists of people too young to have experienced war. History teaches that a continuation of the kind of inflation and economic instability that we are currently facing can lead to the outbreak of war. The last years before World War II were marked by a snowballing accumulation of events that brought suffering and misery to the people. Such a condition must never be permitted to happen again. Today, thirty years after the end of World War II, the undercurrent of fear of another global conflict has by no means ceased to exist. In stronger terms, I might say that today mankind dances wildly on the brink of a volcano.

Some of us who are apprehensive of what lies at the base of the current situation believe that it is vital to do something about these matters. There are other people, however, who argue that our fears are groundless and that we are anxious for no reason. In spite of what these people say, we must realize that we will be greatly hampered in dealing with a situation if we wait until we actually face it. In too many cases in the past, delay meant disaster. In his *Reply to Toki-dono,* Nichiren Daishonin includes an old Chinese saying to the effect that the truly wise man, even in an apparently secure situation, always looks to the future and spies out danger and crisis before anyone else. The fool, on the other hand, fails to sense danger, even when he is in the midst of it. To the leaders of today, I must say that a person in a position of social responsibility cannot afford to act the part of the fool.

The power to wage war rests in the hands of a few leaders. The way to encourage them to move in the way of peace is for the largest possible number of people to proclaim loudly that peace is the only road they wish to travel. I want all of us to intensify our drive for peace, for this is our responsibility as people living in the world today. In the commentary on the Nirvana Sutra in the *Gosho* occurs a passage telling us that when a society is based on the propagation of Buddhism, it and its people are indestructible, no matter what happens. This sacred precept should awaken us to a sense of responsibility and magnanimity.

One age succeeds another. As with the climate, our times are sometimes fair and sometimes foul. In the future, we will probably have to encounter tempests of hardship and trouble. The important question is whether we have the strength to remain steady and unwavering on our path, with our eyes fixed firmly on the prime point of life. The mission of religion is to plant vitality and steadfastness in the minds and hearts of all peoples.

Various powers in the world—authority, money, brutality—attempt to violate human dignity. The role of Soka Gakkai in society is to employ the spirit that wells from the very depths of life to do battle with such powers. This battle is a starting point for a war of resistance against fascism. In terms of social stability, the value of Soka Gakkai, as an organization championing the human revolution, is certain to increase. Making intimate appeals to each person with whom one comes in contact seems like modest, slow work; but all great tasks take time to accomplish. Establishing the contacts that enable individual human beings to cultivate and refine the life within them cannot be accomplished overnight. But the result of such an undertaking is the diamond of life, which cannot be destroyed by surrounding circumstances, no matter how severe. The only path left for mankind is the one leading through slow, modest work of the kind I have mentioned. And to anyone who would scoff at my proposal, I can only ask: "What solution do you suggest?"

Our society is one of constant daily, monthly, and yearly flux. In this information-oriented society, things important today are forgotten tomorrow. In such times, modest thought and open exchange among human beings are of the greatest importance. Nor should the topics of interest be limited to the solving of the problems of the moment. Instead they must include long-range examinations of the meaning of civilization and true affluence and of the significance of a reason for living. Thought of this kind is urgently demanded by the crisis inherent in the social structure of our times. It is often said that, when one has reached the end of one's tether, it is time to return to the starting point. The eternal starting point for human beings must be the dignity of life and the finest aspects of human nature. I believe that the signpost guiding us into the next century must be the conviction that humanity is centrally important. I am eager to discuss matters from this viewpoint with anyone who is interested, because all of the major themes of our times must be analyzed with an eye to future developments and not from the standpoint of political considerations, which too often lead to conflicts. Today, military and political power form the fearsome background for international politics; while concern for humanity and civilization and culture fades from view. Whenever I think of these circumstances,

I recall the famous *Questions of Menander* (*Milinda-panha*), which is a discussion between the Greco-Bactrian King Menander and the Buddhist monk Nagasena. Menander, who ruled in India in the second century of the Christian Era, possessed a sophisticated knowledge of the rationalist and analytical philosophical traditions of Plato and Aristotle and used his powerful brain to refute the philosophies of India of his time. Only the young Buddhist monk Nagasena stood up to him and, according to the text, converted him to Buddhism. In their dialogues, Nagasena's condition for engaging in discussion was that the king employ the thinking of a wise man, not that of a king. By the "thinking of a king," Nagasena probably meant the authoritarianism that advocates the use of force to convert people who are refractory to its theories. By the "thinking of a wise man," he meant the standpoint of total equality, in which human beings can seek truth and happiness and in which all kinds of solutions, commentaries, criticisms, corrections, and categorizations are permitted in the course of the discussion. Such a search for truth and happiness is the meaning of human dialogue. This is the kind of argument that leads to the elevation of education and civilization. For three days, Menander and Nagasena engaged in harmonious, earnest discussion. The confrontation of the king's rationalism and knowledge by the profound wisdom of Buddhism is recorded in an extremely interesting document, my acquaintance with which convinces me that dialogues based on the fundamental aspects of human nature are the tools with which we can overcome the crisis facing mankind today.

Most people who claim not to understand the meaning of Soka Gakkai would understand it if they were more deeply acquainted with Buddhism. In addition, however, because of pressure imposed on us in the past, we have sometimes built around ourselves hedges that were higher than they needed to be. In our urgency to spread knowledge of our teachings and to build and pioneer, we have not always had the time to remove those hedges. I hope that from now on each member will strive to eliminate all such barriers. Our tradition is still young, and we are immature in many ways. We must give serious thought to our failings. We must modestly and openly listen to good advice when it is offered, and we must move in the direction that we feel is secure and trustworthy. Furthermore, I hope that people in society who are not members of Soka Gakkai will openly express their opinions to us. If we can bring them to understand us, they will see that our world is completely comprehensible in common-sense terms. It is important to discover the points on which we agree with others; it is equally important to find the points on which we disagree. Our age demands deep thought and a forward-looking attitude. But it also demands dialogues based on the fundamental elements of human nature. It is the greatest folly to allow divisions and conflicts to recur because we refuse to look farther than the tips of our noses.

In October 1975, at the age of eighty-six, Arnold J. Toynbee concluded a life filled with great work. I shall never forget the sincerity and severity with which, during one of our dialogues, he said to me: "We must go on with our discussions for the sake of the people of the twenty-first century." Throughout our talks, Mr. Toynbee repeatedly insisted that religion is the fundamental basis of all civilization. I, too, am convinced that only a great religion can enable us to revive the vigor and vitality of civilization.

All that we know of the origins of human civilization consists of a few thousand years of evidence. Darwin's tracing of the development of man from the lower animals in his *Origin of Species* amounts to no more than a fragmentary view of the infinite depths of life. Although science has some hypothetical explanations of the origins of life and of the universe, all of its knowledge arrives no farther than the threshold of Buddhist philosophy. Buddhism interprets everything in the light of eternal life—life without beginning and without end— as the essence. Through religious practices, we have attempted to plumb the depths of Mahayana Buddhism, which has long been a major part of Oriental life and thought. In the light of current conditions, I wish to express my belief that Buddhism and its teachings are clearly capable of surpassing barriers of nation, race, and language to become the treasured common property of all peoples. Furthermore, I believe that it is our duty to cherish this priceless Buddhism and to carry it to all mankind.

Now I should like to say a word about the Soka Gakkai agreement to cooperate with the Japan Communist Party for a period of ten years. On August 20 of this year, at a meeting of representatives of the Men's Division, I said that my intentions in making this agreement did not imply specific actions, but that they did imply a desire to ascertain the points on which both groups—the Communist Party and Soka Gakkai—could see eye to eye. Further, I expressed my belief that we should take ten years to find out how deeply rooted the spirit of detente between the two groups might be. There is no denying the importance of the coexistence of religion and socialism from the viewpoint of civilization. Both religion and socialism must be tolerant and forbearing for a long time. What I have set forth in the preceding few remarks represents my opinions on the issue.

In connection with the conclusion of a peace treaty with China, I should like to make the following remarks. My eagerness for a treaty of amity between Japan and China and my aversion to allowing the threat of war to persist into coming generations have already been clearly stated. Seven years ago, at the eleventh general meeting of the Students Division, I urged the normalization of relations between China and Japan. Six years ago, in volume five of the Japanese-language version of my novel, *The Human Revolution,* I insisted that the time had come for the conclusion of a treaty of amity with China.

As you all know, negotiations for such a treaty have progressed to a certain point but have run afoul on what is called the hegemony issue. I have already expressed my feelings on this point; but, because of the importance of good relations between China and Japan to the peace of all Asia, I feel it is worthwhile to repeat them here. In the joint communiqué issued by the two nations in September 1972, it was said that neither China nor Japan would seek to establish hegemony in Asia or the Pacific region and that both would resist attempts on the parts of any other nation or group of nations to establish hegemony in those zones. I insist that if the two nations would adhere to this same attitude, they could proceed smoothly to the conclusion of a peace treaty.

Since the reopening of relations between China and Japan three years ago, as a representative of Soka Gakkai and on a purely private level I have traveled to China often in the hope of establishing friendly, neighborly contacts. During 1974 and 1975, I visited China three times. I have made many good friends there and have helped bring about considerable exchanges in the interests of education, culture, and peace. For the sake of further exchanges and greater friendship, extending to the times of our children and grandchildren, I insist that the peace treaty between China and Japan must be concluded as quickly as possible.

In the "Voice of the Buddha" in the *Gosho* occurs the following passage: "One letter of the Lotus Sutra includes the merits of Shakya-muni, Taho, and all other Buddhas. One *chintamani* jewel is equivalent to one hundred such jewels. And one *chintamani* jewel can cause unlimited jewels to rain down. If one pill be made from one hundred grasses, that pill or one hundred like it can cure illnesses. One drop of seawater is the coming together of sea currents; it is all sea currents" (*Gosho Zenshu,* p. 1121).

If we apply this text to our conditions of daily life and work, we can see that the one hundred *chintamani* jewels, the one hundred pills, and the great sea are Nichiren Shoshu Soka Gakkai and that the activities of each one of us are comparable to the single jewel, the single pill, and the single drop of water. The sea is no more than the aggre-gation of many drops. Each drop contains the sea itself. A single *chintamani* jewel has the power to bring forth a hundred jewels like itself. A single pill is able to cure all sicknesses. I want each of you to realize that you, as an individual, are Soka Gakkai and that Soka Gakkai could not exist without you. The Buddhism of Nichiren Dai-shonin teaches that each person has this kind of mission and this kind of qualifications.

A certain French writer, in trying to point out the way a person ought to live, tells of a simple marble gravestone in a cemetery not far from Paris. On the stone is carved in simple letters an epitaph that says: "Here sleeps August Charles Colignon. He loved good and tried to do good. Striving to put into practice the morals and precepts of Montaigne's essays and La Fontaine's fables, he lived a happy life." Colignon was a simple citizen; but many noted people, including Ralph Waldo Emerson, have been deeply moved by his epitaph. The French writer I mentioned was profoundly touched that simple French people of town and country should try to pattern their lives and actions on the precepts of men like Montaigne and La Fontaine.

But Soka Gakkai is composed of many simple, unknown people

like Colignon. The important difference is that his life of striving to follow the precepts of great French thinkers terminated with his death. We members of Soka Gakkai, on the other hand, following the teachings of the *Gosho,* through our strivings and actions are making our lives manifestations of the eternal philosophy of Buddhism.

Fidelity as a Friend for Life

Delivered at the First Graduation Ceremony of Soka High School for Girls, held in Osaka, March 13, 1976.

~~~

Like other "firsts" in our lives, a first graduation is an event of great significance. This graduation from the Soka High School for Girls is an important landmark in the history of the institution and its tradition, because it marks the initial completion of a full educational cycle. From the bottom of my heart, I hope that, on this brilliant foundation, the school will continue to grow into an institution of such stature that the entire Japanese world of education will know and be proud of its achievements. Moreover, I hope that each member of the graduating class will engrave this prayer on her heart and that she will love and support her alma mater throughout the rest of her life, no matter what befalls her. All of you have worked hard during the three years that you have been growing here. But you did not work alone. You had your classmates, who encouraged you in difficulties and who took your hands and rejoiced with you in happy days. Such friends are difficult to duplicate.

Fidelity and concern for other human beings are the most important things in life. I feel that it is especially significant that you have been able to develop in these directions, not through theory, but through mutual contacts with classmates and experience. As a parting gift to all of the members of this graduating class, I should like to offer this advice: accept fidelity as the friend of your lifetime. Trusting and being trustworthy are great strengths in life.

In general, all of our lives are similar. Those of you who are not going on to higher institutions of education will go to work soon. Many of those who work will continue to study in one way or another, even after they have taken their places in society. Even those who go to college or other advanced schools will work at some date in the future. Some people will have to wait a year or even two before going on to college, but this is less important than it might seem now. Remember that misfortune can be turned into happiness.

A man must go his way and a woman hers, but as long as neither strays too far from the path and as long as both make the best efforts of which they are capable, they will someday find happiness. Keep this in mind and go boldly and courageously to your new lives.

On its own, the graduating class has formed what it calls the Firefly Association; and the parents of the class have donated Firefly Pond, which is located in the center of the school grounds. It will make me extremely happy if the members of this class come together without fail once a year to exchange news by this pond.

There is a popular opinion to the effect that in each graduating class the top student is important and that everyone else is worthy of much less consideration. This opinion is mistaken. Although top-ranking students have certainly made achievements that I do not intend to minimize, their number is small. And there is no reason to allow their scholastic excellence to blind us to the worth of all of their classmates. A look at recent Japanese history illustrates my meaning. Our nation has its faults; but, in the thirty years that have passed since the end of World War II, we have grown into the nation and the society that you see around you now. This achievement was not the result of the talents of a small group of top students. It was possible only because each person in the nation has his or her own special excellence.

Everyone has strong and weak points. The important thing in life is not to give in to weaknesses and to put strengths to maximum use. In my opinion, the person who does this is the truly outstanding person, the kind of person who makes a mark in actual society. What

I have said about making the best of one's strong points without giving in to one's weaknesses holds true in society as well as in school. I hope that all of you will develop your talents courageously as you go forward in life.

There are many years ahead of you. In all of them, a cheerful outlook and good health will be of maximum value. I sincerely hope that all of you will maintain good spirits and physical well-being throughout life.

Now I should like us all to give a rousing hand of applause to the members of the first graduating class of the Soka High School for Girls as they depart from this hall. Will those of you who remain please give the senior members of your educational community a resounding send-off.

Bright Community Members

*Delivered at the Ninth Entrance Ceremony of Soka Junior
and Senior High School, held in Tokyo, April 8, 1976.*

The cherry trees are blooming; and the small, pale green leaves of the *zelkova* trees are beginning to appear. In your lives too, spring has come. You have passed your troublesome entrance examinations and now, with eyes turned toward a bright future, have entered these schools. It gives me great pleasure to congratulate you on this occasion. I should like to congratulate your parents as well, and I shall take this opportunity to request that the faculty and staff of the schools continue their good work of teaching and guidance. The success or failure of education depends on the unity of teacher and pupil.

Recently I have been noticing articles on schools in various newspapers. It is pointed out in these articles that, with the increase of the populations of the bed-town prefectures around Tokyo—Kanagawa, Chiba, and Saitama prefectures—the number of high-school students is rapidly growing. All public schools have from ten to twelve (fifteen in some cases) classes in each grade. Increases in student numbers mean more teachers. According to surveys conducted by one newspapers, more than thirty percent of all students do not know the names and faces of all of the teachers in their school. A certain principal is reported as having said that under conditions of this kind it is impossible to prevent the efficiency of teaching from dropping.

Today, 300 new students are entering Soka Senior High School, and 200 are entering Soka Junior High School. These numbers are just right. Furthermore, you are students of high quality. In other words, the conditions under which you are entering new phases of education are excellent in comparison with those in the educational field in general. I want all of you to understand this and to do everything you can to develop a feeling of unity with your teachers as quickly as possible.

I have heard that student health here is good in comparison with other urban schools, but somewhat inferior to that in rural schools. In asking myself why this could be, I wondered if perhaps the students are studying too hard. But this does not appear to be the case. The reason seems to have something to do with their eating habits. Most of the students in these two schools live either in dormitories or in privately rented rooms, instead of with their parents. The school authorities take care to ensure good food at meals. But, since all of your are in your peak growing phase, three meals are not enough. When you become hungry between meals, you reach for the fastest and easiest thing, which may take the form of cake, bread, or easy-to-prepare instant foods. This kind of eating might do no harm for a month or for half a year. Continued for two or three years, however, high-caloric, low-nutritional foods can have harmful effects and can be the cause of the inferior health I mentioned earlier. This is, of course, a cause of worry on our part. You, however, are the only people who can do something about the situation. I request that all of you pay attention to the things you eat; ensure that you get the right amounts of vitamins, minerals, and other nutrients; and grow into strong, healthy young men and women.

You are now at the stage at which all kinds of impressions are being made on you. These impressions will enter the realm of your subconscious, where they will exert a controlling influence on much of your later life. During the three or six years of school that you will experience here, I hope you will keep this in mind, struggle against all kinds of evil, and seek the good always. In this way you will grow into fine people of steadfast faith.

One way to do this is to ask and heed the good advice of senior students. I hope that all of you will grow into bright, hopeful members of this educational community.

Sorrow as a Source of Creativity

Delivered at the Sixth Entrance Ceremony of Soka University, held in Hachioji, Tokyo, April 10, 1976.

Educating People to Be First-Class Leaders

Allow me to congratulate you on the opening of your college careers. I hope that the next four years will be a stage on which you can develop the rich and meaningful drama of the formative period of your youth. Thinking about the adventures of the life ahead of you moves me deeply. Youth is a precious, irreplaceable jewel. It is a time in life of such great value and importance that the way it is used determines the way later life will develop. It is a usual human experience for impressionability and sensibility to increase dramatically in young adulthood. Young men's ears become sensitive to the sounds of the subtle changes in the world of nature. Deep emotions of love begin to grow in the hearts of young women. Young people of both sexes have the courage to challenge evil authority, which does not deceive them. Young intellects are eager to create and to assist in carrying on the human heritage. It is the special privilege of youth to fly forward to a hopeful future and to move boldly along the path of self-realization. In my own younger years, I made a voyage of the spirit in ways of deep thought, where I was led by my enthrallment to the mystery of

230

life and the universe. Today, I should like to open a page of my remembrances of youth and to focus your attention on the experiences of one individual whose work influenced me deeply.

One of the people who strongly colored my younger years was the Indian poet, Rabindranath Tagore (1861–1941), whose importance has recently undergone re-evaluation. I should like to take this occassion to give you some of my impressions of him. There are many reasons to honor Tagore highly. He ranks with Gandhi as one of the great heroes of India. He was a poet of worldwide stature and the recipient of the Nobel Prize for Literature. As an opponent of colonialism, he planted much thought in the minds of the people of India. For these reasons he was widely praised during the eighty-one years of his life of creativity and struggle. One of the most impressive parts of his life in my view is the curse that seems to have fallen on his family after he devoted his own funds to the establishment of the Shantiniketan School for Peace at Bolpur. One after another, he lost his beloved wife, his second daughter, and his youngest child. In the midst of successive sorrows, he was forced to become involved in the major political issues of the partitioning of Bengal by the British into Muslim and Hindu zones. Tagore loved his family, especially his youngest child, whose death of cholera at the age of thirteen was a great blow. In his reminiscences, Tagore said that his sorrows at this time of life made him curse his fate.

Tagore, the Poet Who Lived for His Mission

Perhaps the poet did perceive a dark shadow of fate—they often fall on human lives—but he overcame his sorrows because he looked boldly and fearlessly at the great inner sea of universal life. If he had not done this, he would have been unable to manifest the courage to brave the crushing sorrows he experienced and to find a new source of strength. Accepting his own sorrow as a self-imposed trial, he moved courageously forward along the path of his mission for the peace and happiness of all mankind. It is this way of life that I commend most highly in Tagore. A person awakened to his own great mission can overcome grief and use experience as a springboard to the next stage in a creative life. A first-class human being is not a grumbler. Although it was essentially a British strategy to ward off anti-British sentiments, the partitioning of Bengal served only to fan the flame of Indian patriotism. It became the stimulus for an intensified anti-British movement.

Acts Based on Certain and Fervent Faith

In the opposition to the Bengal partition, Tagore assumed the leadership almost as if he were preordained to the task. But he did not act on impulse. His actions were based on a certain faith that he felt throbbing in the inner sea of his heart. The following discussion will make this clear.

When the danger of terrorism arose as the outcome of increasing anti-British feeling, Tagore said that violence was not the way to save India. He believed that constructive work in a spirit of tolerance was the only way to produce desirable results. This was the approach he assumed to calm the terrorists. And this alone is enough to show that his resistance movement was not the product of narrow nationalism, but that it grew from a profound "spirit of tolerance." In order to understand his spirit of tolerance, it is essential to examine some of the experiences of his early life.

His father early recognized Tagore's poetic genius and allowed him to roam free in the world of nature on the many trips the two took together in Northern India. Probably the opportunity to run free and breathe the pure air of a natural environment helped generate and cultivate his spirit of tolerance. At the age of seventeen, he traveled to England to study and, while there, became familiar with Western music. Upon his return to India, he wrote the enchanting opera *Valmiki-prati-vah,* which combines the Eastern spirit with Western reason. People who attended performances of the opera were captivated by it.

One of the most deeply impressive times in Tagore's young life was the period he spent in rural Bengal when he was twenty-three. He helped to improve the agricultural cultivation methods of poor Indian farmers and to increase their harvests by introducing elements of Western scientific civilization. At the same time, while working and sweating in the lap of nature, he reached an understanding of ultimate human truth. In short, he underwent the priceless experience of contact with the life that is the source of all things and that permeates mankind, the world of nonhuman nature, and the entire cosmos. The same driving force that results in the pageant of the changing seasons is the source of the compassion and wisdom in the hearts of the poor, but good, peasantry. The only way to create spiritual union among all peoples is to become aware of and to manifest the eternal life supporting all things and residing deep in the hearts of all human beings. Tagore's spirit of tolerance was rooted in this eternal life.

The experiences of his youth gave Tagore the strength and the greatness of soul to overcome personal sorrows in order to participate in the movement against the partitioning of Bengal and to put his own inner passion and sense of justice to good use in everything from art to social and political movements. His experiences, illuminated by youth, demanded the discovery of an inner life force and helped Tagore walk the path of true human happiness and self-realization. A life of self-realization is a happy life.

In a sense, the eternal life that impressed Tagore is close to the Buddha nature, or Buddha Life, that Buddhism has revealed as the result of penetrating observations. In terms of the ego, this is the greater self that breathes deep inside all of the multifarious lesser selves of the world. The only way a human being can hope to achieve a revolution in his life and, by means of it, cultivate a steady, unchanging harmony in both physical and spiritual aspects is to stand firm in the greater self, regulate his heart by its rhythms, and attune his ear to the inner voice.

When I speak of "self-realization," I mean the greater self, not the lesser self, which is controlled by petty desires. Interpreting the self to mean only the lesser self inevitably leads to selfishness and egotism. The self I speak of is the central, essential self that has universal life as its fundamental basis. It is the greater self that is the source of compassion and wisdom.

The Golden Road of Youth

To discover the greater self and to call upon the energy latent in it demand constant spiritual progress and rich sensitivity. I am speaking to you of the characteristics of youth and of self-realization in the greater self, because youth sees most keenly through all things and is able to perceive the eternal. I know this from my own experience. I should like to re-emphasize my conviction that the primary characteristic of youth is the ability to put to use abundant sensitivity and impressionability and in this way to come into contact with the ultimate core of the universe and life and to attain a lifelong faith, philosophy, and mission. There is no hesitating for a human life that has found its essential mission, no fear of trials or hardships. In the turbulence of society, a person who leads such a life turns toward the future with an ideal in his heart and creates a place where he can manifest his true self.

Some people find eternal truth in the world of nature; other people may discover the inner truth of matter and mind in the pursuit of learning. You women sometimes discover the source of compassionate energy in exchanges of true love. No matter which path you elect, experiences that awaken limitless human happiness—together with your studies during your university career—are certain to become food for development throughout the rest of your life. Experience based on contact with universal life and with the cosmos will find application in your studies and will lead you along the golden road of self-realization. In the following four years, I hope you will absorb as much of the human intellectual heritage as possible here in the beauty of the Musashino natural setting. In addition, I hope that, working together with Chancellor Kazuo Takamatsu and with all of your teachers, you will follow a path of learning even higher than that of intellectual achievements.

Soka University is a place for education; it is also a stronghold of world peace. In short, it is a place of training in which to refine yourselves physically and mentally. Here you will be able to devote your youth to the human revolution, to realize your potentialities, to manifest yourself, and to begin to revolutionize your own way of life. I hope that each of you will lead an active, full life, blessed with the four noble qualities of life: true self, eternity, purity, and happiness.

Soka Gakkai, Its Ideals
and Tradition

Delivered at the Thirty-ninth General Meeting of Soka
Gakkai, held at the Soka Gakkai Sapporo Cultural
Center, Hokkaido, October 24, 1976.

My Master and Hokkaido

Since the present general meeting marks the beginning of the Year
of Study, it is particularly appropriate that it should be held in Hokkaido, where both Tsunesaburo Makiguchi, the first president of Soka
Gakkai, and Josei Toda, the second president, spent their youthful
years and prepared themselves through study for the roles they were
to play later in life.

I have paid countless visits to Hokkaido, but I remember most
vividly the very first one I made. It was in the summer of 1954, and I
had come with my teacher and master, Josei Toda, to visit his childhood home, the village of Atsuta. This, his first opportunity to return
to his old home since his release from prison at the end of World War
II, was an emotion-filled occasion for him. He was fifty-four at the
time, and I was twenty-six.

The hot August sun blazed in a clear sky. Nowadays the road is
paved, and one can get from Sapporo to Atsuta in about an hour. But
at that time, we bounced along over dusty country roads, and, what

with a ferry ride across the Ishikari River, the trip took a good three hours.

Along the way, as we ate some roasted corn, Mr. Toda recounted stories of his youth. He told me that, after classes at primary school, he used to go walking along the seashore with his teacher. At a place called the Ruran Sight, where an unusual rock formation jutted from the sea, they would sit down to rest. Then his teacher would read to him, or they would gaze at the distant, sweeping horizon of the Sea of Japan. "On the other side of the sea lies Asia, crowded with people," his teacher used to say. As he listened, young Toda's head filled with great dreams of the future. I still remember with fondness how delighted Mr. Toda was when he told me such stories.

At Atsuta, where we left our things at our lodgings, Mr. Toda told me to take a look around the village. I set off by myself, going down to the seashore, following along the Atsuta River, and strolling about what impressed me as a small, very poor, seaside village.

Small and poor would also be the most appropriate words to describe Soka Gakkai as it was at that time. We were still a very insignificant organization, the very name of which made people ask with a puzzled look: "The *what* Gakkai?"

As I stood on the cape at the entrance to Atsuta harbor I thought about President Toda's youth and about what the future held for Soka Gakkai. I said to myself: "Just wait and see how things are ten or twenty years from now!" I reminded myself sternly: "The solidarity of the people is the foundation of world peace!" I recall facing the Sea of Japan, alone, and shouting these words at the top of my voice.

I returned to Tokyo, my head filled with impressions and resolutions. The poem entitled "Atsuta Village—Thinking of My Master's Childhood Home" is the result of this visit to Hokkaido.

The following lines refer to President Toda and his father and reflect the resolution I felt at the time:

> March forward, brave man, to face the storms of authority!
> This is the motto, the song of father and son.

Twenty-two years have passed. To my surprise, I myself am now approaching the age Mr. Toda was when we made that visit. I have held firm to the resolutions I made at that time and, along with the other members of Soka Gakkai, have devoted myself wholeheartedly to campaign to achieve *kosen-rufu.* I feel only gratitude and joy about the past.

In 1979 I will be fifty-one, just the age Mr. Toda was when he became president of Soka Gakkai. My work has just begun, and I ask all of you to join me in a spirit of hope and courage, in order that we may carry out the tasks that lie before us. I am counting on your help.

Basic Doctrines

The fundamental concern of Soka Gakkai has been, is, and always will be the fulfillment of the True Law through faith, practice, and study. By *faith* is meant faith in the Gohonzon inscribed by Nichiren Daishonin, the original and eternal Buddha of Nam-myoho-renge-kyo. By *practice* is meant religious practices as taught by Nichiren Daishonin, the Buddha in the Latter Day of the Law. By *study* is meant study of the *Gosho,* the writings of Nichiren Daishonin. For this reason, Gongyo, discussion meetings, and study activities constitute the three absolute and indispensable pillars of Soka Gakkai. Futhermore, the keynote of Soka Gakkai lies in the realization of the spiritual and material happiness of the individual, through such faith, practice, and study, as well as in the advancement of peace and culture for society as a whole.

This is the true spirit embodied in Nichiren Daishonin's essay entitled the *Rissho Ankoku Ron* (On securing the peace of the land through the propagation of true Buddhism). Tsunesaburo Makiguchi and Josei Toda made this spirit their own, put it into practice, and left shining examples for countless ages to come.

As I have stressed again and again, Soka Gakkai seeks to promote peace and culture based upon the principles of Buddhism. Only through such endeavor can Buddhist teachings be applied to society and utilized effectively for its betterment.

I have done my very best to carry on in the spirit and direction laid down by presidents Makiguchi and Toda. And I should like to take

238 · SOKA GAKKAI, ITS IDEALS AND TRADITION

this occasion to say that members of Soka Gakkai must always remember the principles underlying the ideals and practices of these two men.

As a basis for achieving the goals of Soka Gakkai and as a doctrinal foundation for their development in present-day society, I propose the following. If they meet with your approval, we should adopt them as a permanent definition of the Soka Gakkai spirit.

1. Soka Gakkai forever stands on the side of the people.
2. Soka Gakkai devotes itself to bringing about the human revolution.
3. Soka Gakkai walks the great Middle Way of Buddhism.
4. The social aims of Soka Gakkai are to preserve peace and to work for the advancement of true human culture.
5. Soka Gakkai guards to the death freedom of the human spirit and in particular the principle of religious freedom.

In previous meetings, we have discussed various practical problems involved in carrying out these points, which represent a summation of much past thought and deliberation. I should now like to establish them as a formulation of the basic spirit in which we shall proceed in the future.

On the Side of the People

Now I shall elaborate on my first proposal: that Soka Gakkai forever stands on the side of the people. There is a famous passage in the writings of Nichiren Daishonin that reads: "The key to all of Shakyamuni's teachings is the Lotus Sutra, and the key to the Lotus Sutra's practice is expounded in the *Fukyo* chapter.What does the Bodhisattva Fukyo's worship of the people reveal? The purpose of the Lord Buddha's advent in this world lay in his behavior as a human being ("On the Three Kinds of Treasure," *Gosho Zenshu*, p. 1174). In the spirit of these words, Soka Gakkai will support the principle of human dignity and appoint itself guardian of the masses of the common people of the world.

As Nichiren Daishonin often pointed out, he himself was the son of a humble fisherman. Clearly, he was on the side of the common people. He writes of himself: "So too, is it with Nichiren, who in this life was born poor and lowly to a family of the *chandala,* the lowest, class ("Letter fromSado," *Gosho Zenshu,* p. 958). In his other writings as well, he emphasizes his humble birth as the son of a fisherman living on a remote seacoast. All these pronouncements should be regarded as his instructions to posterity. He is telling us that adherents of his Buddhism must always remain among the common people and fight on their behalf.

Furthermore, in terms of practice, he clearly believed that his first duty was to devote his life to saving the common people from the sea of sufferings engulfing them. His attitude is suggested by the volume —over half—of his writings that are letters of guidance to various individuals in the lay community. Excluding fragments, these letters number well over four hundred. And each letter deals with the hardships and cares of a single person. In them, Nichiren Daishonin evinces profound sympathy for the hardships of individuals and vicarious suffering, surpassing that of the actual sufferer and guiding him to a solution of his ills. Nichiren Daishonin wrote these letters in simple Japanese at a time when classical Chinese was the conventional medium for communication among members of the intellectual class, thus indicating that his chief aim was to work among and assist the common people.

The Atsuhara Persecutions, which actually inspired him to inscribe the Dai-Gohonzon on the twelfth day of the tenth lunar month of 1279, were mainly for the group of followers centered on Nikko Shonin, Nichiren Daishonin's successor and the founder of the head temple, Taiseki-ji. Peasant farmers, humble common people without wealth or power, were the people who suffered most in these persecutions. It is profoundly significant that the Dai-Gohonzon should have come into existence in response to the martyrdom of the Jinshiro, Yagoro, and Yarokuro, brothers and peasant believers, who were beheaded at that time. Nichiren Daishonin looked upon hard-working common people—farmers or fishermen—as especially deserving of aid to salvation. Moved by the sight of their selfless faith and conviction, he inscribed the Dai-Gohonzon as an object of worship to be enshrined in the High Sanctuary of True Buddhism for all time.

Human Revolution

Next, I should like to discuss my second point, Soka Gakkai's pledge to carry out the human revolution. Surveying the history of Soka Gakkai up to the present and considering the role it should play in the future, we can say with assurance that the organization's most outstanding characteristic is vigorous advocation of a religion of man.

As many scholars have pointed out, there are two principal types of religion: religions of authority and religions of man. Most of the religious movements of the past have devoted themselves to the worship of some absolute deity or principle of authority to which man has been considered subservient. These are what are known as the religions of authority. The frequent religious wars and persecutions that have darkened the history of mankind have come about as a result—though perhaps an unintentional one—of blindness and prejudice fostered by such religions. In the *Social Contract,* Rousseau condemns such religious wars and the stupidity of fighting in the name of gods. More than two hundred years after Rousseau, however, such follies persist.

To be sure, Christianity and other absolutist religions nowadays no longer exercise over men the kind of authority they once did. But other voices of authority have come forward to take their place: science, state power, or the threat of nuclear weapons. Like their predecessors, these new gods of a godless age demand that mankind bow down before them.

Totally different from other religions or pseudoreligions, Soka Gakkai's "religion of man" reverses the relation between men and religious authority, strives to put man himself in the center of all affairs, and seeks to direct the course of history on the basis of this principle. Historians of the future will certainly praise the movement our religion represents.

The universal life, the Buddha nature, residing within each individual is, and must always be, the source of the authority of our religion. This Buddha nature is the purest, mightiest, and most uplifting principle of authority. The human revolution I have been speaking of is the struggle to call forth and realize the Buddha nature in each individual.

The study movement we are embarking on must be part of the larger revolution of human life. We must study for the sake of the human revolution, for the sake of a revolution of life itself, for the sake of our own broader horizons, and for the sake of the salvation of all peoples, everywhere.

You are all familiar with this passage from the writings of Nichiren Daishonin: "Even a tarnished mirror will shine like a jewel if it is polished. A mind which presently is clouded by illusions originating from the innate darkness of life is like a tarnished mirror, but once it is polished it will become clear, reflecting the enlightenment of immutable truth. Arouse deep faith and polish your mirror night and day. How should you polish it? Only by chanting Nam-myoho-renge-kyo" ("On Attaining Buddhahood," *Gosho Zenshu*, p. 383).

In Buddhist terminology, polishing oneself through faith is known as *sokushin jobutsu*, or realizing one's Buddha nature; in modern terms, it means the human revolution. The process of polishing the mind, "which is presently clouded by illusion," until it is clear represents the unfolding, or realization of the eternal life, the Buddha nature, within the individual.

Manifesting the life of the Buddha nature means firmly resolving to be an individual of integrity, determined to grow and advance upward. The bodhisattva, Jogyo, who leads the bodhisattvas who rise from the earth in the fifteenth chapter of the Lotus Sutra, represents such determination. You must learn to have wisdom and strength to see you successfully through any situation. The Bodhisattva Muhengyo, another of the four major bodhisattvas in the same chapter of the sutra, symbolizes this kind of wisdom. No matter what difficulties you encounter, no matter what predicament you fall into, you must never allow yourselves to be defiled by greed, animosity, or ignorance. You must live your lives in a spirit of joy. The attitudes enabling you to do this are symbolized by the bodhisattvas Jyogyo and Anryugyo in the fifteenth chapter of the sutra. The qualities represented by these four bodhisattvas are inherent in all individual human beings.

In contrast to the other bodhisattvas—Monju, Miroku, Yakuo, and Kannon—who appear in the sutra floating cloudlike above the earth, these four and the other bodhisattvas accompanying them spring from

242 · SOKA GAKKAI, ITS IDEALS AND TRADITION

the earth. The character *gyo*, standing for practical action, is a part of the names of all four bodhisattvas. In other words, whereas Monju, Miroku, and the other bodhisattvas who were instructed by Sha-kyamuni Buddha are incapable of the kind of practical action required of bodhisattvas springing from the earth, these four do have the necessary ability, symbolized by the *gyo* of their names. They have been instructed by the great original Buddha. People who, while considering themselves followers of the Buddhism of Nichiren Daishonin, neglect the practical aspects of that Buddhism, are not true Bodhisattvas of the Earth.

Religious practice, enabling them to break open and manifest the great earth of life itself, is the sole source of the power of these four bodhisattvas. This should make clear the course of action we must pursue to complete our human revolution successfully.

Master-Disciple Relation

The issue of the master-disciple, or teacher-student, relation is of the greatest importance to true human revolution of one's inner and outer selves. Chanting to the Gohonzon and working for *kosen-rufu* bring about a revolution in the individual's fundamental life; but relations with other human beings, both within Soka Gakkai and in places of professional activity, business, or community life, are essential to the human being's further advancement and cultivation.

The guidance of a teacher is imperative to genuine progress in an art, technical skill, or academic study. Such guidance is all the more necessary in the study and practice of Buddhism and its doctrines, which might be called the art, or way, of being a human being. Nichiren Daishonin has written of the importance of the teacher in these words: "Though father and mother sire and bear a child that has eyes and ears, if there is no teacher to give it instruction, then its eyes and ears will remain those of a mere animal" (*Gosho Zenshu*, p. 1248).

Both animals and human beings manifest relations between parent and offspring. Parents nurse and guard their young, who in turn display attachment to their parents. But the master-disciple relation has no counterpart in the animal world. It is known to mankind alone.

Former High Priest Nichijun—for whom President Toda had the utmost respect—once said of Josei Toda: "He carried out the master-disciple relation to the fullest. The correct observance of duties and obligations involved in this relation constituted his entire standard for viewing human life. His scrupulousness in this respect enabled him to attain profound understanding and mastery of the way of Buddha.

"What should Soka Gakkai take as the foundation of its faith? I believe it must begin with a clear recognition of the master-disciple relation and proceed to develop and deepen faith on the basis of that recognition. This is my interpretation of the core of President Toda's teachings. Inherently the student must trust the teacher, and the teacher must guide the student. When these duties are fully performed, it is impossible not to attain the true way of Buddhism.

"No one was more attentive to Mr. Makiguchi, the first president of Soka Gakkai, than his student and disciple Josei Toda. Indeed, Toda was more obedient to President Makiguchi than he would have been if the two of them had been father and son.

"These two men, the first and second presidents of the organization, fully determined the attitude toward faith that members must hold and the direction Soka Gakkai must follow in the future."

Although this quotation is long, it is appropriate, because it shows how High Priest Nichijun regarded proper observance of the master-disciple relation as the foundation of religious faith and the key to the attainment of the Way of Buddha. Further, this passage shows that the master-disciple relation between the first and second presidents established the course and paved the way for the advancement of Soka Gakkai. In short, the high priest is saying that true Buddhism cannot exist without the master-disciple relation, the proper observance of which is imperative to the attainment of Buddhahood.

For those of us engaged in basic cultivation of universal life, fundamental teachers—indeed the only eternal teachers throughout the worlds of past, present, and future—are the Dai-Gohonzon and Nichiren Daishonin, the Original Buddha. But we must always remember that Tsunesaburo Makiguchi and Josei Toda, who taught worship of the Gohonzon to present-day society and, through their words and actions, spread the teachings of Nichiren Daishonin, are our predecessors in the human revolution and our teachers in the drive for *kosen-rufu*.

The Middle Way

The third of my proposals is that Soka Gakkai always walk the great Middle Way of Buddhism. Before going on with this, however, I must pause to explain the meaning of the Middle Way. Buddhist doctrine propounds a principle known as the perfect harmony of the three truths (*en'yu-santai*), which explains the fundamental nature of all phenomena. The three truths are these. *Kutai*, the first, is that of the fundamental nature of all phenomena manifest in such processes of living as, for example, speech in human beings. The second truth, *ketai*, is that of the actual, perceptible forms of human beings; but these are only temporary unions of the five aggregates (i.e., form, perception, conception, volition, and consciousness). *Chutai*, the third truth, is the fundamental unity, or source, subsuming and transcending the duality of the other two. In other words, it is the unchanging principle of life itself. *En'yu-santai* is the wisdom that thoroughly perceives the harmonious nature of these three truths; it is the Middle Way of Buddhism.

In modern terms, *kutai*, a manifestion of wisdom, corresponds to progress or dynamic energy. *Ketai* is the present forms of beings. These are temporary and transient but preserve harmony. Human beings, too, while constantly undergoing the process of change, must preserve harmony among themselves and with nature if they are to survive. As I have said, *chutai* is the immutable principle of life itself, the prime point, the origin from which all entities spring.

Healthy growth or development in present-day society is impossible if any one of these three factors—in modern terms, progress (energy), harmony, and fundamental source (origin)—is lacking. Harmony without a firm foundation leads to facile compromise; whereas harmony without progress results in stagnation. On the other hand, progress lacking harmonizing viewpoints generates distortions and imbalance in society, as our modern, excessively materialistic civilization all too eloquently testifies.

The basic, universal principle, capable of harmonizing all three—

source, harmony, and progress—and thus of supporting better, more vital social development, is the true Middle Way: Nam-myoho-renge-kyo. In his discourse on the Lotus Sutra in *Ongi Kuden,* Nichiren Daishonin says: "What is meant by the 'conciliation of the three truths'? It is that which is called Nam-myoho-renge-kyo." This identification of *en'yu-santai* with Nam-myoho-renge-kyo indicates that all phenomena are no more than countless streams and rivers flowing into the great sea of the Mystic Law (Myoho).

A passage in the Lotus Sutra states that "infinite meanings flow from the single Law." The commentary explains that this is "like a hundred or a thousand branches and leaves that all come from a single root." In other words, the great Middle Way of Buddhism entails perceiving that all human activities, including the evolution of philosophies or ideologies, have one source or root—the single Law—and that all of activities are statically and dynamically sublimated into their proper positions.

In general terms, European thought has experienced certain periods of flourishing spiritual philosophy, like Platonic idealism and the Christian concept of the immortal soul. But, at about the the middle of the nineteenth century, as is well known, concern with spiritual matters gave way to vigorous materialism. After World War II, existentialism displaced both material and spiritual philosophies for a while, but is now apparently giving way to another philosophical approach called structuralism. In my opinion, the process of constant, unending change represented by this transition in Western philosophy indicates a continuing attempt to explain only part of what Buddhist terminology refers to as the "infinite meanings." Of course, in saying this, I have no wish to disparage the efforts of the great men who have labored to produce these systems of thought. Still, modern civilization has arrived at a philosophical impasse, from which there seems to be no escape. Western philosophy is impotent in the face of this dilemma, because it seeks only partial, not complete, explanations and solutions. Only the philosophy of the Middle Way of Buddhism can rescue modern civilization and light the way for its radical renewal, because it teaches that infinite meanings arise from the one single Law, as hundreds and thousands of branches and leaves rise from one root. By means of a tortuous course, our times are moving steadily in the direction of the Middle Way, which is the only viable way for man. I intend to do my best to make the great Middle Way the broad, mighty thoroughfare of all the people.

Preservation of Peace and Advancement of Culture

Now I should like to speak briefly about my fourth proposal, that Soka Gakkai must preserve peace and work for the advancement of true human culture, both of which must be based on recognition of life as the paramount possession. In the part of the *Gosho* known as "The Gift of Rice," Nichiren Daishonin wrote: "Life itself is the most precious of all treasures" (*Gosho Zenshu*, p. 1596). There can be no worse crime than taking life. And as Nichiren Daishonin says elsewhere in the *Gosho:* "The foremost treasure of sentient beings is nothing other than life itself. Those who take life are doomed to the three evil paths. The wheel-turning king, or ideal ruler, adopted as the first ten precepts of goodness, 'never to kill.' The Buddha preached the five precepts at the beginning of the Hinayana Sutras and made the command against killing the first of them. The *Juryo* chapter of the Lotus Sutra describes the merits gained by Shakyamuni Buddha through his observation of the commandment. Those who take life, therefore, are forsaken by all the Buddhas of the three existences of life. Nor are they protected by the gods of the six heavens in the world of desires" ("Reply to Toki Nyudo," *Gosho Zenshu*, p. 955).

Warfare is one of the most hideous forms of killing, and no one with a true sense of the value of life and a clear understanding of the stern consequences of the law of cause and effect could ever engage in it. As Buddhists, our first duty is to awaken men and women everywhere to the stupidity and criminality of killing and to inspire in them the pure life that will impel them to put an end to such crimes. In this way we will fulfill the teachings of the Mystic Law, the ultimate essence of the *Juryo* chapter.

Tsunesaburo Makiguchi defined the purpose of our organization as follows: "The aim of the theory of value creation is to help every human being to attain the highest possible happiness, both as an individual and as a member of society." He also said that ". . . no matter how the level of human culture may advance, if nations continue to ignore moral considerations in their dealings with one another and to occupy themselves with struggles for power and authority, there can be no true happiness for mankind."

As in the time when Makiguchi wrote this, so today nations are dominated by struggles for power and authority and wholly lack the sense of decency and right that human beings ought to have. As in Makiguchi's time, now and always the ideal of Soka Gakkai is to establish lasting peace, based on human trust and mutual respect, and to help every human being in the world attain maximum happiness.

Only a culture based on the happiness of each individual is a true culture. Such a culture is the only proper goal for our *kosen-rufu* drive, which is a movement for cultural betterment. Josei Toda described the mission of Soka Gakkai in these words: "To plan for the kind of peace that will last thousands of years and, in this way, to repay the great debt we owe to Nichiren Daishonin and at the same time to ensure the happiness of countless generations of people—this is the mission of Soka Gakkai."

I, too, have declared my mission to be working for peace and culture and have put forth concrete proposals for the realization of my goals. In my struggle to fulfill these aims I will spare nothing.

Nichiren Daishonin wrote, "Life has an end. Yet you should not be grudging with it. Your ultimate objective should be the Buddha land" ("Reply to Toki Nyudo," *Gosho Zenshu*, p. 955). In the spirit of these words, I resolve to follow my chosen path for the rest of my life. I hope that you will join me on this way to final victory.

Guarding Religious Freedom to the Death

My fifth proposal is that Soka Gakkai guard to the death the freedom of the human spirit and in particular religious freedom. Nichiren Daishonin's *Kaimoku Sho* contains the following passage: "Though I might be offered the rulership of Japan if I will only abandon the Lotus Sutra, accept the teachings of the Kanmuryoju Sutra, and look forward to rebirth in the Western Pure Land, though I might be told that my father and mother will have their throats cut if I do not recite the Nembutsu—whatever obstacles I might encounter, so long as men of wisdom do not prove my teachings to be false, then I will never accept the practices of other sects! All other troubles are no more to me than dust before the wind" ("The Opening of the Eyes," *Gosho Zenshu*, p. 232).

These stirring words of the Original Buddha reveal that Buddhists must hold fast to the ideal of religious freedom and the freedom of the human spirit and be prepared to defend it at all times. The Buddhist must never give in, no matter what persecutions, threats, or enticements confront him. He will be able to remain firm in faith to the end because he knows clearly that the Daishonin's Buddhism is the highest truth.

Trials and persecutions inspired Nichiren Daishonin to make this pronouncement. The previous presidents of Soka Gakkai took it to heart and made it the motto of their lives. Tsunesaburo Makiguchi died in prison, rather than betray this principle. Throughout the two years he was forced to spend behind bars, Josei Toda defiantly declared that, though his body was forced into submission, his heart would never submit. After his release, he devoted the rest of his life to the drive for *kosen-rufu*. In spite of criticism and baseless slander, during my struggles to defend the practice of the Mystic Law, I have remained convinced that we must guard religious freedom and the freedom of the human spirit to the death. We must never give in, no matter what the authorities may threaten. We must never waver, no matter what inducements are offered. We must persevere to the end, firm in faith in the rightness of our convictions. This is the key to the establishment and preservation of the highest human dignity.

Pioneering the Human Future

The world is sinking ever deeper into confusion. But ours is an important time, because now we must find ways to continue the work of past leaders and to pioneer a way for leaders of the last quarter of this century and for the century to come. The great leaders of the recent past have vanished from the scene. We search anxiously for light in the darkness, for guideposts into the next century.

But, though chaos reigns now, I believe that dawn will come. The wisdom of man will discover a new road out of our difficulties and into the future. My most cherished hope is that our Buddhist movement can contribute to the opening of a new chapter in human history. After having survived the vicissitudes of more than seven centuries, the great truths taught by Nichiren Daishonin are spreading to other lands and assuming the status of a world religion. I intend to continue earnest and steadfast in my faith in these truths, because I know they can bring the light of revitalization and understanding into the darkness of today.

Challenge All Obstacles

*Delivered at the Seventh Graduation Ceremony of Soka
Senior High School, held in Tokyo, March 16, 1977.*

On the occasion of the seventh commencement exercises of Soka Senior
High School, may I offer my heartfelt congratulations to those of you
who have now completed your studies and are about to go out into
the world.

Speaking as your representative, I should like first to express my
deep gratitude to Principal Osanai and the other members of the
faculty and staff of Soka Senior High School, who have devoted
themselves with such effort and patience to teaching and guiding you
during your three years here.

Human beings require a base or starting point to return to when
necessary. At times life is filled with worries and frustrations. (Indeed,
they make it stimulating.) But when a person seems to be in danger of
losing his sense of direction, it makes a great difference to have a
frame of reference by which he can re-establish a sense of his own
identity. You have spent your young days on the campus of Soka
Senior High School. If you should ever feel lost and defeated, think
back to the profitable years you spent here and gain courage to make
a new start from your recollections.

You, your teachers, and I, as founder of the school, are bound together by unseen ties. In the years to come, all will become strands in a fabric of friendship and triumph for humanity.

Escapism, runing away from reality, is in fact running away from yourself, refusing to face up to your own identity. "I'm tired! I'm bored! The going is too tough!" One can find many excuses to run away. But if a person begins to neglect his studies or his work, he is simply pampering himself. He is being a defeatist, running from his own identity. With such an attitude, he can never hope to make anything of himself. He is doomed to the grumbling, groaning life of the defeatist.

You who are in your late teens and about to enter your twenties must not run away. You are at the starting point of adult life, the period when you must perfect the foundation for the remainder of your years.

Scientists tell us that the human brain reaches developmental peaks at about the ages of four and ten and that the process comes to completion at the age of twenty. A firm foundation laid at this time gives the individual the potential to develop brilliantly in later life. Build such a foundation; put your best effort into it; and, by facing the stern facts of reality, prepare the way for outstanding future successes. At this crucial moment, when you are ready to enter college or start a career, meet the challenge with courage.

Most people who accomplished great things in the past studied very hard, often under extremely difficult circumstances. The father of Jean Jacques Rousseau, one of the most important thinkers of recent centuries, whose works are still widely read, was a watchmaker—a very lowly occupation at the time. Rousseau's mother died shortly after he was born. His father disappeared when Jean Jacques was still a boy, and the future philosopher grew up without ever knowing what real family life was like.

When he was your age, Rousseau became an apprentice to a watch engraver and endured hardships and harsh treatment. Under these circumstances he gained an understanding of society and developed a passionate hatred for injustice. Later in life he wrote such famous works as *Emile* and *The Social Contract,* in which he strongly emphasized the importance of human dignity. The seeds of his ideas are to be found in the experiences of his late teens.

René Descartes, in a sense the creator of modern philosophy, lost his mother shortly after he was born. At the age of ten, he entered La Fleche, one of the most celebrated schools in Europe. He spent eight years there, graduating at the age of eighteen, just the age you are now. During this period, he studied the classics of Greek and Roman literature and the system of philosophy known as Scholasticism. He was very disappointed when he finally realized that all his studies were of no practical benefit. Nonetheless, his academic work provided the foundation for his later philosophical inquiries. Not content to remain disappointed, he set out to learn from what he called "the great book of the world," traveling all over Europe and continuing his search for truth through action and experience. The rich fund of experience and knowledge he acquired at this time led to the formation of the principles of Cartesian logic, which changed the course of world philosophy, and to his famous pronouncement: *Cogito, ergo sum* (I think, therefore I am).

Both Rousseau and Descartes went through periods of diasppointment and despair, when they were about the same age as you. Yet times of trouble and discontent helped form their then-budding characters and identities. Now, as you pass through the same kind of period, without becoming disheartened or distracted, keep your eyes firmly fixed upon your own identity as it takes shape and challenge reality.

In the months and years to come, you will often feel as though you are facing insurmountable public or private obstacles. You may confront a wall that seems too broad or too high to surmount or circumvent. But do not give up in despair, for, in nearly all cases, you will discover later that the apparently insurmountable wall was actually of little or no significance.

You have probably heard many people tell of going to visit the scenes of their childhoods after they were grown. They were astonished to discover that what had seemed huge rivers were only streams, that the spacious streets were hardly wide enough to let two cars pass, and that whole towns seemed to have shrunk amazingly. Seeing now with the eyes of adults what they had earlier seen as children made everything look quite different.

The time will come when you will realize that the obstacles confronting you are really not so big after all. Not that I mean to make light of such obstacles. But, no matter what they may be, work to surmount them. If you fail in your attempt, keep on trying, and you will get over them in time. They are not insurmountable—they only seem to be.

Many different kinds of experiences lie in store for you in the long years ahead. Whatever comes, however, you must not shrink from reality or try to run away. Live courageously and to the fullest of your ability and remember to care for your parents, brothers and sisters, and all those who have been kind to you. When you stumble, pull yourself up again. Live the kind of life that you feel is most suitable to your particular tastes and abilities, but never let yourself be called a coward or a loser. Never forget the spirit you have learned here at Soka Senior High School and always be a credit to it.

Be a Leader Who Walks
with the People

Delivered at the Third Graduation Ceremony of Soka University, held in Hachioji, Tokyo, March 18, 1977.

～～～

On this bright sunny day, it is a pleasure to greet all you young graduating students and to offer my sincerest congratulations and wishes for your future growth and prosperity.

At the same time, both as founder of the university and on behalf of the graduating students, I would like to express my deep-felt gratitude to Professor Takamatsu, president of the university, and to all the other faculty and staff members for the warmth and diligence with which they have carried out the task of training these young people over the four precious years they have been enrolled here.

You students have attended a university that was only recently founded. You have shared with your teachers the work of building and shaping it and have helped to establish traditions that will impel it on the path to a bright future. I assure you I will never forget the contribution you have made, and I hope you yourselves will take great pride in your accomplishment.

Sound traditions have a power, imperceptible to the eye but worthy of highest gratitude and praise from those who built upon them later. Once more, let me express my thanks for what you have done in these past four years and say how much I appreciate it.

After today, most of you will be going out into the world to work at various occupations. The first problem that will confront you, though some of you may feel it more keenly than others, is the gap that exists between the world of theoretical learning and the actual conditions of society. You may find to your dismay that what you have learned in your years in school is not directly applicable to the work you will be doing or that the workaday world seems to move in a quite different direction from the world you have known here. This is particularly true now, when we are passing through a period of dramatic change such as history has seldom seen. The ordeals that await you will no doubt be commensurate in scale.

I hear it said that nowadays that there is a strong tendency for young people to try to avoid or run away from such ordeals. Even while still in school, there would appear to be some young people who lose all interest in academic pursuits and are concerned only in piling up enough units to graduate. If such assertions are true, they augur sadly for the future of Japan.

I hope you will resolutely resist such tendencies. I hope too that you will never lose your youthful determination to make use of the general and specialized education you have acquired here, whether in the immediate or the distant future, for you have given the best years of your youth to the task of acquiring it.

A journalist friend of mine once remarked, "Youth is not a matter of one's age but of the youthfulness of one's spirit." In other words, it is possible to remain youthful all one's life.

From what I have said, you may think that I place the blame for the unfortunate tendencies I have mentioned entirely upon young people. In fact, however, I fully realize that present-day society, including our academic institutions, is responsible for depriving young people of their passion for learning and their spirit of vigor and defiance. That is why I ask those of you who are graduating today to look carefully at the relationship between learning and society and to make certain that you understand it correctly.

But how should we go about examining society? In answer to this, I would like to cite a very interesting article I read in the paper recently—perhaps some of you read it too. It was by a well-known economist, and this is what he said: "If science is to understand the facts of reality correctly, it must at all times approach them not with simplistic or one-eyed vision, but with a vision that is many-faceted in nature."

The simplistic, the one-eyed, view sees all in terms of the tenets of its own particular system of thought and attempts to force the complex, ever-shifting data of reality into a rigid mold dictated by that system. As a result, it is led to ignore any data that fail to fit nearly into the mold. For example, let us look at economic theory in recent centuries. From Adam Smith to Karl Marx and Alfred Marshall, those who have attempted to explain the principles governing the economic world have accepted as axiomatic the concept of the market. In the market, all that matters is whether prices are high or low, whether goods sell or do not sell, whether one ends up with a profit or a loss. It is upon this concept of market and its values that the various economic theories have been constructed.

But, with the changes that have occurred in present-day society, it is clear that no such simplistic view of the economic situation can suffice. The problem of environmental pollution proves this. If the objective is merely to sell products and turn a profit, then it would seem all right for industries to dispose of harmful wastes in any way they see fit, as long as they maintain levels of production. Yet we now realize that such a procedure can lead to unlimited damage to the natural environment. Such methods of production, whatever their economic justification, can no longer be tolerated.

Industries must adopt measures to prevent environmental pollution and be prepared to bear the cost. In other words, they must take into consideration a factor that cannot be measured by the simple marketplace arithmetic of profit and loss.

Science and learning must be particularly alert in recognizing and dealing with developments that cannot properly be measured in terms of the standard criteria applied in the past. That is what the economist I am referring to meant when he called for multifaceted vision instead of a simplistic one.

There is a profound insight in the point he is making, one that far transcends the subject of economics alone. Every discipline or field of learning is based upon and grows out of the observation of some facet of reality, some body of facts. In this sense, no system of learning, however imposing, can be any more complex than the reality it describes. To determine whether a particular branch of learning is alive and viable, we must ask whether it honestly and at all times seeks to learn from the facts themselves, for they are the soil out of which it grows.

This applies not only to academic learning but also to the most ordinary matters of daily fact and opinion. We speak of conflicts of ideology or differences brought about by the generation gap. But in most cases, at the heart of the matter is not a generation gap or ideological difference, but an attitude of unwarranted hostility occasioned by a tenacious clinging to accepted ideas.

If, through the honest observation of reality, we can acquire not only learning but wisdom as well, we will be able to cooperate with one another and acquire energy to build a better future. The understanding that imparts such ability is what I would call true wisdom. Whatever learning or knowledge one may possess, it becomes of value in terms of human society only when it is supported by wisdom.

Buddhism, which is noted for its profound, subtle philosophy, posits two concepts known respectively as *usa* and *musa*. *Usa* means that which is removed from its native state, something that has undergone conditioning or alteration. In a larger sense, it is used to denote all the phenomena of the natural and human worlds. By contrast, *musa* is that which exists in its native state, that which rejects all conditioning or artificiality. It is the unseen essence of life hidden behind the phenomenal world. According to Buddhist teaching, *musa,* or essence, permits *usa,* or manifest phenomena, to come into being and develop in the proper manner. Learning and knowledge belong to the sphere of *usa.* Wisdom belongs to the sphere of *musa,* for it is the inexhaustible power for the creation of values.

It is my hope that all of you who are graduating today will learn to apply this kind of bold wisdom. Do not let yourselves be frustrated by trials or disappointments, do not let your lives become overcast with discontent or envy. Make use of wisdom and live meaningful lives, devoted to the creation of true values.

I have spoken earlier of the need to observe reality honestly and to learn from it. In concrete terms, just what does this mean? I believe it means being the kind of person who remains in constant touch with ordinary people, who walks side by side with them. Though I speak of reality, I do not mean any fixed set of facts or phenomena. I am thinking of all the varied joys and sorrows that make up the lives of each ordinary human being and of the never-ending changes they undergo. This is the ground out of which grow learning and knowledge, the soil that gives them nourishment. And, when it is separated from or heedless of the common people, learning is no more than a lifeless form.

That is why I fervently hope you will never give in to the arrogance of the elite and never let your academic background and high level of learning lead you to look with contempt on people less fortunate than you. If you do so, the four years you have spent on the campus of Soka University will have been largely wasted.

The German poet Goethe remarks in his maxims that, when young people first begin to make their way in the world, it is fine for them to think well of themselves, that they should believe themselves capable of possessing all merits and exploring all possibilities. But, when they reach a certain stage in their development, they must learn to bury themselves among the mass of ordinary humanity surrounding them, must learn how to live for others and forget their own existence in the pursuit of duty and action. Goethe concludes by saying that only when they have submerged themselves in humanity will they come to understand themselves. This is because the true business of life consists in measuring oneself against others.

You are the kind of young people Goethe describes. It is fine for you to have confidence in yourselves. Members of a generation that seems to have few dreams, you deserve praise for daring to entertain high hopes. But to realize these hopes and ambitions and to make them truly a part of yourselves, you must learn to go out and work among the people, patiently and with perseverance. You must never lose sight of this need.

Friends in Joy and Sorrow

Delivered at the Tenth Entrance Ceremony of Soka
Junior and Senior High School, held in Tokyo, April 8, 1977.

In this beautiful spring season, may I offer my heartiest congratulations to all you young people entering Soka Junior and Senior High School. I know you have worked hard to get here, and I sincerely hope that, from today, you will continue to apply yourselves with vigor to your studies. I know too that your parents and other family members have made many sacrifices for you and have put much time and effort into your education and upbringing so far, and I wish to take this opportunity to thank them for their efforts.

From now on, it will be the duty of the teachers and staff of Soka Junior and Senior High School to carry on the task of education begun by the parents and to continue to develop the potential of these young people, who are destined to be the leaders of the future. I know they will fulfill this duty conscientiously and with distinction.

On this happy occasion, I should like to share a few informal remarks with you and to make three requests.

First of all, I would like to urge upon you the importance of developing a tenacious spirit. I want you to have strength of character, to be made of tough stuff, as the saying goes. We are living in a period when, in material terms, life on the whole is very easy. In fact, we

259

might well say that it is too easy. We seldom have occasion to put forth great effort, to drive ourselves onward in order to accomplish a particular objective or gain a particular possession. As a result, young people often appear not to know how to work for success or how to cope with temporary disappointment or failure. We hear through the news media of young people who allow such frustrations to discourage them from continuing on the proper path or even to tempt them into taking their own lives. Such stories fill me with a sense of pity at the terrible waste of life and opportunity, and my heart goes out to the parents and kin who labored to bring up such children.

When we inquire into the causes of the frustration or despair that led these young people to such drastic actions, we are often astounded at their apparent triviality. A poor school record, failure to pass an entrance examination or to find employment—setbacks, no doubt, but of a kind that is readily remedied in the course of a lifetime. And, from the viewpoint of long-term development, such setbacks may be aids to success, providing opportunities for growth in stature and strength of character.

When I hear of young people who gave in to despair, I want more than ever to urge you students of Soka Junior and Senior High School to develop the tenacity of spirit that will refuse to admit defeat, no matter what happens. When they hear sad stories of disappointed youth, some people try to lay the blame upon the ills of present-day society. Of course, there are things wrong with our society and our age. But the ills of society do not excuse people from the responsibility for their own actions. Pointing out the failings of society, no matter how vigorously, will never help us to grow as individuals or to experience the true nature of life.

Timidity is the greatest enemy of youth. I ask you to put forth every effort during your years here in Soka Junior and Senior High School to develop the kind of strength of character that will allow you to challenge and overcome the ills of society.

The second quality that I ask you to cultivate is emotional breadth and sensitivity. Our age is too fierce. As so many modern thinkers have pointed out, the world is now being turned into a spiritual wasteland; and this process will no doubt continue in the future. But you must not allow yourselves to be carried along with the trend of the times, for, if you do, your lives will be blighted by spiritual grayness. One of your future tasks will be to bring the enriching waters of spiritual value to this arid age. Now, while you are young and open of mind, you must cultivate the mental fertility to carry out that task.

There are various ways to cultivate emotional breadth and sensitivity, but I believe that reading is one of the most important. I urge you to read as many books as possible to deepen your thinking. Reading and thinking, which provide indispensable nourishment to the spirit when one is young, are absolutely necessary if one is to cultivate a strong, worthwhile character.

Some of you may object that you do not have the time for reading. But time is an odd thing: if you really want to do something, you can always make time for it. When I was young, I too had a great many things to do. But somehow I managed to read one book after another. Even now, I make every effort to keep up my reading. Those who do not take advantage of every chance they have to read in their younger years will face defeat in later life. I remember that, when I was young, I tried to read a book a day, no matter how busy I was. And the reading I did in those days now constitutes one of the fondest memories of my youth.

Suppose you set yourselves the goal of reading one book a week. In the space of a year you will have read fifty or more books. And, if you continue this practice throughout your youth, you will store up spiritual treasures that will enrich the entire remainder of your lives. Biographies will teach you about the rich, meaningful lives of great figures of the past. History books will suggest ways that human society ought to develop in the future. Creative literature will open up a wealth of ideas about youth, life, and the nature of the human heart and mind. Such books provide the rich soil needed for the full growth of character and ability.

No tree can grow to full height in arid, stony soil. But with sufficient nourishment from the soil, the sapling sends out strong roots and soars to the sky. I hope that, during your years in Soka Junior and Senior High School, you will cultivate this kind of rich soil, so that in later years you too can grow into great trees, bearing abundant fruit and shading those around you.

My third request is that you make school a garden of friendship.

One of the most troubling aspects of our time is the disappearance of true friendship. We continue to speak about our "school friends," and yet I am afraid that the feelings of true friendship that used to be associated with such a term are nowadays lacking. In a competitive age such as ours, in too many cases friends are pitted against one another and forced to regard each other coldly as rivals. Not only in school but also in society at large, we see the same sad spectacle. When they find that their interests clash, formerly open, trusting friends, suddenly become relentless enemies.

The Chinese character for the word *friend* depicts two hands clasped in a gesture of mutual assistance. This is the true meaning of friendship, but such relationships grow increasingly scarce in present-day society. And this is especially regrettable, because true friendship is among the finest, noblest of human relations.

The term *jihi* (compassion), frequently used in Buddhist writings and thought, includes the character *ji,* standing for the Sanskrit word *maitri* (friendship). More exactly, *maitri* designates the state of time in which one constantly thinks of the happiness, peace, and comfort of others. In Buddhism, this attitude of mind is held up as the highest ideal. One Buddhist scripture states that to have good friends and dwell in the company of good friends comprise the whole essence of the Buddhist Way.

Hi, the other character in the term *jihi,* is a translation of the Sanskrit word *karuna,* which literally means to groan. By extension, it means to heed and empathize with other people's sufferings. Praying for the happiness of friends and sharing their sufferings as though they were one's own represent one of the noblest expressions of the true human spirit.

I hope that all of you will make your school a place where such friendship, characterized by both elements in the word *jihi,* prevails and that you will treasure happy memories to brighten all your years. And I hope that you will maintain the friendships you make here throughout the remainder of your lives.

To sum up my requests, I ask you entering students to grow into fine and effective leaders, fully capable of shouldering the burdens of the future. I pray that the years you spend here will be rich and fruitful ones. I am sure that the members of the faculty and staff will do all within their power to help you to make them so. I hope that, resting assured that you are in good hands, your parents and other family members gathered here will continue to watch over you and over Soka Junior and Senior High School.

Tireless Seekers of Knowledge

Delivered at the Seventh Entrance Ceremony of Soka University, held in Hachioji, Tokyo, April 9, 1977.

It gives me great pleasure to welcome all of you entering students. May I express my congratulations and best wishes for your future here. You have four precious years ahead of you. I hope you will spend them wisely and with enthusiasm, making the most of your opportunities for study, for extracurricular activities, and for close association with your teachers and fellow students. I hope, in short, that you will make this one of the most meaningful periods of your life.

I should like to take this opportunity to ask President Takamatsu and the other members of the faculty and staff to put forth their best efforts —as I know they will—in guiding these young people and helping them to develop their full potential as scholars and human beings.

All of you have succeeded in surmounting the very difficult hurdle of entrance examinations. I have no intention of belittling your achievement or dampening your hopes; but I ask you to face up realistically to the fact that life, in every sphere and age, is at best very uncertain. Your entrance examination is an example at hand. No doubt, as a result of hard work, you succeeded in passing it. But for each of you seated here today, there are many other young persons who, though they tried their best, just as you did, failed that examination and now must face bitter disappointment. I hope that they will not become disheartened, but will find the courage to confront life anew.

I remind you that, although you have surmounted the difficult obstacle of the entrance examination, this by no means signifies that the rest of your life will proceed smoothly. In the long decades ahead, you will encounter far more difficult obstacles than entrance examinations. Some people still believe the old idea that graduation from a first-rate college ensures entrance to a first-rate company or professional position. But, I assure you, such a view is completely obsolete.

Life is not that easy. During your college years and later, when you make your way in the rough-and-tumble life of society, you are bound to encounter bad times as well as good times. When times are good, it is wise not to be lulled into false security and to keep careful watch on where you are going. And, when times are bad, you must not allow yourselves to be daunted or disheartened but must call up all the energy you have to overcome obstacles and keep moving ever forward.

Recently a television baseball commentator, who was a well-known pitcher in his youth, remarked that you can tell a first-rate pitcher by the way he pitches when he is in poor form or suffering bad luck. Anyone can pitch a good game when in top form, but a mediocre or inferior pitcher will go to pieces when slightly out of form. A first-rate pitcher uses both effort and skill to keep his pitching at an acceptable level until he is able to get back into stride again. These remarks on pitching contain a truth that applies to all of human life. In the priceless years of youth, you must not settle for a second- or third-rate way of life, in which you are tossed about like a leaf with every little change in fortune.

Look at the way some great men have lived their lives. Luther, who revolutionized Christianity, produced his epoch-making translation of the New Testament while living in seclusion in the mountain castle of Wartburg. Lenin was in a prison camp in Siberia when he wrote his famous work on the development of capitalism in Russia. And Mao Zedong wrote his *Maotunlun* and *Shijianlun,* works that provided the motivating force for the entire Chinese revolution, while living in the remote caves of Yen-an.

Oddly enough, adverse conditions may be more conducive to creativity than favorable ones. In the end, whether the circumstances are favorable or unfavorable, what counts is the stance you take in facing them. That is the reason why, several times in the past when I have addressed the students of the entering class, I have emphasized the importance of living a creative life, of being a creative person. Acquire the tenacious wisdom and forceful vitality that will help you resist being led astray by favorable conditions or disheartened by unfavorable ones and allow you to rise to your feet again, no matter how hard a blow fate deals.

According to an interesting theory I heard recently, present society is moving from a "how" period to a "why" or a "what for" period. In a "how" period, there is general agreement about the goals of human life and society as a whole. The goals themselves are viewed as axiomatic and beyond question, and the only question is how to reach them. To take an example from my earlier remarks, such a period would assume that, for young people like yourselves, the most desirable life is to graduate from a first-rate college and move into a first-rate company or professional position. In the decades just past, when there was much talk about Japan's rapid economic growth, this philosophy prevailed. Behind it lay the assumption that the most important thing for Japan was to achieve a high gross national product; and, in pursuit of that goal, other needs of society were more or less neglected. In such a period, then, there is never debate about the worth of the objective itself. All attention is focused upon the question of how to attain it most rapidly and effectively. In a literal sense, therefore, it is a "how" period. Efficiency counts for everything, and the method of attaining the goal most efficiently represents the highest value.

But the violent, unexpected changes that have occurred in our society in the last few years have proved this philosophy to be a brittle one. Faith in the almighty power and worth of the GNP has collapsed, presenting society with a hopeless impasse and upsetting all our previous values. Now we must earnestly question whether the goals we accepted axiomatically in the past really represent the highest value after all.

For persons of your age group, the questions are: Why go to

college? Why take a position with a first-rate company? Why strain to be a model employee? We have left the era of "how" behind and are in the era of "why" and "what for."

Questioning the meaning of study, work, and life itself is laudable, because it is essentially investigating the basis of one's actions. Any learning, occupation, or way of life that fails to take into consideration the basis for all individual actions is bound to be ineffectual and ephemeral. It was with this thought in mind that I had the bronze statue I dedicated to the university inscribed with the motto: "For what purpose should one cultivate wisdom? Always ask yourself this question!"

And what is the basis for the action I have been speaking of? It is, or should be, the human being himself. From the mid-nineteenth century until the end of World War II, military considerations dominated Japanese society, while human beings were relegated to a place of secondary importance. In the thirty years since the end of the war, economics have assumed prime importance; people are still in the background. The error inherent in such a scale of values has brought the country to an impasse from which it is all but impossible to escape. It is absolutely imperative for Japanese society in the future to place human beings in the forefront and to make them the basis for all action.

Unless we can find a firm, convincing answer to the questions of "why" or "for what purpose," we cannot establish the proper standards to guide us into the twenty-first century. In founding Soka University, I chose the phrase "human education" as the keynote of its policy. It is motto that fits the times and will continue to do so in the future.

Buddhist philosophy expounds the concept of *ichidaiji,* or one great affair. Through Buddhism, the term has passed into everyday speech and is widely used to designate a matter of grave importance. For those of you here today, the "one great affair" in your recent lives has been passing the entrance examination. The famous Edo-period statesman, Okubo Hikozaemon, is well known for having described each crisis that arose as a *tenka no ichidaiji* (a matter of life and death for the state).

In Buddhist terms, the word *ichi* (one) designates the basis, or starting point. It indicates the existence of a philosophy that can serve

268 · TIRELESS SEEKERS OF KNOWLEDGE

as the basic guiding principle in the life of a human being. *Dai* (great) refers to the life and wisdom that derive from this starting point and expand to become manifest in human society, the natural world, and the universe as a whole. The word *ji* (affairs) indicates the actual events or objects created by life and wisdom manifest, translated into action. Therefore the two terms *dai* and *ji* in the expression *ichidaiji* may be said to refer to the activities of our mental and material lives. The *ichi* is the principle or entity that supports these activities. It is, in other words, the basis for them. Because I am a Buddhist, I have explained the matter in terms of Buddhist philosophy, but the concept does not apply to Buddhism alone. Any branch of learning, any philosophy or system of thought must develop from some fixed basis or starting point. Although the exact angle of view may differ from case to case, the starting point will invariably involve concern for the human being.

Soka University is an academic institution, where human beings gather to devote themselves earnestly to the pursuit and broadening of knowledge. Those who do not exert themselves in the search for knowledge and truth are false to the spirit in which this institution was founded. If such persons graduate from Soka University and go out into society, they will undoubtedly become targets of criticism. Others will judge the entire school on the basis of such persons alone and will say that Soka University has no real academic standing. I hope, therefore, that you will not be the kind of students who reflect unfavorably on those who come after you at Soka University.

By the time the twenty-first century arrives, you will be in your forties and at the peak of your powers. It is my fervent hope that from among this group will emerge the leaders of the century to come. For this reason, I shall continue to watch you from the sidelines and to offer words of encouragement from time to time. I pray with all my heart that you will spend the coming four years devoting yourselves with all the energy you have to the acquisition of knowledge.

Personal Observations on China

Delivered at Beijing University, April 22, 1980.

I would like to begin by saying what a great honor it is for me to be able to address you today and state a few of my personal beliefs. May I extend my sincere thanks to Vice-President Ji Xianlin, Vice-President Wang Zhuxi, and the other members of the faculty and student body for making this opportunity possible.

A few weeks ago, Dr. Kojiro Yoshikawa, a leading Japanese authority on Chinese literature, passed away. I am sure there are many people in China who are acquainted with him and his work. In one of his books, he describes China as a country with a "godless civilization." It is certainly true that nothing in the Chinese civilization or culture corresponds to the Christian or Islamic concept of God. Asian countries, such as Japan and India, have from early times preserved and handed down a vast body of myths. China, on the other hand, seems to have been one of the earliest countries in the world to divest itself of mythology. Confucius, the *Analects* tells us, "never talked of prodigies, feats of strength, disorders or spirits"; and the same attitude has been typical of Chinese civilization as a whole. In this sense, the phrase "godless civilization" strikes me as extremely apt.

But what view does Chinese civilization take with regard to man

269

himself and the world in which he lives? If I may venture to generalize on the basis of my very inadequate knowledge of the subject, I would suggest that the phrase, "viewing the universal in the light of the particular" sums up the Chinese approach.

Let me give an example of what I mean. At the beginning of the biography section of his *Shiji* (Records of the historian), Ssu-ma Ch'ien cites the popular belief that it is Heaven's way to have no favorites, but always to be on the side of the good man. He then questions this view by giving examples from history of good men who were destroyed and evil men who flourished. He expresses his own reaction to the situation in the famous words: "I find myself in much perplexity. Is this so-called Way of Heaven right or wrong?" This passage is very familiar, even to readers in Japan.

I do not intend to go into the question of just what is meant by the term "Way of Heaven." No doubt, it is influenced by both Confucian and Taoist philosophy and, from the viewpoint of our present age, smacks of feudalistic thought. At the same time, however, the very existence of such a concept testifies to the desire that people of the time felt for a definition of universal principles. Of course, the longing to discover a universal law or principle underlying and linking both man and the natural world is by no means peculiar to the Chinese people: it is common to human society everywhere.

In the passage I have just mentioned, Ssu-ma Ch'ien questions the validity of the "Way of Heaven" as a universal principle, in the light of particular instances from history. As I am sure you all know, Ssu-ma Ch'ien was condemned to be castrated, because, in the presence of the emperor, he spoke out in defense of his friend Li Ling, a general who had been forced to surrender to the enemy and in doing so aroused the ire of the ruler. The bitterness and resentment that he felt as a result of the punishment meted out to him are reflected in numerous places in his writings. The Li Ling affair and its consequences inflicted a terrible blow upon Ssu-ma Ch'ien. This extremely personal event forced him to make an individual evaluation of good and bad, right and wrong. When he posed his question concerning the "Way of Heaven," he was not doubting the principle as a whole, but was attempting to decide whether his particular "Way of Heaven"— the tragedy that had befallen him as an individual—was right. In this sense, Ssu-ma Ch'ien illustrates the Chinese tendency to view the universal in the light of the particular.

In contrast to this, societies wherein the concept of God is all-important tend to view the particular in the light of the universal. God directs the destiny of the world from a realm far removed from that of human beings. Man can only observe how the absolute, universal deity manifests his divine providence in the world in which we live. The relationship is one-sided; man's role is strictly passive. In such a system, it is unthinkable for a human being to question the nature of the "Way of Heaven" in the manner that Ssu-ma Ch'ien did. In European history, such questioning became possible only in the late years of the nineteenth century, when the "death of God" had been openly proclaimed.

Accordingly, in Europe in the past, when men contemplated the human and natural worlds, they inevitably viewed them through the prism imposed by the concept of God, which, though perhaps valid for them, did not transplant well in nations differing from Europe in history and tradition. The coercion to which Europeans resorted to force their God on others resulted in an aggressive and racially biased colonialism, thinly disguised behind a veil of religious zeal.

Obviously, in the light of their prevailing tendency to view the universal in terms of the particular, the Chinese have avoided pre-imposed prisms—like the European concept of God—and have attempted to extract underlying principles of universal validity directly from reality itself. In his late years, the British historian Arnold J. Toynbee, with whom I was well aquainted, predicted that China would become a focal point of world history in the future. To support his prediction, he cited the world-mindedness the Chinese people have developed to a high degree throughout the long course of their history. Critical of Christianity, Toynbee saw in the venerable Chinese tradition the beginnings of a kind of cosmopolitanism, or universalism, quite different from the aggressive European universalism.

I am not trying to gloss over the harsh realities of Chinese history. Everyone knows that China, too, has had internal dissensions, revolts, foreign aggressions, repeated floods, and droughts, all of which have brought untold misery to its people. I am perfectly aware that the

272 · PERSONAL OBSERVATIONS ON CHINA

object of the repeated revolutionary movements that have occurred in China in the present century has been not only to throw off colonial domination but also to rid the nation of the old feudal system, which, like a persistent disease, poisoned the hearts and minds of the people for a long time.

The Chinese people possess certain basic spiritual propensities that have evolved over the course of the centuries. It is neither easy nor always advisable to change these propensities. They should be carefully directed into constructive and beneficial directions, so as to make valuable contributions to the future of China, Asia, and the world as a whole.

When I look at portraits of the famous writer, Lu Hsun, I sense that with his clear eyes he was able to perceive the basic propensities that characterize the Chinese people. He sought to put aside all prisms and to observe naked reality just as it is. And, when he came to portray human beings, he stripped away every trace of pretense and superficial decoration and sought to capture the true likeness of the people. An enthusiastic reader of his works, I find myself especially moved by the conclusion of *A Madman's Diary*, which deals with the shameless ways in which human beings destroy each other, an act that Lu Hsun likens to cannibalism. "Perhaps there are still children who have not eaten men? Save the children . . .," the protagonist of the story cries. The moral thrust to the passage pierces the reader's heart.

Again, in his *True Story of Ah Q*, which depicts the poorest class of farmers, he writes: "But our hero [Ah Q] was not so spineless. He was always exultant. This may be a proof of the moral supremacy of China over the rest of the world." This simple passage is a striking portrayal of the true nature of the common people, who, in the midst of ignorance and poverty, manage to make their way through life like tough weeds.

The strength and innate honesty of Lu Hsun's characters remind me of the childish Parisian delinquent in whom Victor Hugo, in *Les Misérables*, perceived a kind of incorruptibility born of the ideas that filled the Paris of his time.

Lu Hsun's literary movement cannot necessarily be said to have succeeded. Yet I am certain that the tasks that concerned him throughout his life are being faithfully carried out in the new China of today.

The writer Ba Jin, whom I had occasion to meet recently in Japan, has declared that he wrote "in order to combat my enemies," a statement that impresses me greatly. He went on to say, "What are my enemies? Every kind of old, traditional concept, every irrational system that impedes social progress and the expansion of the human spirit, everything that destroys love." These words reveal Ba Jin to me as a fellow fighter, together with Lu Hsun, in the battle against any one or anything that would bring harm to the people. I might to a step farther and say that I have been much impressed by the fact that slogans such as "Serve the People!" or "Be a Servant of the People!" have appeared so often in China in the period since the end of World War II. I see in them the image of a new kind of people, who will play a vital part in the history of the future.

Perhaps the current slogan, *shishi qiushi,* "to seek the truth in reality," has something in common with the Chinese tendency to view the universal in the light of the particular. At least it would appear to follow the same pattern as Ssu-ma Ch'ien's query on the nature of the Way of Heaven and to be intimately related to one of the finest elements in the spiritual legacy of China: the conviction that one must confront reality directly and, on that basis, decide how reality can best be reconstituted.

We are living in a period of profound change and upheaval. The late premier Zhou Enlai remarked that the last quarter of the present century is a period of crucial importance. In times like these, unless the peoples of the world form bonds transcending national boundaries, they may be visited once more by the horrors of war. As Joseph Needham says in the introduction to his monumental *Science and Civilisation in China:* "We are living in the dawn of a new universalism, which, if humanity survives the dangers attendant on control by irresponsible men of sources of power hitherto unimaginable, will unite the working peoples of all races in a community both catholic and cooperative."

To play the leading role in this universalism, we must have a new type of people, a new image of the common man. And I firmly believe that China, with its long history and devotion to reality, possesses the boundless energy needed to help open a new era of the future.

Thoughts on
the Mexican Poetic Spirit

Delivered at Guadalajara University, March 5, 1981.

As the founder of Soka University and president of Soka Gakkai International, an organization dedicated to the promotion of peace, culture, and education on the basis of true Buddhism, I have traveled to a number of countries and now have the pleasure of coming to Mexico for the first time in sixteen years. During my one-week stay, I have met His Excellency, President Lopez Portillo; Señora Maria del Pilar Galindo Lopez Portillo de Cordero, director of Claustro Sor Juana, Central University of Human Science; Dr. Octavio Rivero Serrano, rector of the Universidad Nacional Autonoma de Mexico, and others, in connection with exchanges between Mexico and Japan in areas relating to culture, education, and the peace movement. We have, to a limited degree, deepened mutual understanding between our two nations. At the unofficial level, I have held a joint Mexican-Japanese cultural festival.

Today, on the last day of my visit, I should like to thank Dr. Enrique Zambrano Valle, rector of Guadalajara University, for giving me this opportunity to speak and to convey my thanks to all the members of the faculty and student body who have gathered here to listen to me.

In the past, I have had occasion to speak at Beijing University on the topic "Some Personal Remarks on China," at Moscow University on the topic "A New Road to East-West Cultural Exchange," and at the Los Angeles campus of the University of California on the topic "Toward the Twenty-first Century."

Today, while reviewing in brief the history of friendly relations between Mexico and Japan, I should like to deliver a few remarks that might be summed up in the title "Thoughts on the Mexican Poetic Spirit," with perhaps the subtitle "Indices of Mexican Culture." Outlining some of my views, particularly as they relate to our mutual desire of striving for peace in this time of increasingly complex international relations, I shall—with your permission—speak for about an hour. Mr. Kimiro Yoshida of Japan will be my interpreter.

As I am sure you are all aware, relations between Mexico and Japan are by no means a recent innovation. In the early years of the seventeenth century, a powerful feudal lord of Japan named Date Masamune dispatched his retainer, Hasekura Tsunenaga, as the head of a mission to Spain and Rome. On the way to Europe, the party passed through Mexico, which was then under Spanish rule. Recently, an author who is well known in Japan has written a novel entitled *Samurai,* the hero of which is modeled on Hasekura Tsunenaga. The novel has aroused much discussion, and as soon as I heard about it, I quickly purchased a copy and read it, to see what picture it gave of the Mexico of that time.

You may also be aware that in 1888, not long after Japan emerged from isolation, it signed a trade treaty with Mexico. This was the first treaty Japan was able to conclude with a foreign nation in modern times that was based on terms of equality between the signers.

Fortunately, in the years since the end of World War II, relations between Mexico and Japan have become very close in the political, economic, educational, and cultural fields. Yet the development of mutual understanding between the peoples of the two countries—not their governments—is still in the initial stage. Therefore I have determined to do all in my power to construct bridges in the fields of culture, education, and the pursuit of peace, to serve as lines of communication between our peoples.

Late last year, the International Congress for the Study of Asian

Peace was held in Yokohama, Japan. Many distinguished persons from Asia and other parts of the world attended it; among them was Mr. Ivan Illich. As you may know, Mr. Illich is at present the director of the International Cultural Information Center of Mexico. I find some of his ideas, such as rejection of conventional education, extreme and difficult to accept. But I was strongly impressed by some of his words quoted in the Japanese press: "My concern is that people should be poetic, that they should tell jokes and learn to smile."

It is an unpretentious remark; yet, in relation to matters concerning education, culture, and peace, it has something important to teach us, because the poetic spirit and a smiling face are the most telling indications that the lines of communication linking the minds and hearts of people are open and functioning. Though we may talk of peace and cultural exchange, unless there is true communication among people's hearts and minds, such talk is virtually meaningless. This is the meaning of a famous passage in the UNESCO Constitution: "War is born in the hearts of humankind. Therefore we must build fortresses of peace within the heart."

Why does Mr. Illich, a scholar born in Vienna, place so much emphasis on the poetic spirit and a smiling face? There are no doubt many reasons. But, though I am only guessing, I suggest that a principal reason is related to his experiences in Mexico, where he has lived since 1960. On the basis of my limited knowledge of Mexican history and culture, I have formed a clear mental picture of the temperament of the Mexican people, a temperament marked by joviality, by smiling faces and poetic spirits, by a special kind of generosity. I do not think my image of Mexico as the "land of sunshine and passion" is a mere superficial impression. I believe that, with their love of fiestas and their strong desire to enjoy whatever life may bring, the Mexican people are determined that, no matter what trials they are called upon to face, they will never abandon their essential gentleness and sunniness or the courage underlying these qualities.

I cannot help recalling an episode recounted in *Mexican Revolution,* a vivid piece of reporting by the American journalist, John Reed. In 1923, when government forces and the revolutionaries were engaged in sporadic fighting, and the situation was in exterme confusion, Reed determined to brave the danger and to enter Mexico. Near the southern border of the United States, he encountered many refugees fleeing from the fighting and seeking safety in America. The border guards were subjecting them to careful inspection for weapons, examining both men and women with a roughness and a thoroughness far exceeding anything the situation called for.

Reed reports that he was standing nearby when he saw a woman holding up her skirts and wading across the shallow water. She was wrapped in a heavy shawl, in which she seemed to be trying to hide something. The front of the shawl bulged suspiciously.

"Hey you! Wait a minute!" shouted one of the officials. "What's that you've got under your shawl?"

The woman slowly opened the shawl a little and then with perfect composure replied, "Señor, how can I tell? It may be a girl, but then again it may be a boy."

Under such tense and frightening circumstances, to be able to make a joke of the matter and to reply with guileless humor show a firmness of nerve that would put a man to shame. The woman handled the situation magnificently.

Another episode connected with the Mexican revolution sticks in my memory. It concerns the revolutionary hero, Pancho Villa, who is still remembered today with respect and affection by the Mexican people. It took place in March of 1913, when Torreon, an important strategic point, was under attack by revolutionary forces. Villa and his men had reached Yermo, to the north of Torreon; and all preparations had been completed for launching an attack on Torreon, when suddenly Villa, the leader of the expedition, was nowhere to be found. His officers waited impatiently for four days, until at last he appeared, tired and muddy. He explained that, having promised to attend a friend's wedding, he had slipped surreptitiously away from the encampment. For the past four days and nights he had been engaged in traditional Mexican style, feasting and dancing in honor of his friend's wedding. Probably things were very different in those days. If any of you were to slip away from classes and go on a four-day holiday, you would find yourselves in serious trouble with your teachers.

When I first read this anecdote, I couldn't help smiling to myself. It seemed to convey so vividly the personality of this romantic, courageous man, the wealth of human feeling that made him refuse to be bound by the rules of military discipline. Though the incident no doubt reflects Villa's own particular character, it is profoundly related to something in the character of the entire Mexican people, something evident in the action of the woman at the American border too: the quality, I previously characterized, somewhat clumsily, I fear, as joviality, smiling faces and poetic spirits, and a special kind of generosity.

There is nothing mawkish or sentimental in that character. The Mexican revolution, like so many other revolutions, was won through the struggle and sacrifice of the people of the nation, and was paid for in their blood. It is said that not only men but, in many cases, women as well took up arms and went into battle. Doubtless many tragic stories could be told of those battles. And yet the two episodes I have recounted show that, in the midst of hardship, people managed to hold on to their poetic spirits, their smiling faces, their senses of humor. That is why they are precious to me. It is precisely this keen sensitivity to human feelings and values that has made possible the respect for human rights and the dedication to freedom, equality, and independence that characterize this nation today.

In 1967, the treaty to ban nuclear armaments from Latin America was drawn up; and an international organization known as OPANAL was set up in Mexico City to implement its provisions. I am told that these steps were taken as a result of strong initiative on the part of Mexico. Such an undertaking must be regarded in a different light from that of the treaty against nuclear-arms proliferation drawn up at the initiative of the United States and the Soviet Union, an operation that exists purely on a political level. Mexico's action is much more deeply related to a positive, independent spirit of choice on the part of the Mexican people.

As we all know, nuclear arms constitute a more frightful, devastating type of weaponry than has ever been known before in history. No greater outrage against the spirit of humanity can be imagined. Because recourse to such weaponry could well lead to the destruction of all humankind, I take every opportunity to call for the banning and abolishment of nuclear arms. On the occasion of the first Special Session of the United Nations General Assembly on Disarmament in

1978, I sent letters to Secretary-General Kurt Waldheim and General Assembly President Lazar Mojsov, in which I made a number of proposals that could lead to the reduction and abolition of nuclear weapons. Among these was a proposal that the United Nations take the initiative in establishing and, in time, enlarging, nuclear-free zones. I am especially grateful for the continuing efforts of the Mexician people to create such a nuclear-free zone in Latin America.

These efforts represent a positive, independent spirit of choice and, consciously or unconsciously, reflect the Mexican people's keen concern for human rights and values and their determination to establish the kind of framework of freedom, equality, and independence that will allow men and women to live as human beings should. I have no doubt that this same concern for human rights led the Mexican people to give warm and continuing support to the Popular Front in its struggle against fascism at the time of the Spanish Civil War.

True, we may talk all we want of freedom and equality and independence, but fully realizing these ideals is difficult. Modern Mexican history can best be described as a process of trial and error, marked by frequent setbacks and frustrations. Many political, economic, and other kinds of problems remain to be solved. All of you here today must exert your efforts and take constructive steps to solve them. But I cannot help but believe that the tenacious soul of the Mexican people, which somehow managed to remain alive during three hundred long years of colonial oppression and which has now been trained and tempered in the experiences of independence and revolution, will do great things in the future. I am convinced that this country will have major contributions to make—not only to Japan, the Latin American countries, and other countries of the Third World but also to all human society—on a scale with those already made in the international art world by the leaders of the Mexican Renaissance: Rivera, Orozco, Siqueiros, and Tamayo.

A painter friend of mine who is well acquainted with Mexico tells me that in your country, when welcoming a guest, it is customary to say, "My house is your home, too." It is a wonderfully warm and friendly kind of greeting, and I feel it conveys the temper of your country very well.

Buddhist scriptures contain a parable that expresses a similar meaning: the parable of the two reed-bundles. (Long ago, in India, it was customary to bind twenty or thirty long, slender reeds together into a bundle.) Shariputra, a disciple of the Buddha, who was noted for his unparalleled wisdom, first employed the following parable.

"Let us suppose that there two bundles of reeds," he said. "As long as the two are leaning against each other, they stand up. In the same way, because there is a 'this,' there can be a 'that,' and because there is a 'that,' there can be a 'this.' But, if we take away one of the bundles of reeds, the other will fall over. In the same way, if we take away 'this,' 'that' cannot continue to exist; and if we take away 'that,' 'this' cannot exist."

The parable is designed to teach the very important lesson that people cannot exist in isolation but must depend upon each other for help. The greeting that you use to guests—"My house is your home, too"—embodies the same profound, wise understanding of human interdependence.

As we enter an age of increasing internationalization and interdependence among nations, we will see a more lively degree of cultural exchange, not only between Mexico and Japan but also among all the countries of the world. We are approaching a time when nation and nation, race and race, must meet one another on terms of complete equality and mutual consideration. To achieve this, lines of communication must link hearts and minds of the peoples of all different countries. It is my hope that my present visit to your country may in some small way serve to further the realization of that goal.

In closing, I would like to address a word to all you students who have gathered here today. Each of you will soon be called on to employ your intellect and fervor in facing the challenges of the twenty-first century. It is my sincere prayer not only that you will become worthy leaders of the Mexican nation but also that each one of you will become a responsible and dedicated supporter of the cause of world peace and will do your very best to advance that cause.

About Daisaku Ikeda

by Yasuji Kirimura
Director of Doctrinal Studies, Soka Gakkai

For the nineteen years between his becoming third president of Soka Gakkai, in May 1960, and his appointment to the position of honorary president in April 1979, Daisaku Ikeda devoted himself to spreading the philosophy of Buddhism, managing an immense organization, and guiding millions of Soka Gakkai members. Indeed, he was largely responsible for making Soka Gakkai what it is today. His outstanding leadership and operational assistance helped take the Soka Gakkai movement to various countries of North and South America, Southeast Asia, Europe, and Africa, where independent organizations were established, incorporated, and set functioning on their own. During that time, he has delivered many stimulating, suggestion-filled messages on such matters of vital current interest worldwide as politics, economics, science, education, and culture. All of his pronouncements have been firmly based on the Buddhism of Nichiren Daishonin (1222–82), which is the basic belief of Soka Gakkai.

To borrow a botanical metaphor, Mr. Ikeda's efforts have been concentrated on strengthening our drive to spread Nichiren Daishonin's teachings, the tree trunk, while causing the branches and leaves of culture and learning to flourish and produce seeds to be planted and cultivated in all parts of the globe. Though he has enjoyed the assistance of many colleagues in this work, Daisaku Ikeda alone has stood at the helm, evolved major policies, cultivated and placed the personnel to carry them out, and encouraged all around him to proceed with the task. No one else could have done what he has done, nor is it likely that any one capable of such accomplishments will appear in the future.

Though he has now delegated the duties of president to others and is honorary president of Soka Gakkai, Mr. Ikeda is still too busy to rest. His duties as president of Soka Gakkai International take him all over the world, assisting friends in the faith in other lands by guiding their activities and organizations. This compilation of several of his vast collection of speeches and addresses is especially timely in connection with this international work. The speeches have been carefully chosen for ease of comprehension by the average reader.

The Buddhism of Nichiren Daishonin is the trunk of the Soka Gakkai tree. Political, educational, scientific, artistic, and other endeavors are the branches and leaves producing fruit and ultimately seeds to be sown in other lands. This is the overall picture; but, when activities in various fields are examined in isolation, they tend to become fixed and formalized. The connections with the basic trunk of our philosophy and system are obscured. Judging Soka Gakkai on the basis of its undertakings in any one given field is tantamount to judging the plum blossom on the basis of the early winter bud. Since Daisaku Ikeda's writings and thought correspond to the general broad picture of Soka Gakkai itself, for the sake of those who are coming to them for the first time or for those who have encountered his work only in fragmentary form, this essay attempts to give the overall picture of the way his philosophy has evolved, especially in connection with the Buddhism of Nichiren Daishonin.

Early Stages

Born on the Omori shore of Tokyo in 1928, Daisaku Ikeda is the son of a family that dealt in edible seaweeds. In the general turmoil following World War I, Japan was attempting to develop as a wealthy country with a powerful military and was already moving in the direction of the militarism that led to the catastrophe of World War II. Mr. Ikeda spent his young years in an environment that impressed him painfully and deeply with the distress that social disruption and foolish leaders—especially foolish militarist leaders—can inflict on ordinary people. Worldwide depression brought hard times to his family, as it did to almost everyone. And, like many other young men he knew, his younger brothers were drafted. His still-forming intellect was confronted with the official, ultranationalist, educational doctrines on the one hand and with literature in the free democratic spirit of the Weimar period on the other. Early familiarity with democratic principles through this literature made Mr. Ikeda especially open to American democracy when it was introduced after the defeat of the militarists at the end of World War II in 1945. This had a determining influence on the formation of his personality and philosophy. His happiness at the freedom made possible by postwar democracy and his rebellion against suppressive militaristic policies during the war stimulated in him a profound respect for arts and letters and a determination to work for world peace.

But all of this would have ended in nothing more than vague ideas if Mr. Ikeda had not come into contact with the Buddhism of Nichiren Daishonin and with Josei Toda, the man who became his teacher and mentor, as well as the second president of Soka Gakkai. These encounters gave Mr. Ikeda profound religious and philosophical endorsement for his ideas, stimulated him to become one of those people who create the age they live in, and suddenly awakened in him the need to act in the name of the movement he believed in.

After first meeting Josei Toda in August 1947 and accepting faith in the Buddhism of Nichiren Daishonin the following year, Mr. Ikeda went to work in a business firm run by Mr. Toda, who instructed and guided him in many fields. The firm published a children's magazine, of which Ikeda was soon appointed editor. This work gave him a deep love for young people and cultivated the habit of always thinking in terms of what must be done to help them to bear the heavy burdens of the future. It is concern with youth that causes him, as president of Soka Gakkai International, to accept with pleasure invitations to lecture at schools and universities in many countries, where he always makes a deep impression on his audiences.

But the most important and priceless thing Mr. Ikeda learned from Josei Toda was faith in the Buddhism of Nichiren Daishonin and an understanding of the importance of its application and study. The depth with which Mr. Ikeda understands the teachings, the power and relevance with which he puts his beliefs into practical action, and the scale of his actions and thoughts in connection with it surprised even Josei Toda himself.

In 1951, when Mr. Toda became its second president, Soka Gakkai had a membership of a few thousand households. Josei Toda brought the number up to 750,000 households before his death in 1958. Daisaku Ikeda was a powerful driving force in successive membership campaigns leading to this increase. In 1960, he became the third president and led the organization to a growth many times that which had previously occurred. Extending beyond education alone, this growth and development brought a deepening and expansion in many fields and cultivated and employed the right kinds of people necessary to carry out the work. Here again, profound faith and understanding of Nichiren Buddhism, broad awareness of learning and culture, and above all else love and subtle understanding of human nature enabled Daisaku Ikeda to succeed.

The Buddhism of Nichiren Daishonin

The Buddhism of Nichiren Daishonin, in which Daisaku Ikeda and Soka Gakkai believe, differs from the Buddhism founded in India by Shakyamuni and from the various other Buddhist sects that developed in China and Japan from Shakyamuni's teachings. However, Nichiren Buddhism is not entirely separate from Shakyamuni's Buddhism.

Shakyamuni did not provide people with a completed way to enlightenment but left much up to rigorous, self-conducted meditation and discipline to be performed by believers themselves. Two thousand years after Shakyamuni's death, ordinary mortals were no longer equal to the task required for the attainment of such enlightenment. In this period, called the Mappo Era (the Era of the Latter Day of the Law), a complete and perfect way accessible to all had to come into being. The perfect way is explained in the Sutra of the Lotus of the Mystic Law, which is said to be a sermon actually preached by Shakyamuni.

The Lotus Sutra clearly states that Shakyamuni was enlightened at some time in the infinitely distant past but leaves unexplained the nature of the Law to which he was enlightened. In the fifteenth chapter of the sutra, bodhisattvas spring up from fissures in the earth and vow to teach the ultimate Law in the Mappo Era, when the Buddhism of Shakyamuni will have become ineffectual. The perfected Buddhism that, as prophesied in the Lotus Sutra, appeared in the Mappo Era is the teaching of Nichiren Daishonin, who established the Law of Nam-myoho-renge-kyo and the Three Great Secret Laws.

The Three Great Secret Laws are these: Honzon, mandala representation of the Law of ultimate enlightenment; Daimoku, the chant Nam-myoho-renge-kyo, which is a practical training method for ultimate enlightenment; and Kaidan, the sanctuary or Buddha realm where the Honzon is enshrined, the Daimoku chanted, protection from evil granted, and suffering eliminated.

The most important significance of the Three Great Secret Laws is best explained in relation to the Buddhism of Shakyamuni, in which believers must undergo severe, prolonged self-discipline and training in order to attain enlightenment. From the standpoint of ordinary human beings, Shakyamuni's Buddhism is abstract and difficult. The Three Great Secret Laws of the Buddhism of Nichiren Daishonin offer concrete, readily understood goals—faith, practice, and study—and thus open the way to enlightenment to all peoples. It is impossible to overstate the significance of this religious development. For this reason, Nichiren Daishonin is rightly called the true Buddha of the Mappo Era.

Training in his Buddhism is very simple and clear, consisting as it does of three elements: faith, practice, and study. Faith means that the believer knows that Nichiren Daishonin is the true Buddha of the Mappo Era, who appeared on earth for the salvation of all mankind, and that the essence of his teaching is embodied in the Dai-Gohonzon mandala enshrined at Taiseki-ji, the head temple of Nichiren Shoshu.

Practice consists of two major parts. The first is morning and evening performance of a service called Gongyo and consisting of readings from the second ("Expedience") and the sixteenth ("Life of the Tathagata") chapters of the Lotus Sutra and chanting of Daimoku (Nam-myoho-renge-kyo). The second is introducing the teachings of Nichiren Buddhism to as many people as possible. As has been explained, chanting Daimoku enables the individual to attain Buddhahood; but this alone would be a purely selfish act inconsonant with the true spirit of Buddhism. This is why practice must consist of both the self-oriented act of chanting Daimoku and the altruistic act of bringing others to the teaching that promises them Buddhahood and happiness. In other words, practice must be directed toward the benefit of others as well as to one's own advantage.

Study is necessary to strengthen and deepen faith, to ensure correct practice, and to enrich one's own abilities to convince people of the importance of awakening to the truth of Buddhism by studying and understanding the maximum about Buddhist doctrines and their theoretical bases.

Soka Gakkai strives to deepen the faith of each of its members by encouraging practice and study and to achieve the universal propagation of the faith (*kosen-rufu*), which Nichiren Daishonin entrusted to posterity. This was the core of Daisaku Ikeda's philosophy and actions while he was third president of Soka Gakkai and continues to be the basis of all he does as president of Soka Gakkai International. (A brief comment about a point that often gives rise to misunderstanding is warranted here. Soka Gakkai is a lay organization devoted to faith in the teachings of Nichiren Shoshu Buddhism. Its president leads the membership in the faith, practice, and study of that Buddhism and stimulates movements to take the teachings to the widest possible audience. He is not, however, the founder of a religious sect. Like all other presidents of Soka Gakkai, Daisaku Ikeda was a commentator on, not a creator of, Buddhist doctrines.)

Trust in Humanity

There is a general tendency—especially among Western intellectuals who know only primitive or Hinayana teachings, the early doctrines of Shakyamuni—to interpret Buddhism as a pessimistic philosophy. It is true that, in his early teachings, Shakyamuni emphasized the inconstancy of everything and the unpleasant, futile aspects of human existence in order to help people break free of attachments to self, desire, and the material world and thus to develop a desire to know the truth. In its first phases, Mayahana Buddhism too taught that ultimate truth was a paradise located in some distant western realm and adopted a pessimistic view of reality and humanity.

The true and essential Mahayana doctrines, however, are found in the Lotus Sutra, which teaches that the immutable, ultimate, peerless truth does not exist apart from the world of actual things and actual human beings. The truth is universally present behind and beyond the apparently inconstant and ugly world of reality. In other words, the Buddha nature can be found equally in all human beings, all of whom are equally capable of manifesting it. Furthermore, as a crystal flashes different lights according to the illumination of its surroundings, so the apparently ugly life and all its operations can radiate loveliness when viewed in the light of the profound universal Buddha nature. This is the interpretation of mankind found in the Lotus Sutra; it is permeated with all-pervasive trust and faith in mankind.

The spirit of faith in the Buddha nature within all human beings is vividly symbolized by the Bodhisattva Never Despising (*Jofugyo-bosatsu* in Japanese), who says to the people he addresses, "I profoundly respect all of you because you are all on the bodhisattva way leading to ultimate Buddhahood." He then bows to everyone.

A consistent article of faith with Daisaku Ikeda is faith and respect for all human beings. He insists that no differences—no matter whether they spring from the generation gap, racial or national prejudices, or domestic quarrels—are unsolvable as long as the parties involved maintain mutual faith in humanity. Differences of opinion, emotional clashes, conflicts of interests are almost inevitable in daily life; but mediation can always bring adjustment and conciliation as long as it rests on mutual faith and trust. If it does not, however, hatred makes discussions of the problems impossible; and animosity and suspicion can be aggravated into cruel conflict.

Daisaku Ikeda's program for avoiding the catastrophe threatening mankind today because of the unprecedented power and destructiveness of the weapons at our disposal is mutual trust and respect in all matters from family squabbles to issues affecting all international society. He is fully aware of the dangers in blind faith, which can lead to the destruction of the innocently trusting person. Ikeda does not condone blind faith in all instances. He does, however, insist that when the individual is forced to choose between trusting and doubting, trusting is the wiser choice.

Making the choice often entails a fierce inner struggle with suspicion and fear. But the truly courageous mind can overcome its own doubts and move bravely in the direction of trust and respect for man, the indispensable ethical basis for all humanity. This concept underlies everything Daisaku Ikeda says.

Unflagging Creativity

Daisaku Ikeda believes with all his being that creativity should characterize everything we do, no matter what the circumstances. As has been explained, creativity distinguished the earliest stages of his life. And, during his nineteen years as president of Soka Gakkai, his creative efforts and their results were virtually superhuman. It was Daisaku Ikeda who completed the interior and exterior organization of Soka Gakkai; who inspired and guided overseas expansion; and who undertook an immense construction project to perfect the facilities of Taiseki-ji, the temple that is the core of Nichiren Shoshu Buddhism.

The very name of the organization Soka Gakkai means Value-Creating Association. (The original name of the organization was Soka Kyoiku Gakkai, or Value-Creating Educational Association. This title, devised by the first president Tsunesaburo Makiguchi, was altered to Soka Gakkai by Josei Toda.) In other words, the creation of value, which ought to be the goal of all human undertakings, is the main purpose of Soka Gakkai. And Buddhism is the religious philosophy the organization employs in the creation of human values.

Each human being is endowed with the Buddha nature and with the power to manifest it. By bringing the Buddha nature to the forefront in all actions, each life can gleam radiantly. This teaching of the Lotus Sutra is the key to creation of value in the lives of all individuals. Unmanifested in actions, however, the Buddha nature cannot bring light into life or cause its potential to flower. This is why practical training and action are essential.

One aspect of Buddhist training and discipline is overcoming the self; that is, a constant struggle against suspicion, egoism, and slothful yearnings to preserve the easy status quo. This struggle is an inner revolution leading the mind of the individual from selfishness to altruism and from mistrust to trust. In this connection, Daisaku Ikeda has strongly urged the importance of what he calls the human revolution.

Because of associations between ordinary revolutionary movements and destructiveness, a few people entertain misgivings that Daisaku Ikeda's human revolution too entails the danger of harm. But these misgivings are unfounded. It is true that certain Hinayana teachings and the doctrines of the Mahayana Pure Land sect lead to harm. In Japan, the Pure Land sect, which promises salvation to anyone who calls on the name of the Buddha Amida, who dwells in a paradise in the west, flourished and became a leading doctrine from about the twelfth century. The effect of its popularity was baleful, since believers in the Pure Land teaching gradually lost the will to face and cope with the contradictions and sufferings of actual life and concentrated solely on the paradise they hoped to reach after death. One of the most popular Western concepts about Japan has to do with hara-kiri ritual suicide and fearlessness in the face of death. This apparent bravery is less courage coming from facing and overcoming fear of death than a perversion, a kind of mental paralysis, arising from the Pure Land teaching.

In contrast to these destructive attitudes, the Lotus Sutra teaches that, if the priceless Buddha nature present in every human being is made manifest, even the inconstancies and uglinesses of life become glowingly beautiful. By the single act of manifesting, everything in life becomes radiant. Nothing requires exclusion or elimination. Nothing needs to be denied: All life, as it is, becomes beautiful. The human revolution based on the Buddhism of the Lotus Sutra is accompanied by no destruction. It is creation in the truest sense— creating that requires no preliminary destructiveness.

Human life ought to be creative. Each second of the present should be filled with creative acts for the future. Every human being has a mission, a reason for living. People who consider their existence a burden are unable to see their missions. Once their missions become clear to them, the burden vanishes. All our efforts ought to be directed toward creating, not destroying. This is a fundamental tenet in Daisaku Ikeda's philosophy, as a glance at the speeches in this book makes perfectly clear.

In the Name of World Peace

The primary goal of Daisaku Ikeda's thought and action—as they have been described in the preceding pages—is lasting peace in the world. History shows that, when a sound period of peace has been established, it has been under the forcibly imposed aegis of a mighty imperium—like the Roman Empire. During the dialogues he and Mr. Ikeda conducted a number of years ago, the late Arnold J. Toynbee said that he suspected any future world peace would come about as the result of the formation, by force, of a political global empire. Daisaku Ikeda, on the other hand, insisted that world peace must be achieved on the basis of a federation of independent states, something like the federation currently evolving in Europe. He believes that peace under an empire would last only so long as the empire itself survived. Furthermore, the attractions of authority and power would invite certain elements to strive to topple the empire in order to set up a different rule of their own. Finally, since power and authority are corrupting, a forcibly imposed peace by empire would contain the seeds of its own ultimate downfall. The kind of peace through federation that Daisaku Ikeda envisages would be built on mutual understanding and trust. Instead of peace through force, it would be peace through reason and faith.

From the time when he was president of Soka Gakkai, Mr. Ikeda has frequently conducted peace-promotion visits to the United States, China, and the Soviet Union—the great powers in whose hands the keys of peace rest. In addition, he has discussed these important matters with many world leaders including secretaries-general of the United Nations. In harmony with Mr. Ikeda's ideas and ideals, the Youth

Division of Soka Gakkai sponsored a peace petition against nuclear weapons that was signed by ten million people.

Now that he is honorary president of Soka Gakkai and president of Soka Gakkai International and has thus expanded the range of his activities to include the whole world, he will doubtless combine his leadership and encouragement of fellow Nichiren Shoshu believers in other lands with intensified activities in the name of lasting peace.

Continuing the tradition of dialogues for peace that began in talks with Arnold J. Toynbee, Mr. Ikeda has already held conversations with René Huyghe, of the Academie française; with Aurelio Paccei, president of the Club of Rome and Professor Brian Wilson of Oxford University, they are underway; and with Dr. Karan Singh of India, dialogues will soon begin. Peace cannot be achieved in a day, and, once achieved, it demands fervor and wisdom to sustain it. In his dialogues with the men just mentioned and with other leaders from the United States, China, and the Soviet Union, Daisaku Ikeda is contributing to the creation of a vitally important, long-term heritage of wisdom for peace that will be a lamp to many generations to come.

Peace is one of the most significant things Buddhism can bring to the world. As is well known, the famous king Ashoka, who was a devout Buddhist in the India of the third century B.C., established ideal peace in his own realm and even sent envoys on peace-promoting missions to such distant places as Greece and Egypt. In Japan in the thirteenth century, Nichiren Daishonin wrote a famous tract entitled *Rissho Ankoku Ron* (The security of the land through the propagation of true Buddhism), which contains his plea for peace and is addressed to the political leaders of the day. *Rissho Ankoku Ron* insists that true Buddhism must be the foundation of peace. Of all his voluminous writings—about half are letters to private individuals, and many are concerned with future developments—Nichiren Daishonin publicly issued only this one. Obviously, he put maximum stress on peace.

Daisaku Ikeda's total dedication to work for peace is more than a personal matter. It arises from his sense of mission to spread the Buddhism of Nichiren Daishonin as widely as possible and to allow its spirit to shine strongly over the whole world.

Glossary

Alaya: the Eighth Consciousness; literally, a repository; an unconscious realm where impressions, or karmic effects, are stored and new mental actions, or internal causes, originate. *See also* Nine Consciousnesses.

Amala: the Ninth Consciousness; literally, immaculate; unlike the Eighth Consciousness, which may produce causes for both good and evil, the Ninth Consciousness is free from all karmic impurity. It corresponds to one's eternal Buddha nature. *See also* Nine Consciousnesses.

Amida Sutra: the most widely known of the provisional teachings, i.e., the teachings preceding the Lotus Sutra.

Anryugyo: one of the four major Bodhisattvas of the Earth appearing in the fifteenth chapter of the Lotus Sutra.

Ashura (Shura): a devil who is extremely pugnacious. He can be used to symbolize Shura, one of the ten states of life. Shura is the condition of anger and refusal to do what is correct, even when the right way is shown.

Bodhisattvas of the Earth: the bodhisattvas who appeared in the fifteenth chapter of the Lotus Sutra and pledged to propagate the Mystic Law in the Latter Day.

Buddhahood: the highest of the Ten Worlds. According to Nichiren Daishonin, Buddhahood is an awareness of the real existence and basic nature of the greater life on which rest all the other nine worlds of life.

Buddha World: the paramount of the Ten Worlds. *See also* Buddhahood, Ten Worlds.

Butsugen: the Eye of Buddha, one of the Five Eyes.

Chian-tzu-wen: See Thousand-character Classic.

Chih-i: See T'ien-t'ai.

Chutai: the third of the three truths; the fundamental unity, or source, subsuming and transcending the duality of the other two (*kutai* and *ketai*); the unchanging principle of life itself. *See also* Three truths.

Chintamani: a fabulous gem capable of fulfilling all wishes (*nyoihoju* in Japanese).

Chuang Tzu: a famous Taoist philosopher, who is thought to have lived from 369 to 286 B.C.

Dai-Gohonzon: *See* Gohonzon.

Daimoku: (1) Title of a sutra, in particular, the title of the Lotus Sutra, Myoho-renge-kyo. (2) The invocation of Nam-myoho-renge-kyo, one of the Three Great Secret Laws, chanted as a means of attaining Buddhahood.

Doshi: leader or master.

Egen: the Eye of Wisdom, one of the Five Eyes.

En'yu-santai: the perfect harmony of the three truths, i.e., the Middle Way of Buddhism.

Esho funi: the concept of the indivisibility of living beings and their environment, one of the basic principles of Nichiren Daishonin.

Five aggregates: form, perception, conception, volition, and consciousness. In Buddhism, these five compose a sentient or human being.

Five Eyes: the various powers of perception—the Physical Eye *(nikugen),* the Heavenly Eye *(tengen),* the Eye of Wisdom *(egen),* the Eye of Law *(hogen),* and the Eye of Buddha *(butsugen).*

Five pollutions: the corruptions of (1) the age, (2) people and society, (3) desires, (4) thought, and (5) life itself. People of the Latter Day of the Law inherit these pollutions and cannot get rid of them until they practice the true Buddhism.

Four Sufferings of life: birth, aging, sickness, and death.

Fukyo: bodhisattva who appears in the *Fukyo* (twentieth) chapter of the Lotus Sutra; the "BodhisattvaWho Does Not Disparage," he does not condemn, but helps to salvation even those who have slandered the Buddhist Law and who have persecuted him.

Gohonzon: the major object of worship and veneration for believers in Nichiren Shoshu.

Gongyo: the services of prayer and chanting performed by believers of Nichiren Shoshu for attaining Buddhahood.

Gosho Zenshu: collected writings of Nichiren Daishonin, considered to be the "actual words of the original Buddha and the supreme teaching for the Latter Day of the Law," the basic scripture of Nichiren Shoshu. Followers of Nichiren Shoshu are taught to apply the precepts contained in these religious theses and letters to their everyday lives.

Hinayana Buddhism: One of the two main streams of Buddhism; literally, the "lesser vehicle." Also known as Theravada Buddhism.

Hogen: the Eye of Law, one of the Five Eyes.

Hung-chieh: an annotated edition of T'ien-t'ai's *Mo-ho-chih-kuan* (Great concentration and insight). This annotation was written by Miao-lo.

Ichidaiji: the Buddhist concept of "one great affair," or a matter of great importance, especially implying the purpose of a Buddha's appearance in this world.

Ichinen Sanzen: a profound Buddhist truth illuminating all aspects of the basic nature of life in a systematic philosophical interpretation of the phenomena of the universe. The term *ichinen,* literally "one thought," refers to the ultimate nature of life; *sanzen* means all universal phenomena. The doctrine expressed by the combination of the two words is that the ultimate nature of life is endowed with all universal phenomena, in all their stages and variations.

Issai shujo: literally "all living or sentient beings."

Issho jobutsu: the attainment of Buddhahood during the lifetime of the individual human being.

Itai doshin: "many in body, one in mind," or unity of people with a common cause; in this Buddhism, with faith in the Gohozon and the common cause of *kosen-rufu.*

Jigage: Verse section, which concludes the *Juryo,* or sixteenth, chapter of the Lotus Sutra.

Jitai-kensho: the Buddhist theory of the realization of the true self.

Jogyo: leader of the Bodhisattvas of the Earth who appeared in the fifteenth chapter of the Lotus Sutra and vowed to propagate Myoho-renge-kyo in the Latter Day of the Law.

Jyogyo: one of the four leaders of the Bodhisattvas of the Earth who appeared in the fifteenth chapter of the Lotus Sutra.

Kannon: (Sanskrit: Avalokiteshvara) a bodhisattva who appears in the Lotus Sutra floating cloudlike above the earth. According to the sutra, he assumes thirty-three different forms to save the people.

Kegon Sutra: according to T'ien-t'ai, compilation of the teachings of Shakyamuni expounded during the first three weeks following his enlightenment.

Ketai: the second of the three truths; that of the actual, perceptible forms of all existence.

Kosen-rufu: literally to teach and spread (Buddhism) widely; also to secure lasting peace and happiness for all mankind through the worldwide propagation of Buddhism.

Ku: the void, nonsubstantiality, latency.

Kutai: the first of the three truths; that of the nonsubstantial nature of all phenomena manifest in such processes of living as speech in human beings and blossoming in flowers.

Latter Day of the Law: *See* Mappo Era.

Life Expressions: the dynamic aspects of life's movement and actions.

Lotus Sutra: the ultimate of all Buddhist teachings. It is generally divided into twenty-eight chapters, the most important of which are the *Hoben* and the *Juryo*. Nichiren Daishonin often used the words "Lotus Sutra" in his writings to indicate its essence, Nam-myoho-renge-kyo.

Mahayana Buddhism: one of the two major streams of Buddhism; literally the "greater vehicle." The Mahayana teachings are concerned with individual salvation and also stress the importance of leading *all* people to enlightenment.

Makiguchi, Tsunesaburo: founder and first president of Soka Gakkai.

Manas: the Seventh Consciousness; the realm of abstract thought, reason, awareness of self. *See also* Nine Consciousnesses.

Mappo Era: the Latter Day of the Law. Traditionally, the time following the two millennia after Shakyamuni's death—our own times—in which people are enlightened only by the teachings of Nichiren Daishonin. *See also* Zoho Era.

Miao-lo: (Japanese: Myoraku) a great T'ang-dynasty Chinese priest, who is credited with a revival of T'ien-t'ai Buddhism. He restored the sect and interpreted the three great works of its founder.

Middle Day of the Law: *See* Zoho Era.

Middle Way: the ultimate reality that gives rise to all phenomena; the law of Nam-myoho-renge-kyo. See also *en'yu-santai*.

Miroku: (Sanskrit: Maitreya) a bodhisattva who appears in the Lotus Sutra floating cloudlike above the earth.

Mo-ho-chih-kuan (Great concentration and insight, *Makashikan* in Japanese): One of the three major works of T'ien-t'ai. It clarifies the deep meaning of the Lotus Sutra by propounding the concept of Ichinen Sanzen.

Monju: a bodhisattva of wisdom who appears in the Lotus Sutra floating cloudlike above the earth. He represents the virtue of wisdom.

Muhengyo: one of the four major Bodhisattvas of the Earth.

Musa: that which exists in its native state; that which rejects conditioning or artificiality. See also *usa*.

Myo: a character that stands for *mystic,* as in Mystic Law; implies "beyond the realm of ordinary human understanding."

Myoho: *see* Mystic Law.

Mystic Law: (Japanese: Myoho) ultimate law of life and the universe, the law of Nam-myoho-renge-kyo.

Nam-myoho-renge-kyo: expounded by Nichiren Daishonin as the essence of the Lotus Sutra. Simply put, it means devotion to the ultimate law of the universe.

Nembutsu: to worship Amida Buddha and recite his name.

Nichikan Shonin (1665–1726): teacher and writer, the twenty-sixth high priest of Nichiren Shoshu.

Nichiren Daishonin (1222–82): the founder of true Buddhism.

Nichiren Shoshu: the orthodox school of Nichiren Daishonin's Buddhism.

Nikko Shonin: the second high priest of Nichiren Shoshu; the closest disciple of and immediate successor to Nichiren Daishonin.

Nine Consciousnesses, Theory of: classification of the spiritual functions of perception. The first Five Consciousnesses are the perceptions of the five senses: sight, hearing, smell, taste, and touch. The Sixth Consciousness enables one to integrate the perceptions of the five senses and form judgments about them. The Seventh Consciousness, or *manas,* is the realm of abstract thought, reason, awareness of self, and so on. The Eighth Consciousness is called *alaya,* meaning a repository, an unconscious realm where impressions, or karmic effects, are stored and new mental actions, or internal causes, originate. The Ninth Consciousness is called *amala,* meaning immaculate. Unlike the Eighth Consciousness, which may produce causes for both good and evil, the Ninth Consciousness is free from all karmic impurity. It corresponds to one's eternal Buddha nature or essential self.

Nirvana: in the Buddhism of Nichiren Daishonin, an enlightened condition of life in the real world, based on faith in the Gohonzon. In the Hinayana sutras, it meant to attain enlightenment by annihilating one's consciousness and reducing one's body to ashes.

Ongi Kuden: the compilation of the oral teachings of Nichiren Daishonin on the Lotus Sutra that were delivered to his close disciples. Written by Nikko Shonin and approved by the Daishonin.

Rissho Ankoku Ron (The security of the land through the propagation of true Buddhism): treatise written by Nichiren Daishonin.

Sanzen: See Ichinen Sanzen.

Setsuna jodo: attaining Buddhahood in a single moment; the state in which a human being attains Buddhahood while still in his mortal body (*sokushin jobutsu*).

Shakubuku: the "compassionate act of introducing people to true Buddhism"; propagating true Buddhism by refuting another's erroneous or prejudiced ideas and leading him to the correct Buddhist teachings.

Shakyamuni: also known as the Buddha or Gautama Buddha; the first historical Buddha, who, according to Buddhist tradition, lived about 3,000 years ago in India.

Shikishin funi: the Buddhist philosophy of the indivisible oneness of mind and body.

Shin-Ju: the Life Expressions.

Shin-O: the Sovereign of Life; the "principal axis of all activity."

Sho-Hondo: the Grand Main Hall of Taiseki-ji, the head temple of Nichiren Shoshu.

Shura: *See* Ashura.

Sokoshin jobutsu: manifesting one's Buddha nature. See also *setsuna jodo.*

Sumeru, Mount: In ancient Indian cosmology, the highest of all mountains, which stands at the center of the world.

Taho: A Buddha who praised Shakyamuni for teaching the Lotus Sutra and gave credence to its validity.

Taiseki-ji: head temple of Nichiren Shoshu.

Taishaku: One of the two tutelary deities of Buddhism, Indra (the other being Bonten, or Brahma).

Ten Worlds: According to Nichiren Daishonin, and life exists in ten worlds, all of which are eternally inherent in life and emerge in response to one's interaction with his environment. They are Hell, Hunger, Animality, Anger, Humanity, Heaven, Learning, Realization, Bodhisattva, and Buddhahood.

Thousand-character Classic: an ancient summary of Chinese history and Confucian philosophy written in 1,000 characters, none of which is repeated *(Chian-tzu-wen)*.

Three Treasures: the Buddha, the Law, and the Priesthood.

Three Truths: *kutai, ketai,* and *chutai,* the perfect harmony of which explains the fundamental nature of all phenomena in Buddhist doctrine. See also *en'yu-santai.*

T'ien-t'ai: another name for Chih-i, founder of the T'ien-t'ai (Japanese: Tendai) sect.

Toda, Josei (1900–1958): successor to Tsunesaburo Makiguchi to become the second president of Soka Gakkai.

Usa: that which is removed from its native state; something that has undergone conditioning or alteration; also means phenomena of the natural and human worlds. See also *musa.*

Zoho Era: the Middle Day of the Law. The second millennium after Shakyamuni's death, which saw the birth and growth of T'ien-t'ai Buddhism. *See also* Mappo Era.

The "weathermark" identifies this book as a production of John Weatherhill, Inc., publishers of fine books on Asia and the Pacific. Book design and typography: Miriam F. Yamaguchi. Composition: Samhwa Printing Co., Seoul. Printing: Kenkyusha, Tokyo. Engraving and printing of the monochrome plates: Kinmei, Tokyo. Binding: Makoto Binderies, Tokyo. The typeface used is Monotype Bembo.